Greenspan's Fraud

Also by Ravi Batra

The Crash of the Millennium
Stock Market Crashes of 1998 and 1999
The Great American Deception
Japan: The Return to Prosperity
The Myth of Free Trade
The Great Depression of 1990
Surviving the Great Depression of 1990
The Downfall of Capitalism and Communism
Muslim Civilization and the Crisis in Iran
The Pure Theory of International Trade
The Theory of International Trade under Uncertainty
Prout and Economic Reform in India

GREENSPAN'S
FRAUD

HOW TWO DECADES OF HIS POLICIES HAVE UNDERMINED THE GLOBAL ECONOMY

RAVI BATRA

palgrave
macmillan

First published in 2005 by
PALGRAVE MACMILLAN™
175 Fifth Avenue, New York, N.Y. 10010 and
Houndmills, Basingstoke, Hampshire, England RG21 6XS
Companies and representatives throughout the world.

PALGRAVE MACMILLAN is the global academic imprint of the Palgrave Macmillan division of St. Martin's Press, LLC and of Palgrave Macmillan Ltd. Macmillan® is a registered trademark in the United States, United Kingdom and other countries. Palgrave is a registered trademark in the European Union and other countries.

ISBN 1–4039–6859–4 hardback

Library of Congress Cataloging-in-Publication Data

Batra, Raveendra N.
    Greenspan's fraud : how two decades of his policies have undermined the global economy / Ravi Batra.
        p. cm.
    Includes bibliographical references and index.
    ISBN 1–4039–6859–4 (alk. paper)
    1. Greenspan, Alan, 1926– 2. Government economists—United States—Biography. 3. Board of Governors of the Federal Reserve System (U.S.) 4. Monetary policy—United States. 5. United States—Economic policy—1981–1993. 6. United States—Economic policy—1993–2001. 7. United States—Economic policy—2001– I. Title.

HB119.G74B38 2005
332.1′1′092—dc22   2004065030

A catalogue record for this book is available from the British Library.

Design by Newgen Imaging Systems (P) Ltd., Chennai, India.

First edition: May 2005

10 9 8 7 6 5 4 3 2 1

Printed in the United States of America.

In the memory of my late teacher
P. R. Sarkar

CONTENTS

ACKNOWLEDGMENTS

In completing this project I gratefully acknowledge help from the group of ten (the G-10): first and foremost, my wife, Sunita, without whose prodding and inspiration this work might still be in incubation; Airié Stuart, my editor at Palgrave Macmillan, who read, edited, and accepted the work enthusiastically; my agents Michael Broussard and Jan Miller at Dupree Miller, who led me to Airié; Abdullah Khawaja for timely research assistance; Chris Hartman of United for a Fair Economy (UFE.com) for permission to use a graph; my copyeditor, Bruce Murphy, and production editor, Alan Bradshaw, for forcing me to add more explanations in the text; Ellis Levine for checking out the legalities, and, last but not least, Melissa Nosal, Airié's assistant, for never being too busy to take my call.

Many books and articles have provided the supporting material. Among them are: *Alan Shrugged: Alan Greenspan, the World's Most Powerful Banker* by Jerome Tuccille; *Greenspan: The Man Behind Money* by Justin Martin; *Maestro: Greenspan's Fed and the American Boom* by Bob Woodward; *Dot.con: The Greatest Story Ever Sold* by John Cassidy; *Origins of the Crash* by Roger Lowenstein; *Bull!: A History of the Boom, 1982–1999* by Maggie Mahar; several newspapers such as *The New York Times, The Wall Street Journal, The Washington Post, The Dallas Morning News, The Financial Times, The Boston Globe, The San Francisco Chronicle, The Christian Science Monitor, The Daily Telegraph, The Guardian, The Irish Examiner, The Buffalo News, The Toronto Star, The Pittsburgh-Post Gazette, The Ottawa Citizen*; several magazines including *Time, Newsweek, The New Yorker, The Nation, The Economist, Forbes, CNN/Money*; above all, I am grateful to that amazing contraption called the Internet, which was indispensable in providing speedy information.

1

THE TWO FACES OF ALAN GREENSPAN

October 19, 1987, is known as Black Monday, the day the New York Stock Exchange suffered the worst crash in history, with a bang that echoed around the world. The Dow Jones Index (the Dow in short) then sank 22.6 percent, almost double the single-day drop in the notorious crash of 1929. From Toronto to Tokyo, London to Sydney, Buenos Aires to Brasilia, share markets shed tears, mourning the demise of the Dow. Wall Street and investors across the globe agonized over a bleak future. They had been caught off guard, because no financial wizard had foreseen the debacle. But in one of financial history's biggest ironies, Black Monday launched the brilliant future of someone named Alan Greenspan. It propelled him into glory and celebrity, giving him unprecedented influence over the global economy.

Barely two months before the disaster of the Dow, with large bipartisan support, Greenspan had been appointed the chairman of the Federal Reserve (the Fed in short), a coterie of 12 regional banks that control the levers of money supply in the United States. He came with no banking experience; his credentials as an economist were considered by some to be mediocre, but he had foresight and business acumen that few can develop from their scholarship alone. He had not done any path-breaking work in economics, at least none that was commonly cited. Yet he was savvy enough to know when to open and shut the money pump that lubricates financial markets. He had made his mark through business forecasting, which had brought him close to big firms on Wall Street.

Actually, Wall Street's first choice in 1987 was not Greenspan but Paul Volcker, who had been selected as the Fed chairman by President Jimmy Carter in 1979. Volcker had done such a good job of taming inflation, which had plagued the globe since the early 1970s, that the financial world had come to adore him. But an inflation fighter is rarely popular with politicians, because he tends to keep interest rates high and raise the rate of unemployment. Volcker was not on amicable terms with the reigning president, Ronald Reagan, who preferred his pal and adviser, Wall Street's second choice, Alan Greenspan.

Following his swearing-in ceremony as Fed chairman in the month of August, Greenspan must have disappointed the president, as he raised the interest rates a notch, presumably to display his own credentials as an inflation fighter. This appeared to be a clear attempt to woo Wall Street, which was uneasy with Volcker's departure. Within weeks of Greenspan's arrival as the head of the Fed, financial brokers felt reassured. But then the stock market, which had been soaring since 1982, roared into a frenzied crash, shaking investors around the planet. Everyone wondered: Would the new chairman be up to the Herculean task of stabilizing the markets?

With the shareholder world in shambles, Greenspan swung into action to prevent the kind of economic collapse that had followed the much leaner 1929 crash. As Fed chairman, he had enormous power over interest rates and commercial banks. He flooded the financial world with money, made loans cheaply available to investors, and persuaded bankers across continents to follow his lead. The rest is history. Share prices stabilized around the globe in a matter of weeks, and economic calamity was averted. In fact, the Dow, along with global stock indexes, ended the year with a gain, mocking the October Massacre.

Black Monday presented one of the stiffest challenges to Chairman Greenspan, but he rose to the occasion, becoming a celebrity in the process. Henceforth, he became the darling of Wall Street and investors all over the planet. Greenspan had remained calm amidst financial jitters. Alan Murray of *The Wall Street Journal* commended Greenspan for "Passing a Test." Later, *Forbes* and other influential magazines described his handling of the crisis as "Greenspan's Finest Hour. He got on the horn and told the banks they had to lend money to Wall Street. Then he dropped money market rates and long-term rates fell sympathetically."[1] Still later, the Associated Press recalled: "The 1987 crash occurred only two months after Greenspan was sworn in as Fed chairman. He received a large amount of praise for his handling of that financial crisis."[2]

However, for Greenspan this was just the beginning of his climb to stardom on the global stage. Countless articles were written about his personality and life, heads of central banks envied him, politicians kowtowed to him, experts and economists, including Nobel laureates, lauded him.

Greenspan became a kind of cult figure. The world was infatuated with him, as the international media credited him with steering the globe through one economic disaster after another—the Mexican crisis, the Asian crisis, the Russian default, Brazil's crippling debt burden, and so on. His words became gospel to millions of people involved with share markets. With the world shaken by Russia's default on foreign debt in late 1998, *The Economist* headlined: "All eyes on Al," assuming that everyone knew "Al" meant Alan Greenspan.[3] On May 4, 1999, *The New York Times* enquired: "Who needs gold when we have Greenspan?"

In March 2000, *Time Europe* posed a silly question: "How many Federal Reserve chairmen does it take to change a light bulb?" Then it offered a tongue-in-cheek answer: "One. Greenspan holds the bulb, and the rest of the world revolves around him."[4] The same year, France decorated Greenspan with its highest award, the French Legion of Honor. Two years later, Queen Elizabeth II knighted him "in recognition of his outstanding contribution to global economic stability and the benefit that the UK has received from the wisdom and skill with which he has led the US Federal Reserve Board."[5] Like heads of state, kings, and princes, he received the red-carpet treatment wherever he went.

People called him maestro,[6] a visionary, the best economist ever. But who was this person who had catapulted into the spotlight from virtually nowhere? Did the world really know Alan Greenspan? Was there another side to his life and accomplishments, one that was not so pretty? In looking at his early influences, could you find a pattern of beliefs that lay underneath his choices? What were the hidden motivations behind his actions? Behind the soft outward face was there another, the face of a charmer, an opportunist, a social climber? It could explain how he had advanced so far without sufficient credentials; how his extraordinary career appeared to derive crucially not from merit but from favoritism and connections.

Greenspan first came into the national limelight when President Gerald Ford appointed him as the chairman of the Council of Economic Advisers (CEA) in 1974. Greenspan did not even have a Ph.D. at the time; nor had he penned anything pioneering to earn the recognition of his peers; yet he was able to rise to a position normally held by star economists, who usually hold a doctorate and are acclaimed for their original publications. The CEA chairman in 2004, for instance, was Dr. N. Gregory Mankiw, a Harvard University stalwart.

Greenspan's main credential in 1974 was his intimate friendship with then–Fed chairman Arthur Burns, who recommended his pal to the recently vacant position at the CEA.[7] Burns was once a professor at Columbia University, where Greenspan enrolled for his doctorate from 1950 to 1952. The pupil and the teacher grew close because of their ideological affinity. But Burns was an eminent economist, renowned for his seminal work on the business cycle, whereas Greenspan dropped out of school after two years of laborious night classes. Thus the student and the teacher were a study in contrast—one had gained worldwide recognition for his scholarship, the other was interested in becoming a business-man rather than an erudite professor.

Despite their differences, the two grew so close that Greenspan even held the first mortgage to Burns's home in Washington in 1970, playing the role of a banker.[8] When he was nominated as Fed chairman to become the world's foremost banker, this type of relationship proved more impor-tant than his meager banking experience. Greenspan, according to finan-cial journalist Maggie Mahar, won the nomination "first and foremost because he was a Republican."[9] Thus it can be argued, favoritism, not merit, nor genius, started Greenspan off to political prominence that eventually took him to stardom. Even Bob Woodward, a great admirer who called Greenspan maestro, could not help but note:

> Greenspan had long had the habit of reaching out to the politically powerful. . . . Greenspan cultivated relationships with any number of people involved with politics, always making people think he was on their side. . . . Greenspan's attentiveness—his willingness to take a phone call immediately, arrange breakfast or a private meeting the next day— left many with the feeling that they had an exceptional relationship with the chairman. He had *dozens of such relationships*.[10] (My italics)

Apparently *"dozens of such relationships"* with key people helped build the case for Greenspan in the minds of those who mattered, and enabled him to stay in power long enough to become by far the most celebrated Fed chairman ever. Greenspan can be seen to have two faces, one that reflects his true genius accurately, and the other that takes advantage of opportunities. This book focuses on the Greenspan that has managed to stay almost completely hidden from the world despite his public stature.

I will show you the real impact of Greenspan's influence, how he unwittingly effected a global crash and spread economic misery on our planet; my emphasis is on the duplicity underlying his actions that affect people in America and elsewhere. Whether it is Social Security, taxes, industrial deregulation, or financial markets, Greenspan sways it all. He has towered over far more than the world realizes.

This book is biographical but it also aims to be more. I will explore the economic theory and policies of this powerful man, including his legacy to us and to posterity. I begin with a chapter on Social Security, which charts a history of the effect of his tax proposals on the American people. The book goes on to describe his early life and the ideas that shaped his thinking and career. What I hope emerges is a more complete picture of Greenspan—an important figure in the financial world, yes, but also a proponent of an extreme form of rational selfishness, the stuff of his mentor, Ayn Rand—and of the extent of his power.

Once you get to know the real Greenspan, I think you will wonder along with me how he became such a powerful figure in the world, towering over heads of state for almost two decades; how he secured high-level positions and obtained the approval of Democratic senators, while opposing almost everything they cherished.

In the pages that follow, you will see a slow erosion of the gloss adorning Greenspan and discover the man's real views. You will see how he operates, and be privy to key moments in his business and political career, such as when the chairman cheered his mentor for denouncing President John F. Kennedy as a fascist dictator; paid lower wages to young female employees while getting personally involved with some and (in his own words) getting "better quality work" from them; denounced antitrust laws as "utter nonsense"; regarded big business as "America's persecuted minority"; and even enhanced the credibility of security analysts, some of whom later drew hefty fines from New York Attorney General Eliot Spitzer for research fraud. Throughout his suspect actions and views, he has nurtured ideas that blatantly contradict history. For instance, he backed the claim of supply-side economists that low income tax rates nourish economic growth, even though the decades with the highest post–World War II growth rates also had by far the highest tax rates in U.S. history.

Few of the chairman's theories, I will show, stand the test of history. For example, Greenspan would even abolish the minimum wage, claiming that it creates job losses, even though the 1960s, the decade with the highest minimum wage—$8 per hour in terms of 2004 prices—also had the lowest rate of unemployment since World War II, at 3.5 percent. The contrast should be apparent when you realize that the hourly minimum wage today is a pitiful $5.15, with a jobless rate in excess of 5 percent.

Few have any idea that Greenspan's theories blatantly contradict logic and historical facts. Not surprisingly, they first created a share-price bubble, and then hurtled the world into a devastating stock market collapse at the birth of the new millennium, wiping out, at one point, over $7 trillion of wealth.

Such discoveries and conclusions about Greenspan came as a shock to me, and I think they will shock you as well. I wondered how this man of intensely extremist views frequently bypassed the careful vetting process through which the Senate and the media normally examine the credentials of a president's nominee.

Chairman Greenspan has actually been actively involved in framing U.S. policy for more than three decades. People only know about him as the head of the Federal Reserve since 1987, but he shaped tax legislation as President Reagan's economic adviser from 1981 to 1983, and, as mentioned above, served as the CEA chairman under President Ford from 1974 to 1976. Greenspan has outlasted at least five presidents, and, in the process, become a legend—a folk hero to investors and lawmakers, but also an anathema to a growing number of critics. Some say he even dwarfs the president of the United States in terms of worldwide influence.

This book is a critical examination of the variety of contributions that Greenspan has made to the American and world economy. There is no doubt that he was and is a controversial figure, but so far no one has accused him of committing fraud. This is not fraud in the legal sense, but in the sense of trickery that seriously afflicted the finances of millions of families in America and, possibly, around the world. Few understand that the chairman has swayed U.S. tax laws as much as the supply of money and interest rates.

I will demonstrate that Greenspan has personally benefited from his tax policies, for which millions of Americans have paid the bill. This is not to suggest that his proposals were motivated purely by self-enrichment, but that the legislation and policies born from his advice brought him gains at the expense of working families.

Throughout the book I take great care in assigning motivation to Greenspan's actions. While it's difficult to read somone's intent, it's also true that actions mirror one's mind. There is a well known dictum in eco-nomics: Choice reveals preference. In the same way our endeavors reveal our thoughts and goals. Sometimes the circumstantial evidence behind a case is so copious and compelling that it easily leads us to definitive con-clusions. My claims regarding Greenspan are supported by his own words, actions, and, occasionally, by similar opinions voiced by others.

Greenspan's economics has extracted trillions of dollars in taxes from the American middle class and sharply enriched the rich, who are essentially people like himself and his friends—multimillionaires, politicians, and businessmen. Furthermore, I will argue that he, more than anybody else, is responsible for the prolonged stagnation in which the United States has been mired since the start of the new millennium. His policies have led to the pooring of America as well as the world, while a tiny minority has raked in millions, even billions, in profit. He may be a legendary figure in the eyes of many, but when you carefully explore what he has wrought, the aura of public reverence around him can evaporate quickly.

This book will show that because of Greenspan's beliefs or support for certain policies family income and real wages have declined for a broad swath of Americans, while CEOs have earned millions in stock options and capital gains; U.S. manufacturing has been decimated and the country is saddled with more than half a trillion dollars of trade deficit per year; nearly two million lucrative jobs have vanished since 2000, and millions of people have been downsized.

Many economists blame President Bush for the sorry state of the U.S. economy since 2001, but Greenspan's legacy is far longer and durable than that of the president. George Bush, in my opinion, has stran-gled the economy only in recent years, while the Fed chairman has been going at it since 1981, more than two decades ago.

In this book I will show that Greenspan has committed two types of fraud through his policies—one financial and the other intellectual. How has he gotten away with it? With, as financial writer John Cassidy says, "cozy links with the rich and powerful": "His [Greenspan's] ability to impress influential people, although rarely remarked upon is, in many ways, the key to his success."[11]

According to Cassidy, "Greenspan has told colleagues that he regards Clinton and Nixon as the two smartest presidents he has dealt with." This statement speaks volumes for the man's character and judgment, because in my view intelligence and integrity go together. As we all know, both of Greenspan's smartest presidents happen to be the only elected chief executives ever tainted by impeachment: Nixon resigned under the threat of impeachment, and Clinton was actually impeached.

In this book I will show how Greenspan's financial fraud began in 1983, when he persuaded lawmakers to overtax the American worker in advance and create a surplus in the Social Security Trust Fund that would meet the pension needs of baby boomers, who were expected to retire in large numbers around 2010. But the Trust Fund, after collecting $1.5 trillion of extra taxes from working families over two decades, has no surplus cash. Greenspan's financial or tax fraud actually had its origin in the massive tax cut of 1981 that he supported. That tax cut eventually had global consequences and led to regressive taxation in Europe and Canada, oppressing the poor.

Greenspan's intellectual fraud will also be explored. I will show how he apparently changed his theories, opinions, and statements time and again for his personal benefit, i.e., to stay entrenched as the chairman of the Federal Reserve, led the world into a stock market bubble, and lured millions of gullible savers and pensioners into share markets, which collapsed in the end. With the help of his intellect, he secured power for himself, but penury for countless others. Some of his theories lacked consistency and common sense.

All this constitutes the biographical part of this book; but there is also an analytical part, which examines the economic impact of Greenspan's Social Security and intellectual fraud, and shows that the fraud doubly hurt Americans. It imposed higher taxes on working families and also decimated their real wages and savings over time. For Europeans, it led to higher unemployment and the share price bubble, which burst disastrously in the end.

Greenspan, of course, has views on almost everything that matters to an economy. I will show that they are mostly suspect. He says he believes in free markets, yet, on closer examination, it looks as if he believes not in free markets but in free profits. He is a protectionist par excellence, because his proposals and beliefs almost always enhance the profits of big business, while shafting the average American. His policies have occasionally protected bankers and speculators from their own mistakes that threatened bankruptcy for some of them.

In almost every crisis that Greenspan has managed, speculators emerged with a smile and a fat bank balance. They earned high returns from risky investments in emerging markets, and when those investments soured, Greenspan dutifully stepped in and bailed out businesses and the afflicted countries.

Greenspan even rationalized the growing U.S. trade deficit, although it partly arises from the protectionist policies of America's trading partners. The deficit enriches big business and is an integral part of Greenspan's version of free trade as well as free profit. However, the idea of free profit is very different from the notion of free markets.

Greenspan rails against the minimum wage, and holds it partly responsible for joblessness. I will show that whenever the minimum wage went up in America, employment generally rose. The chairman argues that the share market euphoria of the 1990s resulted from the Internet revolution and high productivity growth; I will show that it resulted mostly from his policies that caused people's wages to lag behind productivity gains. There was, after all, no market mania in the 1950s and the 1960s, when GDP (gross domestic product) growth was much stronger.

Greenspan argues that the U.S. living standard has risen under his stewardship of the economy over two decades. I will use figures from the *Economic Report of the President* to demonstrate that the real wage of 80 percent of Americans fell in the 1980s and stagnated in the 1990s even though per-capita GDP went up. Even that rise pales before the corresponding rise from 1950 to 1970.

Greenspan asserts that budget deficits and excessive money growth raise long-term interest rates and thus harm the social interest. I will argue that he is right, but he has ignored his own views and pumped so much money into the economy in recent years that inflation could return in the near future. He used to be a deficit hawk like most Republican conservatives, and worried that tax cuts generally exacerbate the budget imbalance, but he would still like to perpetuate the Bush tax cuts that he once conceded were partly responsible for today's mega budget deficits.[12]

Greenspan even says that the stock market crash of 2000 and 2001 was not his fault. I will show you that I had predicted the exact timing of this crash in a 1999 book entitled *The Crash of the Millennium*, and said in advance that the economy, especially employment, would stagnate during the 2000s. Now I will argue that Greenspan's economics must be abandoned to raise American wages and jobs and restore prosperity around the world. In fact, I will offer a new economic paradigm to cure the global stagnation that has resulted from tax, trade, and monetary policies inspired by Greenspan. What I hope to accomplish is an urgent wake-up call about where we are headed; we need to open our eyes to who is at the helm of the global financial world and examine the effects of faulty economic policy in order to bring about reform.

On May 18, 2004, President Bush renominated Greenspan for yet another four-year term, and the Senate confirmed him a month later. By law the Fed chairman has to be a member of the board of governors of the Federal Reserve, with each governor's term limited to 14 years. After first serving out Volcker's board term, Greenspan was appointed a Fed governor in January 1992. So his term will terminate 14 years later in January 2006, but if the president chooses not to nominate anyone else, Greenspan could stay on as interim chairman till 2008. Until then, in view of what the man has already wrought, the global economy could remain stagnant and possibly be in a free fall. We need to act now, and introduce economic reforms to undo the vast damage that Greenspan has done.

At the point of this writing (February 2005), the United States, in the words of *The New York Times*, is "a country that needs to borrow $2 billion a day to stay afloat."[13] Yes indeed, two billion dollars every day. The country needs to borrow this much daily to support the dwindling living standard of the working American. Such is the vast economic misman-agement plaguing the nation and the global economy today. This is Alan Greenspan's chief bequest to the world. As business writer Louis Uchitelle puts it: "Foreigners are helping to make the indebtedness possi-ble by subsidizing consumer credit through more than $600 billion a year in loans to the United States. . . . America's mounting deficit in its over-seas transactions and its growing indebtedness to foreigners cannot be sustained."[14]

We have to diagnose the ailing U.S. economy and prescribe reforms. It is in this spirit that this work is presented to the public. The reforms that I offer are based on logic, history, and, above all, common sense. The first ten chapters present my prognosis of our economy's illness, and the final one, chapter 11, offers prescriptions. In short, we will have to aban-don a significant number of Greenspan's ideas to bring a semblance of sanity to our economy.

2

THE SOCIAL SECURITY
FRAUD

ccording to the Random House Dictionary, the word "fraud"
signifies a variety of meanings, including deceit, trickery, sharp
practice, or breach of confidence used to gain some unfair or
dishonest advantage. If this is all it takes to prove fraud, it will now be
shown that Greenspan has committed fraud on the American nation, by
which is meant the vast majority of people. I will demonstrate that
Greenspan has personally benefited from his tax advice and policies, for
which millions of workers have paid the bill. This is not to suggest that his
proposals were motivated purely by self-enrichment, but that the legislation born from his persuasion brought him gains at the expense of
working Americans.

If fraud is said to occur when a person promises one thing but then
turns around and acts to defeat that promise, then Greenspan is guilty of
perpetrating one. If two friends make a deal with you, and later join hands
to break it, then think of Greenspan as one such friend. In fact, in his case
the fraud turns out to be flagrant, because, as we shall see presently, it
started on the same day his assurances were enacted into law, and continues to this day.

Suppose your financial adviser earnestly told you some 25 years ago
to invest more money in his brokerage firm, so you could enjoy a decent
living upon retirement. You had misgivings about his advice, especially
because you could not afford the increased payments year after year, but
went along, willy-nilly, fearing that you could run out of money in your

old age. After all, there are plenty of sob stories regarding people facing hard times in their golden years. So you agreed to make certain sacrifices in your youth, and parked growing amounts of money in the financial firm controlled by your adviser. "Your money," he declared sincerely, "is totally safe and will only accumulate over time. Otherwise, you could face a bleak future, at a time when you're old and fragile."

Now, a quarter century later, he informs you he won't be able to pay you the promised benefits. He simply doesn't have the money. Instead of investing your savings into income-producing assets, he has mostly frittered away the funds by giving hefty paychecks to himself and his friends. You are shocked, to say the least. You cry foul: this is bloody murder, an outright fraud. "How could I have been duped by this charlatan? Why did I keep my eyes closed for all these years, while a robbery was plainly being committed?"

Believe me, something like this has happened to the Social Security Trust Fund, the popular pension program that you count on for retirement. And the master culprit, who made it all possible, is none other than the legendary figure, Bob Woodward's "maestro"—Alan Greenspan. Of course, the maestro had plenty of help from multihued politicians—from President Reagan to Democratic speaker of the House of Representatives Tip O'Neill, to the Republican Senate majority leader Howard Baker. But Greenspan was the ringleader, and over the years politicians came and went, but his star only grew brighter until he became arguably the most powerful man in the government of the United States.

Greenspan started a multiparty scheme that ended up fleecing the American people, involving the media, the Democrats, and the Republicans, who did not question or foresee its ill effects. Sadly, the scheme turned into a scam that has continued to this day, and could last as far as the eye can see, unless the public screams foul and compels lawmakers to repeal it.

Here's how it all began. Let's backtrack in time and return to the year 1981, with high inflation, unemployment, and growing budget shortfalls in the background. Upon President Reagan's urging, Congress had just enacted the famous, or infamous, tax cut of 1981. The legislation, which arose from a hard-fought battle between the Democratic and Republican members of Congress, trimmed the income tax rates by an average of 25 percent over the next three years. In addition, the legislation cut the corporate income tax slightly, from 46 percent to 45 percent, but businesses got enough breaks that their tax burden declined sharply.

During the election campaign the year before, with Greenspan among others advising him, Reagan had asserted that he would cut taxes, increase defense spending, and still balance the government budget. The inflation surge of the 1970s had put a broad swath of Americans into higher tax brackets, and people felt oppressed by the rising tax burden. But with high joblessness, tax receipts fell perennially short of government spending, thus swelling the budget deficit. At the same time, the Republicans customarily accused the Democrats of neglecting the nation's defense needs even as the Soviet Union grew stronger. It was against such a backdrop that Reagan made his promises to capture the White House.

Some, especially George H. W. Bush, Reagan's rival in the Republican primaries, had regarded such promises as "voodoo economics," but in 1981 the president got his wish list with the help of Congress, which at the time was a chamber divided, with Republicans controlling the Senate and the Democrats controlling the House. However, the laws of arithmetic were not as kind to him as the lawmakers. He had inherited a budget deficit of some $74 billion, or 2.5 percent of the GDP, from his predecessor, Jimmy Carter. Following the tax cuts enacted in mid-1981, the deficit, contrary to the president's rhetoric and expectations, began to soar and ballooned to over $200 billion by the end of 1983.[1]

The budget shortfall was, and is, unprecedented. It soared to as much as 6 percent of the nation's output. The government borrowed 25 cents for every dollar it spent. Financial markets were especially alarmed at these numbers, and interest rates went sky high. Business and mortgage loans were hard to get, and unaffordable.

Most economists blamed the budget shortfall for those giant interest rates, which led to the worst recession since the 1930s. Some of the budget shortfall occurred because of a lingering recession that Reagan had inherited from his predecessor, Jimmy Carter, but a large portion arose from the massive reduction in taxes paid by wealthy individuals and corporations. The president needed revenues to trim the deficit, bring down the interest rates, and improve his chances for reelection.

Enter Alan Greenspan, who was an affluent New York businessman-cum-economist at the time. He had served as the CEA chairman under President Ford and was very popular with Republican bigwigs and politicians. He had also helped draft Reagan's economic-agenda speech during the election campaign. Few realize that voodoo economics was partly the handiwork of none other than Mr. Greenspan, who was perhaps the most influential among all of Reagan's economic advisers, both before and after the election. He was constantly sought-after on the lecture circuit and delivered as many as 80 speeches a year, his fee ranging from $10,000 to $40,000 per lecture.[2] In today's dollars, that fee averages some $50,000.

Greenspan headed his own consulting firm, Townsend-Greenspan, and was on the corporate boards of Alcoa, Mobil Oil, Morgan Guaranty, and General Foods.[3] Because of his enthusiastic and influential support for the Reagan program, before and after the election, the tax law of 1981 should be called the Reagan–Greenspan tax cut. See what columnist Steve Rattner wrote about the maestro's role in that legislation: "In the week or so surrounding the disclosure of President Reagan's economic package, Alan Greenspan, by his own account, made five separate trips to Washington, appeared on seven television news programs and attended countless White House meetings, [and] has emerged as a major outside influence on Mr. Reagan's economic policy."[4] (The importance of this point will become clear later.) At the time, in jest, Greenspan was known as Reagan's "out-house" adviser, in contrast to an in-house adviser.[5]

In December 1981, the president selected Greenspan to chair a blue ribbon commission, ostensibly to save a popular retirement program, called the Social Security system, which was supposedly facing a grave crisis. The selection was somewhat odd, because Greenspan was not particularly fond of the Social Security program. He made this clear to *The New York Times* in 1983 when he blurted out that he did not "like the present Social Security system," and found the institution unnecessary for an "ideal society."[6] He was also known as a critic of the New Deal, of which the retirement program was perhaps the foremost accomplishment. He was clearly not an ideal choice to head the Social Security commission.

But Reagan needed a man who shared his beliefs; the president was confident that Greenspan, who had been his economic consultant and a rich man himself, wouldn't do anything to harm the interests of the affluent, whose taxes had been trimmed just six months before. Even though the economy had started to recover toward the end of 1982, the unemployment rate exceeded 10 percent, and the federal deficit had jumped by 75 percent over its level in 1980.

Social Security is perhaps the most popular program that the government offers to the American people. It owes its origin to the Great Depression, when millions of people were homeless, pensionless, and unemployed. It was the brainchild of President Franklin Delano Roosevelt (FDR) in the 1930s. FDR signed the Social Security Act in 1935 and founded a system that has been a lifeline to the elderly ever since. The act established a program to ensure that retirees will never again have to starve or live in the streets. It provided for a payroll tax designed to build a trust fund and to make the program self-sufficient.

A lot has changed since 1935. The program started out small, but grew tall, taller, and tallest. Today it is the bedrock of the American retirement system. A Social Security pension can mean a difference between life and death for the elderly, who, in general, have meager savings of their own. When the program started, the payroll tax was just 2 percent, shared equally by the employer and the employee. It was imposed on the first $3,000 of a worker's earnings. With such a low tax rate, the system was not an undue burden on employees at its beginning, but the tax gradually rose over the years as people retired in growing numbers.

The Social Security Trust Fund, by and large, had been running a small surplus ever since its inception, its tax receipts usually exceeding its payment in retirement benefits. However, the same was not true of the general federal budget, which was increasingly in deficit from the early 1950s. At first this deficit was small, but after 1965, when the Vietnam War came into full swing, the deficiency became embarrassingly large for the government.

From 1969 on, the Social Security surplus was included in what is known as the unified budget, which then showed a smaller shortfall. Such a transformation of the budget process meant that the government's deficit looked smaller than it really was. But it also meant that the retirement program, being a part of the unified budget, could call upon the government's general revenues available from other taxes. In 1969, for instance, the unified budget showed a minor surplus of $3 billion, but without the Social Security cash, it would have been in arrears for half a billion.

The Greenspan commission was a motley assembly of 15 men and women with diverse interests, beliefs, and constituencies. It was bipartisan, consisting of eight Republicans and seven Democrats. Besides union leader Lane Kirkland, it included two well-known senators, Robert Dole and Daniel Patrick Moynihan, and two business leaders from major corporations. Its initial assignment was to save the Social Security system, but as the general budget went into an unprecedented shortfall, it became clear that revenues were desperately needed not just for Social Security but also for the federal government, whose deficit was actually ten times the deficit of the retirement program.

In 1982, the Trust Fund borrowed $12 billion from another federal agency to pay its benefits, but the government borrowed $128 billion from financial markets to cover its deficiency. Apparently it became the commission's job to find new sources of revenue without reversing the income and corporate tax cuts.

Greenspan faced a grand task from the beginning. His commission went nowhere for the first 12 months. Some of its members, mostly the Democrats, wanted to raise taxes; others, mostly Greenspan and the Republicans, sought cuts in benefits; some felt that the Treasury should use general revenues, which meant either using the income tax receipts or borrowing from credit markets. This last option was ruled out by Greenspan. As an economist he believed in laissez-faire, minimum, if any, government regulation, a balanced federal budget, and, if possible, small income tax rates. The ballooning budget deficit had required some rise in taxes even in 1982, but the income levies had been spared. Reagan called these new taxes "revenue enhancements," perhaps because they taxed gasoline but not incomes.[7] This way he could never be accused of raising taxes.

By early 1983, however, Greenspan was convinced that the solvency of the retirement program lay in a combination of increased Social Security fees and lower benefits. Reduced benefits alone were not going to bring the long-term deficit into balance. Columnist Deborah Rankin affirmed his position in this way: "Alan Greenspan said a week ago that faster payroll tax increases and reduced cost-of-living adjustments for beneficiaries are needed."[8]

The Reagan–Greenspan theology required that the income levies remain small even if it became necessary to coax money out of the destitute, because this is essentially what the commission proposed in 1983. Instead of the general budget that actually faced a massive deficit, the commission insisted that the Social Security Trust Fund faced a giant shortfall, some 30 to 75 years into the future, when baby boomers would retire in large numbers. Never mind that in 1983 itself, the Trust Fund's receipts began to rise because of rising employment, while the general budget suffered an even larger deficit of $208 billion.

In fact, by the end of the year, the Fund earned a small surplus. But the Greenspan commission relied on "forecasts" that showed a gargantuan deficit looming in the Fund, not five to ten years hence, but more than half a century later. It proposed eliminating the Social Security deficit expected from 1983 all the way to 2056 by overtaxing workers in advance, and generating an adequate surplus in the process.

Until then the Trust Fund had been a pay-as-you-go system. Basically, the government collected and paid out roughly equal amounts of money in Social Security taxes and benefits. This kept the payroll tax burden manageable for small businesses and their employees. Greenspan and his cohorts suggested that the Social Security fees be raised sharply, so that enough funds could accumulate to meet the projected shortfall in the twenty-first century. They, in effect, proposed to enhance the taxes for those who could least afford them.

The Social Security tax applies equally to the minimum-wage earner and millionaires. Of all the levies, this is the most regressive, because it has a fixed rate and a ceiling on the taxable wage base. In 2004, for instance, someone who earned a wage base of $87,900 was taxed at the rate of 6.2 percent, forking out $5,450 in the process. But financier Warren Buffett, with millions of dollars in income, also paid the same amount of tax.

The Greenspan proposal would prove to be a crippling burden for the poor and the self-employed, because it sought to lift rates over and above those provided by a 1977 law. Today, a full-time minimum-wage earner, working for 2,000 hours annually at a wage of $5.15 per hour, earns about $10,000 annually. On that she has to pay a Social Security and Medicare tax of 7.65 percent, or $765, which leaves her with $9,235. Add to this a state and local sales tax averaging 8 percent in big cities, and she forks over another $739 to meet her minimal consumption.

This sum of over $1,500 in taxes can make a difference between homelessness and living in an apartment, between three meals a day and malnourishment, between a doctor visit and living with illness. This is why the commission's tax proposals amounted to coaxing money out of the destitute, i.e., the millions who subsist on the minimum wage.

A worse outcome awaited those working for themselves. Today, a self-employed individual, earning $30,000 a year, has to pay nearly 15 percent in Social Security taxes. Once $4,500 is deducted in self-employment contributions, an individual is left with little to support a family, especially when his income is subject to the sales and income tax as well.

Somehow Greenspan was able to convince his bipartisan commission and then Congress to go along with his scheme. So it was that, despite the somewhat muted objections of the poor and middle-income taxpayers, his tax proposals were enacted as Social Security Amendments in April 1983. It was a major overhaul of the system. The legislation postponed cost-of-living benefit increases for six months, changed the indexing of benefits to once a year instead of twice, raised the payroll tax slightly but the self-employment tax sharply, forced new federal employees to join the system, increased the retirement age gradually from 65 to 67 by 2027, and imposed the federal income tax on part of the Social Security benefits of high-income retirees.

The Social Security tax called FICA (Federal Insurance Contribution Act) is the sum of two tax rates, one for hospital insurance (HI) and the other for retirement and disability (OASDI, or Old Age Survivor and Disability Insurance). The HI rate applies to a person's entire earned income, whereas the other rate applies to a certain wage base. Actually the OASDI rate was set to rise in steps from a 1977 law, but its increase was accelerated by a year in the 1983 law. This itself was not a major change; what the 1983 act also did was to sharply increase the tax rate for the self-employed.

In 1980, the payroll tax applied to the first $25,900 of a person's earnings. So the maximum taxable wage base that year was $25,900, which jumped to $87,900 by 2004. Thus the OASDI tax increase of 1977 and 1983 hit the average worker with a double-edged razor. It accelerated the tax rate schedule on the one hand, and increased the maximum taxable earnings on the other. The wage base was also linked to the growth of the average wage per year, ensuring that a worker's Social Security contribution could rise annually. With prices rising year after year, salaries have been consistently increasing for most employees, and so has the taxable wage base.

No wonder the Trust Fund produced over $1.5 trillion surplus in just two decades, between 1984 and 2004, and if it had been properly invested, say, in AAA corporate bonds, which offered double-digit yields in the 1980s, it could have earned another trillion by now.

FICA applies equally to employers, who in 2004 had to pay the same 7.65 percent rate on the first $87,900 of an employee's earnings. For the self-employed, the Social Security tax has become a crippling burden, because their incomes are subject to an almost double rate, or 15.3 percent, coupled with rebates that are tiny enough to be ignored. FICA and the self-employment tax are two different types of levies, but today they are generally lumped together as payroll taxes.[9]

The 1983 legislation also stipulated that starting from 1992, the proceeds of the Trust Fund would be separated from the general budget and not made part of the unified budget. It reconfirmed the long-established principle that the government was merely a middleman collecting levies from workers and then transferring them to retirees. The Fund thus was not the government's property, but belonged to average Americans, and its projected surplus was to be preserved for the baby boomers, who were expected to retire in large numbers after 2010.

Even though the new Social Security act had vocal bipartisan support, the Democrats were somewhat subdued, while the Republicans were euphoric. At its signing ceremony, President Reagan hailed it as "a monument to the spirit of compassion and commitment that unites us as a people. . . . The changes in the legislation will allow Social Security to age as gracefully as all of us hope to do ourselves, without becoming an overwhelming burden on generations to come." Democratic House Speaker Tip O'Neill, who stood nearby, pitched in and echoed the effusive spirit of the congregation: "It shows, as the president said, the system does work. This is a happy day for America."[10] It would actually turn out to be a day of infamy.

WHY THE FRAUD?

Tax increases occur all the time, and are seldom declared fraudulent, even though some of them bear heavily on the poor. The sales and gasoline taxes are cases in point. Everybody has to pay them equally regardless of their income levels. Then why was this, the 1983 tax act, a horrendous deception?

Normally, tax revenues are used for their avowed purpose. When Houston needed to build a stadium for its football team, it imposed a special sales tax and used the revenue to build the façade. When a city such as New York raises its school tax, the money goes to improve the curriculum. In other words, the taxpayers fork out money from one hand, and receive benefits from the other. But if the sales tax was raised for the public benefit and its proceeds went into the pockets of city officials, then it would be fraud. It would also be fraud if the money made little improvement to the schools but was diverted to reduce the taxes paid mainly by the class of people who had financed the election of the authorities.

This is essentially what happened with the Trust Fund. From the moment the new Social Security tax went into effect, its surplus revenue was used primarily, if not completely, to pay for the shortfall in the general federal budget. Indeed this was done as a matter of routine.

All the promises that Greenspan, Reagan, and Congress had given with great sincerity to the American people were forgotten in a hurry. There was no lockbox in which the Social Security money could be stashed away from predatory presidents and lawmakers to accumulate for future retirees. As a result, the Fund today has a few billion dollars of cash to meet its current obligations. For the rest, it has $1.5 trillion of non-marketable government IOUs, while the government itself has a deficit of nearly $420 billion. In other words, after the government overtaxed the average American worker for more than two decades, we are back to where we were in 1983.

How do we know this happened? Let's go to the website of the Social Security Administration—www.ssa.gov—to get the answer. Once inside the website, click on "Social Security Trustees 2004 Report" in the side-bar to the left, then on "text on portable document," then on "Table of Contents," and finally on "VI. Appendicies." It takes a little effort to find the information, but the reward is well worth it to get to the bottom of the issue in question.

Scroll down until you come across Table VI.A5, which deals with assets of the OASI Trust Fund, in thousands (OASI stands for Old Age Survivors Insurance and is part of the OASDI fund). The leftmost column reads as "Obligations sold to the trust fund (special issues)." These are all special securities that the United States Treasury sells to the Social Security Administration in exchange for its revenues. They are special all right, because they cannot be sold in the bond market for cold cash. Such are primarily the assets of this trust fund. The retirees, of course, have to be paid in cash, which appears way at the bottom of this table as "undisbursed balances." At the beginning of 2004, such balances amounted to $219 million, out of the total assets of $1.36 trillion.

Going to Table VI.A6 yields the same information about the DI (Disability Insurance) Trust Fund. Its undisbursed balances were $182 million, with total assets of $175 billion. The combined OASDI Trust Fund thus had about $1.5 trillion in assets, of which undisbursed balances totaled less than half a billion dollars—just shy of a day's worth of hard cash benefits. In other words almost the entire amount was and is worthless, because the government itself lives in hock, with a total debt exceeding $6 trillion, rising by nearly half a trillion a year. A trillion here, a trillion there, and soon you're talking about real money.

Such is the pitiful state of the combined Social Security Trust Fund. Most Americans nowadays live from paycheck to paycheck. So does their retirement system. Where has all the money gone?

A lot has happened since the "revenue enhancement" of 1983. The tax system has been churned time and again, in the name of promoting the social good, which has usually meant more dollars for the opulent. From all this churning, one point is crystal clear. The Social Security surplus simply financed the tax cuts of rich individuals and corporations. Greenspan paid lower taxes, and so did Mr. Reagan, the lawmakers, and their financiers, but millions of other Americans—the destitute, the middle class, the self-employed, the needy—saw a giant rise in their tax bills.

The likes of GM, IBM, Exxon, Enron, and their bosses wallowed in the government's largesse, while the downtrodden and the penniless, including those earning the subsistence wage, footed the bill. The purpose of the 1983 tax act was to accumulate funds over the coming years so Social Security would remain solvent, but from day one, it was used to enhance the after-tax income of Mr. Greenspan and those in his income class.

Greenspan knew, or should have known, that the projected surplus in the Trust Fund would be spent immediately to pay for the federal short-fall, which was unprecedented at the time. He knew that the government, hungry for revenues, would spend every penny of the projected Social Security surplus. Has the U.S. government ever saved money? In August 1983 itself, shortly after the enactment of the tax increase, Greenspan lamented that the government has "a regrettable tendency to spend revenues when we have them."[11] Its short-term surpluses, rare and evanescent, have always been used primarily to finance the tax cuts of wealthy individuals and corporations. This happened in the 1920s, and more recently between 2001 and 2003.

The retirement system was looted from the first day the surplus came into being, because the 1983 act itself gave Congress a free hand to spend the Trust Fund's money until 1992, when the Social Security finances were to be separated from the unified budget. This provision in fact contradicted the Greenspan commission, which had said that

> a majority of the members of the National Commission recommends that the operations of the . . . Trust Funds should be removed from the unified budget. . . . The National Commission believes that changes in the Social Security program should be made only for programmatic reasons, and *not for purposes of balancing the budget*. . . . The majority of the National Commission believes—as a broad general principle—that it

would be logical to have the Social Security Administration be *a separate independent agency*, perhaps headed by a bipartisan board.[12] (My italics)

Thus Greenspan and his commission, in my view, made in effect a solemn promise not to use the retirement system's funds to balance the general budget. Yet the promise was broken by all parties involved in the subsequent legislation the day it went into effect.

The very fact that the law allowed the government to include the Social Security surplus in the general budget for eight long years from 1984 to 1992 itself meant that politicians had a secret agenda that was not disclosed to the public. Yet Mr. Greenspan went along with this provision, which was pivotal to his recommendations to create and preserve the surplus for retiring baby boomers. In a Congressional hearing, he had testified that most members who backed the commission's recommendations were uneasy about them, but in the end they compromised and supported the provisions as a package. Even though "all of the individual components" of the plan were not acceptable to them, he had said, "we support them" in their entirety.[13]

Greenspan himself had favored amending the cost-of-living formula to trim the future growth of benefits, but the commission had rejected his plea.[14] His testimony that "we support them" implied that he no longer insisted on adjusting the inflation formula.

The Social Security act was a legal and moral compact between the politicians and the average American worker. The lawmakers and other supporters of the legislation, in effect, declared: "You pay higher taxes now in exchange for guaranteed benefits at the time you retire." Whatever reservations any lawmaker or a commission member had were to be forgotten from the day the new law was signed.

First by making recommendations, and then by testifying on their behalf, Greenspan made a solemn promise to the Americans, calling on them to make sacrifices to secure their retirement future. He had effectively offered a deal to the people that their benefits would be protected in exchange for sharply higher taxes. See what columnist David Francis wrote on October 3, 1983: "Worrying about your Social Security pension? Don't, says Alan Greenspan."[15] *The Washington Post* had already declared him a hero "in the fight to rescue Social Security."[16]

Greenspan glowed in the limelight of the so-called Social Security reform, because he seemed to have saved the pension system from "collapse." At least, that's what the public believed. The retirement legislation was his baby, from start to end. Even though Greenspan had only made some recommendations, and then testified for them later, he was, more than anyone else, responsible for the Social Security act of 1983. His assurances and suggestions, mostly embodied in the law, acquired an aura of solid promises that earned him tremendous prestige. He became one of the most sought-after men in America. The media courted him; beautiful women dated him even though he was nearing 60; and audiences paid big fees to listen to him. He was the man of the hour, who had solved the thorny Social Security dilemma.

Alas, just six months after the enactment of new taxes, Mr. Greenspan reneged on his solemn promise. He began to lament that the federal budget was out of control because of the soaring cost of pension programs. On October 26, 1983, reporter Harry Ellis quoted Greenspan: "The budget deficit is the symptom of a more deep-seated problem—the breaking down of the fiscal process in this country." So, what was the solution? "One step, says Greenspan, would be to reduce benefit increases in all entitlement programs," by indexing them "to the consumer price index minus 3 percent. . . . This, he says, would result in a 3 percent benefit reduction in real terms for social security and federal pension recipients, compared with the present system."[17]

Greenspan's rush to reduce the Social Security benefits seems to have crossed the limits of outrage. The ink from the president's signatures on the 1983 bill is still wet, and the chief proponent of that law already wants to trim the purchasing power of the benefits by as much as 3 percent a year. Politicians had effectively crushed the spirit of the Greenspan commission's report by postponing the separation of the Trust Fund from the general budget by eight years, and here Greenspan talked about undermining that law even before it went into effect in 1984. The commission had rejected his plea for amending the inflation-indexing formula, and in his Congressional testimony he had supported the entire compromise package, but now that new taxes had been enacted, he felt free to break the deal he had made with the American people. Thus Greenspan wanted the government to have its cake and eat it too.

Millions of American workers including the destitute were already doomed to face soaring tax bills that could mean homelessness and malnourishment for some, and Mr. Greenspan was busy reneging on his promise with impunity. Why? Why did the maestro seek to undermine a major provision of the new legislation?

There was a pressing reason. Greenspan was convinced that the budget deficit had to be trimmed immediately to bring down the interest rate. The Social Security act would bring in new revenues but not right away, and it could take a long time before tax receipts were high enough to make a dent in budget shortfalls that were projected far into the future. However, if benefits could be trimmed even as new revenues appeared, the budget deficit would fall faster and thus accelerate the interest-rate fall.

This is precisely why Greenspan called for a cut in retirement benefits even before the new law went into effect. It didn't seem to bother him that he was breaking all the pledges he had made in his Congressional testimony and the commission's report, because higher payroll taxes had been enacted already, and he could safely, even though erroneously, blame the gargantuan budget deficit on the high cost of Social Security.

This was just the beginning of his vitriol against the retirement system. On January 3, 1985, reporter Jonathan Fuerbringer wrote that Alan Greenspan among "three top Presidential economic advisers told Congress today that a cut in the cost-of-living increase for Social Security recipients must be part of any package to reduce the Federal deficit."[18] But why? Social Security was and is an independent program financed by its own taxes; it had nothing to do with the general budget deficit, which was the byproduct of the income and corporate tax cuts of 1981. And what about the legal and moral compact between the government and the American people?

SOCIAL SECURITY TAXES AND THE BUDGET DEFICIT

Now you can see what the real purpose of the Social Security act was in Greenspan's mind. It was primarily to lower the federal budget deficit, which worried him because it kept the interest rates high and thus crippled the economy. In 1983, the federal budget was in the red by over $200 billion. The 30-year mortgage for a home was close to its peak, a hefty 15 percent. Few homes and cars were selling, and the unemployment rate exceeded 9 percent.

Most economists blamed the economic malaise on the federal deficit that seemed to be out of control, and it was clear it had to be trimmed to lower the long-term interest rate. Interest rates are also determined by the nation's monetary policy, which is in the care of the Federal Reserve System (in short the Fed). In the early 1980s the Fed chairman was Paul Volcker, who could have opened the money pump, eased credit conditions, and possibly brought the interest rate down. But Volcker's hands were tied by giant inflation rates prevailing at the time.

President Reagan had inherited a lousy economy from his predecessor, Jimmy Carter. The country was ravaged by stagflation, which combines a stagnant economy with high inflation. Most experts believed—and rightly so—that the deficit financing of the 1970s along with giant rises in oil prices had basically crushed the American economy, which in 1980 faced a jobless rate of 7 percent plus an inflation rate of 13.5 percent. This was a double whammy, and few painless cures were in sight.

Deficit financing occurs when the Fed prints money to finance, wholly or partially, the government's budget deficit. Since such policy had already ravaged the economy, a further dosage, in Volcker's view, could prove suicidal. That's why the gigantic interest rates of the early 1980s got no help from monetary policy.

The only alternative left was to eliminate or cut the budget deficit and thus lower the demand for borrowing in credit markets. This would trim the interest rate, which is the price of credit, because when the demand for something falls, its price also falls. Thus falling government demand for borrowing, especially in an inflationary environment, means visibly lower interest rates, and conversely.

This is what in fact Reagan had promised to do during the election campaign. He wanted to trim the budget deficit, but he and his like-minded advisers such as Greenspan, Jack Kemp, and Martin Feldstein, among others, thought the solution for the budget imbroglio lay in huge cuts in corporate and income taxes. After such cuts were enacted in 1981, the deficit, not surprisingly, went up and up, because the income and corporate tax receipts simply plummeted. Add to this the minor Social Security deficit, and the government red ink soared to unprecedented heights, which could not but lift the already lofty interest rates.

Reagan's revenue enhancement of 1982 through new excise and gasoline taxes was merely a band-aid to the festering wound, and did little to ease the budget mess, which kept swelling. In 1981, the government borrowed 12 cents out of every dollar it spent; in 1982, it borrowed nearly the same; but in 1983, it borrowed as much as 25 cents for a dollar of spending. Such was the background in which the Greenspan commission and the lawmakers operated to solve the Social Security problem, which was minor and clearly paled before the horrendous budget shortfall.[19]

The Trust Fund had a series of deficits from 1975 to 1981, but they were miniscule relative to the federal deficit. The Social Security arrears arose for two reasons. Benefits soared because of raging inflation, as they were linked to the cost-of-living; at the same time, revenue fell because of increasing unemployment, and both reasons tended to compound the Social Security arrears.

But by December 1982, the inflation rate over the previous 12 months had declined sharply to just 3.8 percent, so the Social Security deficit was beginning to cure itself. In fact, as inflation fell dramatically and jobless-ness slowly, the Fund's deficit turned around and moved toward a surplus even before the infamous Social Security act of 1983 went into effect the following year. The Fund did not even have to borrow money from credit markets, because its assets had generally remained positive. This cushion had steadily dwindled after 1975, but it was not negative.[20]

Even the Greenspan commission put the cost of salvaging the Trust Fund from 1983 through 1989 at just $168 billion, which meant that, even if the economy remained stagnant, only $24 billion per year was needed to meet the Social Security short fall until the end of the decade.[21] This could have been done through minor and temporary adjustments in the laws already passed to raise more revenue or through public borrow-ing, rather than the massive and permanent tax rise of the 1983 act. If the government could borrow $200 billion for operating expenses, it could have easily borrowed another $24 billion for the retirement program.

In any case, by itself the Trust Fund swiftly moved toward solvency after 1982, as the economy began to expand. It was the federal budget that faced a massive shortfall, especially after 1981, when the Reagan–Greenspan tax cuts were enacted. It was the federal government that needed to borrow vast sums, not the retirement program. But, as best-sell-ing author David Johnston reminds us: "In 1983, though, public atten-tion was diverted from the immediate fiscal crisis by reports out of Washington that Social Security was in trouble, deep trouble."[22]

Why was the government so alarmed not by its own insolvency but that of the Social Security program? We can only speculate at politicians' motives from what transpired, because lawmakers are seldom accused of openness and clarity.

Apparently both the Democrats and Republicans conspired for their own reasons to make a mountain out of the molehill of the Social Security issue. For the Republicans the relentless drumbeat about the pension problem and the subsequent establishment of the Greenspan commission provided a diversion from the budget mess they had exacerbated with their tax cuts. Reagan's pre-election promise to balance the budget through his tax plan had turned on its head as the federal red ink soared. So the Social Security issue offered the public a convenient distraction.

To the Democrats the Social Security dilemma presented a thick club with which they could bludgeon their opponents during debates and election campaigns. In fact, this is what they did to great advantage as they accused the Republicans of doing nothing about the Social Security problem and reaped a net gain of 26 seats in the House in the 1982 mid-term elections.

Members of both parties had conspired to give birth to the Social Security "monster," which they had to tame or else risk dethronement from mobs at the ballot box. This is precisely why Democratic Senator Moynihan and Republican Senator Dole, along with President Reagan, kept prodding Greenspan to offer a compromise package for the so-called Social Security reform that was totally unnecessary at the time. Once the genie had been let out of the bottle, there was no alternative but to pacify it, even if it meant fooling the gullible public and the media. The Social Security issue was phony, pure and simple.

A *Washington Post* article by Juan Williams and Spencer Rich captures the ethos underlying the compromise offered by the Greenspan commission report:

> For some Democrats, the decision to seek a compromise was fueled by fear they would be seen by the public as blocking a compromise for political reasons. . . . White House willingness to compromise was sparked by fear that Democrats would use the issue to continue attacking the president as the foe of Social Security. Another White House motive was a desire to . . . *lower the federal deficit.*[23] (My italics)

The italicized part of this quote brings us to the purpose of the entire Social Security campaign, namely to lower the budget deficit by means of raising anything but the income and corporate tax. This was the main reason why both parties, along with Mr. Greenspan and the president, enthusiastically endorsed the recommendations of the Greenspan commission. How can we be so sure about their motives, when they are always disguised? Actions speak louder than words. Their motives would become crystal clear later, in 1990, when both parties rejected a proposed bill to lower the payroll tax.

The federal budget was running amuck following that fateful Reagan–Greenspan tax cut (see note 19 and accompanying Table N.3). The Republicans stealthily wanted to raise taxes to bring the budget under control, but they would have to swallow their pride by conceding they had made a fatal mistake in 1981 by slashing the income and corporate tax. Their ideology was also dead set against such action, but the payroll tax rise could be presented as salvation for the entire Social Security system, which would then solve their ideological dilemma. In fact, President Reagan usually avoided mentioning the term "payroll tax," preferring to emphasize the solvency of the Social Security program. In public the Republicans categorically rejected the payroll tax hike, but they hoped covertly that the Democrats would demand one to protect the retirement benefits.

The Democrats were unable to see through the Republican ruse, and did indeed insist on higher Social Security taxes, so long as the benefits were preserved. They too had supported the 1981 tax cut and, as mentioned above, were afraid of the consequences of non-compromise. As columnist David Broder put it: The compromise "represented a stark fear of the implications of failure. 'How many more disasters can we afford?' was the rhetorical question of one commission member, Sen. Daniel P. Moynihan."[24] What disaster? The Trust Fund was on its way to mending itself. Its red ink was the result of high unemployment, which lowered its revenues, and high inflation, which increased its cost-of-living benefits.

In the long run, spanning almost two centuries, the U.S. jobless rate has approximated 4.5 percent, and the inflation rate 3 percent. Both sources of the minor Social Security problem would have vanished over time either automatically or by means of suitable monetary and fiscal policies. In fact, as the economy created new jobs in 1983, the Social Security deficit vanished in a hurry. Congress had already passed the Reagan–Greenspan tax cut, which was designed to create jobs and bring inflation under control. That legislation itself could have solved the Social Security crisis over time. There was absolutely no need to create a phony issue, alarm the public and frighten it into accepting a gargantuan rise in payroll taxes.

What about all those baby boomers retiring in large numbers in the twenty-first century? The pay-as-you-go Social Security system had worked with minor glitches until 1983, and it could have done the job in the future as well. We will discuss this issue in detail in chapter 11.

For now, let's say that the program's deficit in 1983 did not portend disaster for the future of the retirement system. It was a short-term blip that at most would have required the Social Security Administration to borrow from the public for a few years, until its finances improved.

Senator Moynihan, somewhat unintentionally, let the ugly secret of the Greenspan commission out in an op-ed piece in *The New York Times* in May 1988. He described how Reagan's budget director, David Stockman, had issued a somber warning in January 1983 that Social Security was about to face the "most devastating bankruptcy in history," a groundless warning that had found a lot of believers; how "a scare campaign of vicious proportions" had been occurring for some time; how that had prompted some commission members to huddle together for 12 days in Blair House, a presidential office; and how they had come to an agreement on the day the commission was supposed to issue its final report. He went on:

> Almost everyone involved knew by then that the Administration had got the nation's finances in terrible shape. . . . There would be $200 billion budget deficits "as far as the eye could see." The national debt would triple in eight years. And President Reagan was not going to do anything to prevent it. *And so we would.*[25] (My italics)

The commission's secret was finally out. It was all about balancing the budget and controlling the national debt on the back of the American worker; "the nation's finances were in terrible shape," and the president couldn't care less, so they had to raise the payroll taxes. Dire warnings about Social Security's solvency issued by David Stockman and the Greenspan commission were mere pretexts, but they petrified a lot of people. So the commission had to act.

The Greenspan commission fooled a lot of Americans and the media, but the foreign press saw its recommendations for what they were. Take a look at what London's *Financial Times* wrote:

> Advocates of lower budget deficits and higher taxes in the U.S. Administration have won their biggest economic policy victory to date with President Reagan's approval of social security tax increases and benefit reductions which should cut U.S. budget deficits by around $20 billion in each of the next seven years.[26]

The *Financial Times* also explained how the commission's report would remove a thorny issue for President Reagan in view of "the public's perception that the Reagan administration was willing to allow the collapse of the whole social security system." You wonder who created that type of public perception. The Democrats, of course; they vigorously aided in the deception. Yes, the retirement system needed short-term help, but it was not on the verge of collapse. However, what was obvious to the *Financial Times* eluded much of the U.S. media and the public in 1983. Greenspan, in fact, emerged as a celebrity from his subterfuge.

Why did Senator Moynihan accept blatant and oppressive taxation of the poor and the middle class? In the hope that it would eliminate the budget deficit, pay off the public debt, and in the process leave surplus funds for the retirement of the baby boomers. After all, when the debt vanishes, so do interest payments, and that spares government funds for other uses. Moynihan's conclusion in short: Reagan was going to do nothing about the growing public debt and the deficit, so the Greenspan commission set out to accomplish that task for him.

How foolish were these Democrats who fell into the trap carefully laid out by the Republicans, who couldn't admit their fiscal policies had miserably failed? Senator Moynihan, despite all his good intentions, did not recognize the extent of Greenspan's perfidy. He continued to hope against hope, even in 1988, fully four years after the new payroll taxes became effective. The unified budget deficit, after swallowing the Social Security surplus of over $60 billion, was still $120 billion.

Just two months before Moynihan wrote his op-ed article, Greenspan, now the chairman of the Fed, had broken his promise once again. On March 2, 1988, the Associated Press reported that "Alan Greenspan told Congress today that it should consider trimming entitlement programs, including Social Security," in order to reduce the budget deficit.[27] Again you wonder what Greenspan was up to, because the retirement system was now generating growing surpluses year after year, and remember that it was not supposed to be used to balance the federal budget. Why cut the benefits if they were not responsible for the deficit?

By the following year, Mr. Moynihan was completely disillusioned. Since his colleagues and the new Republican president, George H. W. Bush, kept plundering the Social Security surplus, he offered a proposal to repeal the payroll tax rise that was to take effect on January 1, 1990. His proposal would also reduce the tax rate in 1991. In all, his plan would cut the payroll tax by $62 billion over two years, and later bring the pay-as-you-go approach back to the retirement program. He assailed the prevailing system as "thievery" and put all the politicians on the spot.

Finally, Greenspan and company faced a choice between hypocrisy and the social good.

Guess what most of the lawmakers as well as Greenspan did? They chose hypocrisy. The Republicans, who always jump at the chance of cutting taxes, denounced Moynihan's plan. President Bush called it a "charade,"[28] while Senator Robert Dole told a news conference that "he detected no sign of a Republican move toward the Moynihan proposal."[29] The Democrats, who claim to belong to the party of the little people, were equally obstructive. They now had a majority in both chambers of Congress and could have easily enacted the proposal, but, as reporter Andrew Rosenthal remarked at the time, "top Democrats are almost as edgy as the Republicans about the potential fallout from the Moynihan proposal, which would repeal increases in the Social Security tax."[30]

Equally predictable was Greenspan's reaction. The man who had hailed Reagan's income and corporate tax cuts put his considerable weight against the Moynihan plan that called for a slight cut in the payroll tax. He agreed with the senator that the government's use of Social Security surpluses was "most improper," but would not support his tiny tax cut. On February 27, 1990, testifying before the Senate Finance Committee, he offered a tortured argument, and said, "support for the system may well erode when the next generation is asked to take on a tax bill that their parents were unwilling or too short-sighted to assume during their working years." As if the next generation wouldn't have to foot the tax bill any way, after the lawmakers had raided the Social Security surplus, year after year, robbing it of real assets. But there were more pearls of trickery in this testimony:

> I have testified often before committees of the Congress about the corrosive effects that sustained large budget deficits have on the economy and about the way our economic prospects in coming years will hinge on our ability to increase national saving and investment.
>
> One factor that argues for running sizeable budget surpluses by later this decade is the need to set aside resources to meet the retirement needs of today's working population.
>
> Building surpluses in the trust funds also contributes to fairness across generations.[31]

Greenspan still harbored the illusion that surplus payroll taxes would generate actual budget surpluses. Second, he now wanted budget surpluses generated "by later this decade," not right away, even though the government had already consumed the Social Security surplus since 1984. At least this time, Greenspan did not call for trimming the retirement benefits. That, in an atmosphere electrified by the Moynihan plan, would have been too much of an outrage even for the Fed chairman. But, knowing his mindset by now, you know for sure that one day he would be back to push his old theme.

Another lawmaker who railed at the injustices created by the 1983 act was Democratic Senator Ernest Hollings of South Carolina. Appalled by the government's regular looting of the Trust Fund in exchange for IOUs, he castigated the administration in 1989 for masking the true budget deficit and "indulging in *enough fraud and larceny and malfeasance* to land an ordinary citizen in the penitentiary"[32] (my italics). This is a tough but true description of what various administrations have been doing to the nation's finances ever since 1981. Senator Hollings continued:

> Of course the most reprehensible fraud in this great jambalaya of frauds is the systematic and total ransacking of the Social Security trust fund in order to mask the true size of the deficit. As we all know, the Social Security payroll tax has become a money machine for the U.S. Treasury, generating fantastic revenue surpluses in excess of the cost of the Social Security program. . . .
>
> The public fully supported enactment of hefty new Social Security taxes in 1983 to ensure the retirement program's long-term solvency and credibility. The promise was that today's huge surpluses would be set safely aside in a trust fund to provide for baby-boomer retirees in the next century.
>
> Well look again. The Treasury is siphoning off every dollar of the Social Security surplus to meet current operating expenses of the government.[33]

Senator Hollings went on to offer a proposal to ban the use of the Social Security surplus in budgetary calculations. Embarrassed by the truth in the senator's denunciations, the Democratically controlled Congress finally did something and passed the Budget Enforcement Act of 1990, of which section 13301 clearly states:

> Not withstanding any other provision of law, the receipts and disbursements of the Federal Old Age and Survivors Insurance Trust Fund and

the Federal Disability Insurance Trust Fund shall not be counted as new budget authority, outlays, receipts, or deficit or surplus for purposes of (1) the budget of the United States Government as submitted by the President, (2) the Congressional budget, or (3) the Balanced Budget and Emergency Deficit Control Act of 1985.[34]

But the act turned out to be a toothless gesture. It provided Congress and the president, who signed it into law, an amiable cover for ignoring the Moynihan proposal, which had a real bite against Congressional fraud and larceny. As an economics professor, Allen Smith, describes it:

Senator Hollings thought that by making it illegal for the Congress and the president to include Social Security funds in their budget calcula-tions the deliberate deception of the public would come to an end. But he was wrong. The Bush administration and many members of Congress got over this tiny hurdle by simply ignoring the law. They con-tinued their deceptive practices just as they had done before. But there was a difference. Now they were guilty of more than deception. *Now they were guilty of deliberately violating federal law.*[35] (My italics)

So ever since November 5, 1990, the day the president affixed his auto-graph on the Budget Enforcement Act, the lawmakers have been breaking the law with impunity, because every year the Social Security surplus has been used and spent in the federal budget except 1999 and 2000, when the general budget recorded a tiny surplus on its own.

Why didn't the Democrats, whose hearts are with the poor and the downtrodden and who controlled both chambers of Congress in 1990, pass the Moynihan plan and trim the payroll tax? Why did they take cover behind Senator Hollings' bill instead? There are two reasons. First and foremost, cutting the Social Security levy would have forced them to raise revenues elsewhere, especially from the income tax that mostly burdens the wealthy, and that would be blasphemy in a money-dominated society. Second, the budget act enabled them to feed an illusion that they cared and did something. This behavior, or misbehavior, of the legislators reminds you of Mark Twain's humorous and penetrating insight: "It could probably be shown by facts and figures that there is no distinctly native American criminal class except Congress."[36] Mark Twain was perhaps exaggerating, but nowadays Congress routinely breaks the budget law it passed in 1990.

GREENSPAN'S PIVOTAL ROLE IN THE FRAUD

To my knowledge, the maestro rarely, if ever, protested the abuse of the Trust Fund. By 1992, Congress had already spent almost $200 billion of the Social Security surplus. But even after that year, when even by the 1983 law the Trust Fund had to be separated from the unified budget so Congress couldn't borrow from it, Greenspan seldom reminded anyone that the Fund's revenues must be set aside in a vault or invested in AAA corporate bonds so that the government wouldn't use the money for non–Social Security purposes. If this is not fraud, what is!

Of course, other federal officials were also complicit in this, but Greenspan was the ringleader. Best-selling author William Greider puts it aptly: "Alan Greenspan recommended the tax increase and other 'reforms' to insure the soundness of the retirement system far into the century. . . . The terms were now established in the way that the government is financed."[37] Presidents and lawmakers have come and gone, but Greenspan remains ensconced in the seat of power, and it was, and is, his duty to safeguard the Trust Fund for the baby boomers. Given his considerable prestige and power, given his celebrity, he could have lectured and shamed the lawmakers and the president into compliance with the 1983 law. He did not. Instead, he attacked the Moynihan plan.

Greenspan broke his word to Americans in at least two ways. First, even before the 1983 act became effective he advised the lawmakers to trim Social Security benefits, and then reiterated this advice time and again. His advice violated the deal he had made with workers—namely, pay giant taxes in return for slash-proof benefits. Second, he had assured the public that the Trust Fund's surplus would not be used to balance the general budget, and that assurance failed the first day the surplus appeared. In fact, he reneged on his recommendations knowingly, because he suggested that retirement benefits be cut to wipe out the federal red ink. That one suggestion, repeated again and again, broke both his pledges.

Even as he sought to slash benefits, he rejected Senator Moynihan's plan to trim the payroll tax and return to the old, pay-as-you-go system. The president and most congressmen also opposed the senator's proposal, but at least they did not call for cutting the benefits. The lawmakers broke one promise, but Greenspan broke two.

Has any established economist been able to make accurate forecasts about the economy, say, over the next five years? Here, Mr. Greenspan relied on his predictions more than half a century into the future. He and his commission added to the myth that the system would soon go bankrupt and that a massive tax hike was necessary to create a big and growing surplus so future retirees would have a cushion awaiting them. The maestro invented a cure for which no known disease existed in 1983.

Thus, the payroll tax hike became a massive fraud, when its surplus revenue was repeatedly used to pay for the tax cuts of people who were in the same opulent class as Mr. Greenspan himself. In hindsight, the Social Security legislation was just a sham designed to cover the federal shortfall so the pro-wealthy tax cuts of 1981 could be preserved.

The fraud is not that taxes were raised on the poor and the middle class, but that the government, with Greenspan as its chief economist, spent the money to finance the general budget deficit resulting primarily from repeated cuts in income tax rates. Now the State has little money left to pay the promised benefits to future retirees. How is this episode different from the tale of the financial adviser who bilked thousands of dollars from you in return for a comfortable retirement?

More deception was yet to come. Greenspan's trickery didn't end with the Social Security tax hike. During the 1980s, almost every economist was convinced that the government's red ink would last for decades, and they turned out to be right for many years. The 1981 income tax cut was followed by another five years later, and, as a result, the budget remained in arrears all through the 1980s. Can you believe that in 1986 most of those Democrats and Republicans, who would later trash the Moynihan plan to trim the payroll tax by just 1 percent, jumped at the chance to slash the top-bracket income tax rate from 50 percent all the way down to 28 percent?

Greenspan offered only lukewarm support to the new bill: "I'd say net on balance, by a close call, this is a good bill."[38] But he "acknowledged that the measure might raise slightly less revenue than anticipated," and thus increase the federal shortfall.[39] Yet he had repeatedly sought to slash the budget deficit by trimming the retirement benefits.

THE FED CHAIRMAN AND THE TRUST FUND

Greenspan's appointment as the chairman of the Federal Reserve in 1987 portended poorly for the Social Security system. The Fed chairman has historically been regarded as a man of enormous power, no matter what his politics or credentials. Greenspan perhaps was the only person who had helped raise payroll taxes and then quickly turned around to seek lower Social Security benefits. He had been mostly silent even as the lawmakers routinely raided the Trust Fund in order to defray the government's operating expenses. He had also endorsed the 1986 tax cut even if it meant some increase in the budget deficit. Following his appointment as the Fed chairman, the Trust Fund faced a bleak future. He would see to it that one way or another its surplus was squandered in some form of tax cuts for the wealthy.

In 1988 the new Fed chairman, as mentioned above, made another call for slashing the retirement benefits. Then in 1990 he denounced the Moynihan plan to trim the payroll tax, while agreeing in principle that the Trust Fund's surplus should be preserved for future retirees. But his actions, as usual, spoke louder than his words, and the Moynihan proposal went nowhere.

The Moynihan plan had exposed the blatant hypocrisy of all those entangled with the Social Security system. So it was not before 1994 that Greenspan made another serious effort to trim the benefits. Testifying before the president's entitlement reform commission, Greenspan said there was "no alternative" to trimming the growth of the retirement programs including Social Security. He parroted the same old theme but now also expressed concern about the burgeoning Medicare spending, which is a separate issue altogether.[40] The two should not be lumped together because of their historically different evolution.

In 1997, Greenspan told the lawmakers:

> This imbalance in social security stems primarily from the fact that, until very recently, payments into the social security accounts by the average employee, plus employer contributions and interest earned, were inadequate to fund the retirement benefits. This has started to change. Under the most recent revisions to the law and presumably conservative economic and demographic assumptions, today's younger workers will pay social security taxes over their working years that appear sufficient, on average, to fund their benefits during retirement. However, the huge liability for current retirees, as well as for much of the work force closer to retirement, leaves the system as a whole badly underfunded.[41]

Greenspan still showed no awareness of the real problem facing the retirement system, namely the government, which was constantly plundering the Trust Fund's surplus, leaving no cushion for the future. Yet he went on to repeat his favorite theme to cut the benefits.

As blatant as Greenspan had been all these years in contradicting himself about Social Security, the worst was yet to come. The self-contradictions in his testimonies in 1999 and 2001 were beyond description. First, take a look at his 1999 testimony:

> The dramatic increase in the ratio of retirees to workers that is projected, as the baby boomers move to retirement and ever enjoy greater longevity, makes our *current pay-as-you-go* Social Security system unsustainable.[42] (My italics)

Look how he described the current system. It was no longer supposed to be a pay-as-you-go program, but a tax-in-advance program. He would know, because he had designed it in terms of the 1983 law. In a way, he was right. The tax-in-advance system had been reduced to the pay-as-you-go system, because the government had robbed it of its cash. For a pay-as-you-go system is one where there is no surplus to be used in an emergency.

During the 1990s, especially after 1995, the budget deficit, for a variety of reasons, fell rapidly. First, a new president, Bill Clinton, with tepid support from Greenspan, engineered a slight rise in the income tax; the Fed chairman mainly backed the Clinton package for its spending restraint and went along with the tax rise because of its potential to lower the federal deficit and bring down the interest rate.

Second, a Republican-dominated Congress sharply controlled the growth in government spending. These two measures, along with soaring revenues arising from booming capital gains generated by the stock market, brought the deficit down and then created a small but growing surplus in the unified budget. This happened from 1998 to 2000; so great was the share market euphoria that some economists now projected a four-to-five trillion dollar surplus in the first decade of the new millennium.

It is against this background that Greenspan testified about Social Security in 1999. He regarded the "current pay-as-you-go Social Security system unsustainable," because of the dwindling number of workers relative to retirees in the near future. He supported President Clinton's plan to preserve the projected budget surplus for Social Security: "The large surpluses projected over the next 15 years, *if they actually materialize*, can significantly reduce the fiscal pressures created by our changing demographics" (my italics).[43] See how sensible he is here about the dubious nature of predictions, but this wisdom eluded him in 1983, when his commission relied on the certainty of projections over the next 50 to 75 years. Greenspan offered more pearls in his 1999 testimony:

> While a sharp rise in the number of retirees in about ten years seems almost a certainty, the financial and economic state of the American economy in the early twenty-first century is not. We cannot confidently project large surpluses in our unified budget over the next fifteen years, given the inherent uncertainties of budget forecasting. How can we ignore the fact that virtually all forecasts of the budget balance have been wide of the mark in recent years?[44]

So he went on to suggest that Social Security benefits be trimmed:

> There have been extensive discussions of potential changes, such as extending the age of full retirement benefit entitlement, altering the benefit calculation bend points, and adjusting annual cost-of-living escalation to a more accurate measure. Considerations such as these should not be taken off the table.[45]

As you can see from these passages, for once Greenspan makes sense, at least regarding the slippery nature of projections, even though the cut in benefits still contradicts his old promise not to touch them. I have dwelled on his 1999 testimony to show you how this wisdom disappears the moment he sees an opening to cut the income tax.

With the unexpected arrival of the unified budget surplus Greenspan finally had a chance to redeem himself. Here was a godsend for him, where he could have insisted on earmarking the projected surplus for the Trust Fund and fulfilled his 1983 promise to the average American. In fact, this is what Bill Clinton and the Democrats and many others proposed. They sought to create a lockbox, which would hold Social Security revenues and use them only for paying benefits, utilizing any non–Social Security surplus to retire the debt. This is because more than 90 percent of the reliable part of the unified surplus arose from the cash in the Social Security Trust Fund.

However, in January 2001 George W. Bush took over as president and immediately sought to use the projected surplus for slashing taxes for the wealthy. Instead of reminding the new president of the massive future needs of the Trust Fund, Greenspan actually supported him. The Fed chairman could have used his position, prestige, and authority to dissuade the president from cutting the income tax. But he endorsed the Bush administration's forecasts that even after meeting the future needs of retirees, there would be enough left to pay for a $1.35 trillion tax cut. He backed the president's plan and the result was another bonanza to the wealthy people like himself and the president. As usual, low-income groups received scraps, but more than 75 percent of the tax relief went to those earning in excess of $200,000 a year.

Contrast this position with Greenspan's testimony in 1999, where he was thoroughly skeptical of budgetary projections and advised lawmakers to start slashing the benefits because, as had happened recently, budget forecasts could be wrong. But in 2001 his caution evaporated in a hurry, because now the question was one of tax cuts for the wealthy. (There was another, in fact more pressing, reason behind Greenspan's testimony in 2001, and we will examine that in chapter 4.)

As Greenspan's biographer, Jerome Tuccille, reveals: "The statement that Bush's tax plan had Greenspan's 'fingerprints all over it' is based on interviews with sources close to the Bush administration."[46] If true, then the tax cut of 2001 ought to be called the Bush–Greenspan tax cut. This idea is reinforced by what economist Jeff Madrick writes: "Alan Greenspan, chairman of the nation's central bank, publicly supported the tax cut. Such was the prestige of the man at this point that, in my view, his comments were decisive."[47]

We have now come full circle, from the Reagan–Greenspan tax cut of 1981 to the Bush–Greenspan tax cut of 2001. In both pieces of legislation, the affluent came out smiling, while others got scraps. Both ended up creating giant budget deficits—6 percent of the nation's output in 1983, 4 percent in 2004.

Both times Greenspan turned to Social Security for the salvation of the budget. In 1983, he championed a massive rise in payroll taxes; in 2004 he would issue another call for slashing Social Security benefits. Not surprisingly, his backing for the 2001 tax cut derived from a tortuous argument. Jeff Madrick again:

> If he [Greenspan] were consistent with his past comments, his first concern should have been to use any fiscal surpluses to pay down the national debt, not cut taxes. Instead, he put forward a *peculiar justification* for his support of Bush's plan, claiming that these surpluses would accumulate so rapidly that the federal government would be forced to acquire private assets, such as stocks and bonds. This, Greenspan said, the nation could not abide.[48] (My italics)

If anyone deserved a tax cut in 2001, it was the American worker who disproportionately pays the payroll tax. It was the Trust Fund that had an overflowing and reliable surplus, not the general budget, whose surplus was based on projections that easily could be wrong. The income tax on top brackets was 70 percent in 1980, went down to 28 percent under Reagan, and then, after Clinton's legislation, settled at 39.6 percent at the end of the 1990s. So even if the Bush administration's overly optimistic projections about the budget surplus turned out to be accurate, it was the payroll tax, not the income tax rate, that ought to have been lowered. But that would have hardly made a dent in the IRS bills of people like Greenspan and the affluent, and in a money-dominated American political system, such an ethical measure had no chance of enactment.

To his credit, Greenspan has been consistent in his support for uplifting the living standard of the wealthy. When facts fail to justify his self-serving ideas or policies, then his modus operandi has been to rely on a variety of forecasts.

What a cruel joke these forecasts turned out to be to the average Joe. In 1983 Greenspan used public fears about projected shortfall in the retirement program and backed a massive hike in payroll taxes in order to preserve the pro-wealthy tax cuts of 1981, whereas in 2001, he backed the administration's projections to bring about another pro-affluent tax reduction. How convenient was this? Each time he himself was a major beneficiary of the tax cuts resulting from these projections, while knowing that economists' predictions rarely turn out to be right even in the short run, let alone in the long run. Each time the tax reductions were ostensibly meant for the nation's benefit, but actually enriched mainly the rich, including Greenspan himself.

We all know what happened to that ballyhooed budget surplus. Within two years, the Bush administration's forecast of the trillion-dollar surplus turned on its head. In 2004 alone, the unified deficit approximated $420 billion, while the Trust Fund itself had a surplus of $170 billion. Without that Trust Fund, the federal deficit neared $600 billion, or a whopping 5 percent of output. Now the administration hopes to cut its annual deficit in half in the near future.

During the election campaign of 2000, George Bush's mantra had been "compassionate conservatism," which turned out to mean compassion for the conservatives, especially those with mega-bucks and fortunes, who were the biggest beneficiaries of the Bush–Greenspan tax cut in 2001. Before securing his tax cut Bush promised that he would not touch the Social

Security surplus in his budget, but his pledge turned out to be as solid as Greenspan's. So now the retirement program collects $170 billion worth of government IOUs per year, while the government lives from hand to mouth. The Social Security bank is busy lending money, under duress, to a pauper.

Greenspan's outrage against the vast majority of Americans, however, doesn't end here. In February 2004, he again raised the specter of Social Security insolvency and suggested benefit cuts for future retirees to control the mushrooming budget deficit, because there was little money left in government coffers. Yet, in the same breath, he argued that all the Bush tax cuts, including those of 2002 and 2003, be made permanent. Once again, he used his bully pulpit to hit the poor on the head, while giving the affluent a reason to celebrate. In 1983, he had proposed the Social Security tax hike; in 2004, he called for the Social Security benefit reduction, each time to preserve the financial interests of affluent folk.

A closer look at his 2004 testimony reminds you of what he had done in 1983. Proceeding step by step, his first step was to create some kind of alarm about the future of the pension benefits based on someone's projections:

> Today, Federal outlays under Social Security and Medicare amount to less than 7 percent of GDP. In December the CBO projected that these outlays would increase to 12 percent of GDP by 2030 under current law. . . .[49]

His second step was to call for a sacrifice on the part of workers, this time in terms of a cut in future benefits:

> Another possible adjustment relates to the age at which Social Security and Medicare benefits will be provided. Under current law, and even with the so-called normal retirement age for Social Security slated to move up to 67 over the next two decades, the ratio of the number of years that the typical worker will spend in retirement to the number of years he or she works will rise in the long term. A critical step forward would be to adjust the system so that this ratio stabilizes.[50]

Of course, in order to stabilize "this ratio," the retirement age has to rise above 67, which in effect cuts the future benefits of the workers paying excess payroll taxes today. So, it is the same old Greenspan act: create an alarm using projections and then call for workers to make a sacrifice. Who should benefit? This also comes out clearly from the testimony in question.

In view of this upward ratchet in government programs and the enormous uncertainty about the upper bounds of future demands for medical care, I believe that a thorough review of our spending commitments—and at least some adjustment in those commitments—is necessary for prudent policy. . . . I certainly agree that the same scrutiny needs to be applied to taxes. However, tax rate increases of sufficient dimension to deal with our looming fiscal problems arguably pose significant risks to economic growth and the revenue base. The exact magnitude of such risks is very difficult to estimate, but they are of enough concern, in my judgment, to warrant aiming to close the fiscal gap primarily, if not wholly, from the outlay side.[51]

It is clear that Greenspan wants to solve the fiscal mess by cutting retirement programs, and preserve all the tax cuts engineered by President Bush to honor his compassion for the conservatives, mostly the tycoons, who financed Bush's election campaigns of 2000 and 2004. The real cause of the deficit, namely the giant tax cuts, as usual eludes the maestro. He even ignores the contemporaneous projections of the Social Security trustees that the retirement fund could easily pay benefits until 2042.

In 2004 Greenspan worried about the tax increase posing "significant risks to economic growth and the revenue base," but where was this concern when he engineered a massive rise in payroll taxes in 1983, and then denounced the Moynihan plan to cut the payroll tax in 1990? Apparently such concerns bother him only in the case of the income tax, which, when trimmed, disproportionately rewards affluent people and corporations.

Greenspan was hailed as a hero in 1983 for his dubious achievement, but not in 2004, when finally many saw through his shenanigans. Paul Krugman, a distinguished professor of economics at Princeton University and an influential columnist with *The New York Times*, greeted Greenspan's latest tirade against Social Security with these words: "The traditional definition of chutzpah says it's when you murder your parents, then plead for clemency because you're an orphan. Alan Greenspan has chutzpah."[52]

To me, it is more than chutzpah. At the very least, it is a scam. The late Senator Moynihan called it thievery. But Senator Hollings called the looting of Social Security an outright fraud that could land ordinary citizens in jail. Was it fraud? Let us take an overall look at what the maestro has wrought in Table 2.1.

This is what Greenspan's modus operandi has been over almost a quarter century, starting from 1981. First support a massive income tax

Table 2.1. Greenspan's Social Security Fraud Dateline

1981: Greenspan advises the president to cut income and corporate taxes and later agrees to chair the Social Security commission, ostensibly to save the Social Security system.

1982: The Greenspan commission diverts public attention from the real crisis, which is the mushrooming budget deficit, by insisting that Social Security faces a massive long-term deficit.

1983: In January the Greenspan commission advises Americans to accept sharply higher payroll taxes in exchange for guaranteed benefits in the future, suggesting that the projected Social Security surplus should not be used to meet the government's operating expenses.

In April, the Social Security act is signed into law, but Greenspan remains silent even though the Social Security surplus will be used to meet government expenses until 1992, thus contradicting Greenspan's recommendation made in the commission's report.

In October, just six months after the tax rise was passed, Greenspan suggests that Social Security benefits be trimmed to reduce the budget deficit, thus contradicting recent legislation and his commission's plea to guarantee benefits from 1985 on.

1985: Greenspan reiterates his plea to cut Social Security benefits to trim the federal deficit, even though the Social Security program starts to run a surplus.

1988: Greenspan again reiterates his plea to cut Social Security benefits to trim the federal deficit, even though the Social Security program is running a growing surplus.

1990: Greenspan denounces the Moynihan plan to trim the payroll tax, even though the Social Security surplus is being used in non–Social Security spending by the government.

1994: On July 15 Greenspan again recommends slashing Social Security benefits.

1997: Greenspan again recommends slashing the Social Security benefits by amending the cost-of-living formula and by raising the retirement age.

1999: Greenspan warns Congress against relying solely on the projected surplus in the unified budget to ensure the solvency of the Trust Fund, because projections could be wrong. He reaffirms his plea to trim the benefits.

2001: Greenspan supports the Bush tax cut to reduce the projected budget surplus. This time, he is not worried that projections could be wrong.

2004: Greenspan suggests that benefits should be cut for future retirees, because the Bush tax cuts that he supported have created a large budget deficit, even though the Social Security Trust Fund itself is running an annual surplus of nearly $170 billion.

Greenspan's Fraud: (1) Helping to raise the payroll tax to meet the government's operating expenses, but selling the plan as Social Security reform. (2) Supporting tax cuts for the wealthy and asking workers to make sacrifices, using projections not facts. Mark Twain once said: "There are lies, damned lies, and statistics." Greenspan made full use of such damned lies to benefit the wealthy.

cut for millionaires and billionaires, essentially business people like your-self, and when the resulting budget deficit zooms, frighten people about the future, using projections. Second, ask workers to make sacrifices today in order to balance the budget, so that the tax cuts favoring the afflu-ent are preserved and workers make sacrifices to reward the rich. Third, in the process of making all these pleas, repeatedly contradict yourself. Such shenanigans are practiced only by those who are frauds or who commit frauds.

Greenspan's fraud in a nutshell is this: Support tax cuts for the wealthy and ask the average worker to make sacrifices, using projections not facts. He behaves like an insurance salesman who cons people into parking their hard-earned money into phony schemes. Greenspan cried wolf too many times, and now few trust him with Social Security.

Greenspan is anti–Robin Hood—he legally robs the poor and rewards the opulent. A capsule of his fraudulent actions appears in Table 2.1, and captures the ethos of the maestro. Many people blame this fraud on politicians—Republican and Democratic lawmakers—but Greenspan, as mentioned before, was and is the ringleader of the entire scam. Others have come and gone, while he remains entrenched in the seat of power. Let me repeat: Greenspan is perhaps the only influential man who helped raise the Social Security tax and then quickly turned around to issue a call for slashing the Social Security benefits. Other accomplices did one or the other, but not both.

However, it seems that the outrage against the Social Security pro-gram would never end. The same stench of fakery and deception that per-meated economic debate in the early 1980s filled the air in February 2005. Then, as now, the real crisis was in the federal budget, but the government wanted to solve the phony Social Security crisis. Never mind that the program is running a growing surplus at this time, while the government's operating budget gushes red ink. As before the government relies on projections to fool the public about the health of the pension plan, while ignoring the ugly reality of its own deficit. It is promoting Social Security privatization, which will definitely enrich Wall Street, and is manufacturing a non-existent crisis to justify its plan.

For once, let's ignore projections and heed the hard choices facing us now. Look at what the reliance on projections has already done to the federal budget, turning a $5 trillion projected budget surplus into an equivalent deficit. The real crisis is that the government has already plun-dered over $1.5 trillion of the Social Security Fund and continues to squander away the fund's annual surplus. This is the stark reality, which needs to be addressed at this time, not what might happen 30 years from now. Remember what the celebrated economist John Maynard Keynes once said: "In the long run we are all dead." Should we then disrupt our lives just because we are dead in the long run? Likewise, should we disrupt our economy today just because we could face a Social Security deficit two to three decades from now? The projections can be manufactured and abused, but not the prevailing facts.

However under the guise of privatization, President Bush wants to do what Greenspan has preached for a long time—cut retirement benefits while retaining 1983's giant rise in payroll taxes. Today, as in the early 1980s, the Republicans seem to have a hidden agenda, namely to solve the long-term budget mess on the backs of the poor and the middle class—this time by cutting pension benefits. What a sad irony! Those Republicans who warn Americans about the bankruptcy of the Social Security system in 2042 are currently creating the very conditions for its bankruptcy by plundering its surplus. The president has already squandered over half a trillion dollars of the retirement fund's cash to pay for his tax cuts, while promising in 2001 that he would not touch it, and now he apparently wants to make sure that the fund's looted surplus will never have to be redeemed. This would be one way to finance his tax cuts over the long run. For once, let Social Security not become fodder for the rich man's tax reward. For once, let's be practical and not base our policies on uncertain predictions. More will be said on privatization in chapter 11.

3

GREENOMICS: FREE PROFITS DEFINE FREE MARKETS

Alan Greenspan was just nine years old when he first came across a serious book on political economy, one written by someone he knew intimately—his dad. Herbert Herman Greenspan's 1934 work, *Recovery Ahead*, offered a thoughtful endorsement of FDR's New Deal as a way to fight the Great Depression. Alan had been born during the go-go milieu of the roaring twenties, with the stock market breaking records year after year. His father, like many others, made a fortune trading shares, but then lost it all in the great crash of 1929. Humbled by that calamity, the dad foreswore views that tempt people into risking their all in speculation.

In one of the world's great ironies, Alan would turn out to be an exact opposite of his father. The son would become an ardent reader and believer of classical utilitarian philosophy and laissez-faire economics, championed by the likes of Adam Smith, David Ricardo, and Jeremy Bentham. He would castigate the New Deal and all it stood for. He would even go a step further than most classical economists, who believed in small-firm capitalism, as he came to decry any government measure that impedes corporate profits. He would even denounce antitrust laws, such as the Sherman Antitrust Act, as "utter nonsense"; big business, he would come to believe, is America's persecuted minority.[1]

Bob Woodward's maestro, as I mentioned earlier, would cheer his mentor, Ayn Rand, for denouncing President John F. Kennedy (JFK) as a fascist dictator.[2] In short, things that stood in the way of a businessman's profits, ideas that hampered an entrepreneur's acquisitive tendencies, philosophies that even remotely protected anyone from the excesses of corporations became anathema to him. Such was the background and the belief system of Alan Greenspan when he was appointed as the chairman of the National Commission on Social Security Reform in 1981. Even in 1987, when he became the chairman of the Federal Reserve, his views had changed little, as would become clear from the monetary policies that he later followed. Before we plunge into Greenspan's economics, let's delve briefly into the character of the man and the circumstances that molded his life and philosophy. His economic ideology may be described in a nutshell as: "free profits define free markets."

By "free profit" I mean unencumbered profit—an idea that anything hampering the flow of corporate income is bad for the economy: if profits fall or corporate taxes rise, productivity suffers. If the government regulates the economy in any fashion, free enterprise dissolves. If mergers are inhibited, the living standard shrinks. If the government intervenes on behalf of the consumer or worker, production loses efficiency. If taxes rise on those who can afford to pay them, output growth sinks. Such are the tenets of the creed that free profits define free markets. Such, basically, are the beliefs of Alan Greenspan. Greenspan's economics may be abbreviated to Greenomics, which essentially turns out to be Greedomics, signifying a view that nothing should be done to interfere with business greed and the pursuit of profits. Nay, the government should protect businessmen and their riches from their own mistakes.

Greenomics evolved over time. Adam Smith and Ayn Rand provided the dominant strands in Greenspan's thought, but there were other strands as well. Those came from what is known as Keynesian economics, which is the antithesis of all that Smith and Rand stood for. However, Keynesian economics offered something that Greenspan would later use, partly to further the interests of the business class. Thus Greenomics turns out to be a hodgepodge of contradictory ideas; its one common thread is to advance the self-interest of the businessman, using an incoherent stew of Smith's, Rand's, and Keynes's thought, combined with a pragmatism born out of personal benefit. We will now explore its basic tenets, leaving the question of "personal benefit" to the next chapter.

CLASSICAL ECONOMICS

The views that Adam Smith expounded are today known as classical economics. The term was coined by Karl Marx, the celebrated founder of communism, and later popularized by John Maynard Keynes, an economist who became so influential that an entire branch of economic theory, called Keynesian economics, is named after him. Smith championed a free-market system, which displays keen competition among businesses and where information is freely available to workers and consumers alike.

The idea that made Adam Smith a celebrity is called the invisible hand, which appeared in 1776 in his masterpiece, *The Wealth of Nations*. The book offered an elegant defense for what is today called the free-market system. Although industrial revolution had begun more than two hundred years before his birth, capitalism was still in its infancy. Under the pervasive influence of religion at the time, the public generally distrusted the profit motive and the idea of individualism, which was feared for its potential for anarchy. Smith's peers generally championed the interest of the State, not of the people.

Smith offered a new idea that admired self-interest as well as the human quest for money and profit. He argued that self-preservation comes naturally to everyone, so that the pursuit of self-interest and ambition is virtue not vice, and leads to prosperity not anarchy. This is what motivates employers and employees to put capital and labor to uses that are the most productive. A firm seeks maximum return from its investment, whereas a worker chases the highest salary for his or her effort. Facing keen competition from others, a producer has to offer high-quality goods at a low price, whereas to compete with their colleagues, everyone has to work to their best potential. This is how self-preservation works. Smith wrote: "It is not from the benevolence of the butcher, the brewer, or the baker, that we expect our dinner, but from their regard to their own interest."[3]

The mechanism that brings the best out of producers and workers is Smith's invisible hand of a free market. The invisible hand brings consumers and producers to interact with each other. Each party pursues its self-interest, and in the process helps itself and the other attain its goal. Businesses know that people want quality products, so they produce goods and services in demand, using technology and resources in an efficient way to minimize costs and thus prices. Everyone is happy in a free-market economy characterized by intense competition among firms, consumers, and workers. Consumers enjoy superb quality from their low-cost purchases, producers earn adequate profits because they produce goods at minimum cost, and workers enjoy high salaries arising from their hard work.

The pursuit of self-interest by everyone thus ensures that society's resources are put to their best use, generating the highest living standard from available technology. Smith's analysis of a market offered a variety of new prescriptions. How may society maximize its living standard? Smith provided a simple answer. Create keen competition at all levels of economic activity. Make sure there are no monopolies at the level of production or workers. Keep the markets free by discouraging mergers among profitable firms.

Smith assailed various government regulations that generate monopolies and constrict business competition. In his view, small-scale enterprises were a constant source of new competitors. This point is very important, because the CEOs of modern-day giant firms have generally invoked Smith's free enterprise to justify their unseemly incomes. Adam Smith did not decry avarice, which is inherent in most of us, but the State institutions that tolerate mega mergers, restrict competition, and in the process enable some to be enormously wealthy while forcing others into destitution. He justified the profit motive, not profiteering.

The American Republic

It is an irony of history that a pioneer is acclaimed everywhere except at home. Britain, where Smith was born, paid lip service to its brilliant writer, and continued to sanction the State trading monopolies. However, a feisty new republic, the United States of America, which had declared independence in the same year that saw the arrival of *The Wealth of Nations*, heartily followed his prescriptions. Individualism permeated America's freedom fighters, who generally disliked state intervention in private matters such as the hunt for profit in a business venture.

Leaders of the new republic turned out to be worthy disciples of the revolutionary economist, except in his admiration of free trade. Smith usually railed against tariffs, but not in matters of self-defense and retaliation against excessive foreign tariffs. However, American presidents, from

George Washington to Thomas Jefferson to Abraham Lincoln, generally adopted high import duties and protected the home market for manufactured goods. American firms thus faced little competition from foreign producers, but they had more than enough at home. The birth of hundreds of new and small companies generated intense rivalry among businesses even though foreign goods were expensive. Smith's idea of a free enterprise had found a fertile field to prove itself. Most of the preconditions for the triumph of the invisible hand then existed in the United States.

Early ventures by U.S. entrepreneurs were small, unable to dominate any market. Keen competition is a dynamic force that lubricates industrialization and prosperity. The Americans, just like modern Japan, imported technology and capital, combined them with domestically available resources, and sold their goods to domestic customers. The rest is history.

By the turn of the twentieth century, the young republic had come of age. Starting practically from nothing, it had bested the well-established economies of England, Germany, and France. America emerged as the global leader in technology, industry, per-capita GDP, and, above all, the real wage. The invisible hand of Adam Smith had built one of the most visible industrial empires in the world. Henceforth, free enterprise would become gospel for economists, politicians, and the people.

Jeremy Bentham's Influence

Another British writer who influenced Alan Greenspan as well as classical economists was actually a philosopher named Jeremy Bentham, who believed that human actions are guided purely by pleasure and pain, and nothing else. "Nature," wrote Bentham in oft-quoted words, "has placed mankind under the governance of two sovereign masters, pain and pleasure. It is for them alone to point out what we ought to do, as well as to determine what we shall do. On the one hand the standard of right and wrong, on the other the chain of causes and effects, are fastened to their throne. They govern us in all we do, in all we say, in all we think: every effort we can make to throw off our subjection, will serve but to demonstrate and confirm it."[4]

In his view, no one does anything if it does not bring pleasure, or avoids pain. If people could find no joyful activities or feared no discomfort, they would simply be inert, motionless, and lazy. These are the fundamental emotions that underlie all other emotions. Work or effort is basically tedious, and not itself a source of pleasure. A person's innate desire is for ease or comfort, not labor. In other words, workers are basically lethargic and uninterested in doing anything except under the pressure of hunger or for eschewing pain. "The practical outcome of this doctrine," assert economists Hunt and Sherman, "was the widespread belief at the time that laborers were incurably lazy. Thus only a large reward or the fear of starvation and deprivation could force them to work."[5] In economics jargon, pleasure became utility and pain became disutility. The economists came to believe that everyone tries to maximize utility and minimize disutility.

Such utilitarian beliefs form the psychological basis of classical economics and its policy prescriptions. Smith proved that capitalism or free markets formed an efficient system, so that the economy should be left to itself, because government intervention only creates poverty and stagnation. But the creed that laborers would offer little labor unless goaded by hunger led the latter-day classical economists to oppose labor unions and minimum wage laws. This is because if government or union actions raise wages above the subsistence level, workers would withhold their labor, so output and profit would decline.

Therefore, classical economists believed that wages should be kept as low as possible. This, they argued, would also keep workers fully employed, because low wages induce companies to hire more workers, ensuring a high-employment economy. Of course, profits would then be high, but high profits also serve the social interest. From high profits arises capital accumulation, which in turn promotes new technology, raises labor productivity, and causes further increases in profit. This is a virtuous circle that generates high efficiency, high employment, and high growth.

Greenspan's View of Antitrust Laws

You can already see that classical economics and utilitarian philosophy give rise to the view that free or unencumbered profits define free markets, for without high profit the beneficial effects of free markets evaporate like thin vapor. But Greenspan's view of profit is even more generous to the businessman.

Classical economists generally favored the presence of keen competition, which could occur only if the size of firms was small, so that no single producer could corner a market and determine the market price. Capitalism could not be efficient if small firms were replaced by a few dominant firms, which tend to raise their prices by reducing output. But keen competition among businesses tended to squeeze profits, which were still high because of efficient production but not as high as those of a few dominant firms.

American industrialization started out with small firms, but over time, because of collusion and mergers among businessmen, it turned into what may be regarded as monopoly capitalism, wherein a few firms dominate important industries. As companies grew in size and profit, they began to influence politics and elections. The lawmakers were quick to offer legislative favors in return for campaign contributions and bribes. With politics and profits mingling together, giant American corporations throve apace, gobbling up even more of their rivals. The wheeling and dealing that occurred among businessmen toward the end of the nineteenth century earned them the derogatory label of Robber Barons, men who, according to economists Gilbert Fite and Jim Reese, "built poor railroads, turned out shoddy products, cheated honest investors, sweated labor, and exploited the country's natural resources for their own wealth and satisfaction."[6]

Almost every major industry came to be dominated by regional monopolies, which are dominant firms in an industry. The economy might not have grown as fast without these swindlers—which some doubt—but there were distressing side effects of this concentration of economic power on a vast scale—a malady that has afflicted the American economy ever since the end of the nineteenth century. So outrageous were the practices of Robber Barons that by 1889 the entire country was up in arms, leaving Congress with no choice but to take action. The end product was the Sherman Antitrust Act of 1890, which barred any person or corporation from conspiring to form monopolies or to stifle competition in any way.

Companies came to detest this law. What businessmen hate most is competition, because it increases uncertainty and trims profits. They also detest government intervention and regulations that adversely affect their incomes. They welcome regulation only when it cuts competition and ensures a steady and high return. Toward the end of the nineteenth century, while most industries had become concentrated in the hands of a few barons, the railroads continued to face cutthroat competition. In fact, their rivalries were so intense that they themselves demanded regulation from Congress, which was quick to respond. The Interstate Commerce Commission (ICC) was established to regulate the railroads in the public interest, and preserve their profits. Later, some other antitrust laws outlawed price discrimination, requiring some corporate customers to pay more than others.

Most economists endorse the antitrust laws not just in the United States but also in England, France, Germany, and the rest of Europe, because of their stimulus to competition. Classical economists, including Adam Smith, also backed the breakup of monopolies. But Greenspan wrote a stinging critique of the whole idea underlying such laws: "The entire structure of antitrust laws in this country is a jumble of economic irrationality and ignorance."[7] " 'Competition'," he goes on, "is an active, not a passive noun . . . it implies the necessity of taking action to affect the conditions of the market in one's own favor."[8] In other words, if a company's executives swallow other businesses "to affect the conditions of the market in one's own favor," it's all right. If that company turns into a monopoly, it is well and good, even if the consumer suffers from its giant prices or many workers are fired by merged firms. It is fine if the behemoth rakes in mega-profits, because then, the maestro claims, economic efficiency and growth will pick up. In the pages to come we will demonstrate the dubious nature of this and many other claims.

What is consistent with Greenspan's version of competition? "In the early days of the United States," according to Greenspan, "Americans enjoyed a large measure of economic freedom. . . . If two competitors concluded that it was their mutual self interest to set joint price policies, they were free to do so."[9] This is Greenspan's version of competition— collusive behavior to set prices jointly.

In other words, Greenspan's logic would endorse the profit strategy of OPEC (Organization of Petroleum Exporting Countries), which encourages its member countries to routinely collude with each other and fix the price of oil because it is "their mutual self-interest to set joint price policies." It's true that Greenspan applies his argument to companies, not countries, but in a global economy, countries, like businesses, are competitors. If price setting is consistent with inter-firm competition, then Greenspan's logic implies that it is also consistent with international competition.

Greenspan would also endorse Enron's pricing behavior, because his version of competition "implies the necessity of taking action to affect the conditions of the market in one's own favor." Enron is certainly one company that acted to alter market conditions in its own favor. Greenspan does not call such action market manipulation, but others view it differently. Many have concluded that Enron's executives lifted energy prices sky high, paying millions in compensation to themselves. See, for instance, what the *Wall Street Journal* wrote:

> Enron Corp.'s energy traders manipulated California's power system to increase profits during the height of the state's 2000–2001 energy crisis, documents released by federal regulators show.
>
> The internal company documents were the first to provide evidence of what had been suspected through previous inquiries by the Federal Energy Regulatory Commission—that market manipulation was a major factor in sending wholesale energy prices soaring in six Western states.[10]

Electricity prices charged by Enron were so high that even now California is reeling under the burden of debts, which were partly the handiwork of that venturesome firm.

What matters to Greenspan is the existence of a free capital market, which ensures that monopolies, especially those lacking government protection, behave like competitors, minimize their costs and prices, and thus maintain productive efficiency. If they do not, then other entrepreneurs borrowing funds from capital markets will enter the industry and destroy the monopoly position of the company. The competitive outcome is ensured because either the monopolist behaves like a competitor or other firms enter the industry with the help of lenders in the capital market. There is no need for antitrust enforcement, because the system retains its efficiency without that intervention. Free enterprise is thus ensured by a free capital market.

"It's the government, not business mergers," writes biographer Jerome Tuccille, "that creates the conditions for monopoly, according to Greenspan, by providing for franchises, patents and subsidies. It is the government that makes laws against prostitution, gambling, and narcotics, and thus gives rise to monopolistic controls in black markets."[11] Thus Greenspan makes a distinction between two types of monopolies—one aided by government fiat, and the other emerging by outcompeting its rivals through innovation and efficient production.

Greenspan's analysis overlooks reality. First, the monopoly producer has the financial clout to buy up politicians, who are likely to protect the producer's market advantage and make it difficult for new firms to invade his territory. So if the government generates the conditions for monopoly, it is because the dominant corporations buy up the government. Second, even if new firms do succeed in challenging the monopolist, they will be gobbled up by the dominant firm in the absence of antitrust laws.

To be sure, Greenspan chastises private corporations as well for seeking government subsidies and laws that restrict competition. However such criticism displays an evenhanded treatment of the issue, but nothing more. It does not eliminate pervasive corporate influence on the government, which remains beholden to big business, whether or not giant companies actively or passively pursue legislation biased in their favor. Even if monopolies come about independently of government patronage because of their low-cost production and prices, once they have driven the competitors out, they engage in price gouging and have the government pass laws to create entry barriers to new firms.

Look at what has happened in industry after industry in the 1990s. Petroleum, pharmaceuticals, steel, computers, etc., are dominated by a few giants. Microsoft alone had over $50 billion in cash; drug manufacturers like Pfizer and Johnson & Johnson have swallowed small companies, and now charge exorbitant prices for their goods, so much so that people take trips to Canada and Mexico to buy low-priced medicines. The government is in the pockets of drug makers, and does not permit free entry to foreign medicines in the United States, even in these days of official obsession with globalization. Needless to say, the antitrust laws have not been vigorously enforced since 1981 to halt business mergers. If such corporations were broken up, prices would plummet from enhanced competition and raise the nation's well being.

Thus Greenspan's distinction between a monopolist who profits by charging a higher price and the one who does the same through efficient and low-cost production is phony, because they both have the opportunity to bribe the authorities and secure entry barriers. Once monopolies have been formed, they perpetuate themselves, and it may take a long time before their evil effects are thwarted by new legislation. That is why antitrust laws are needed to outlaw monopoly, no matter what its underlying justification.

Greenspan denounced the 1890 Sherman Antitrust Act,[12] which later broke up Standard Oil, the biggest trust of all, into 16 smaller companies including Exxon and Mobil. However, this trust, according to Greenspan, performed a great service by keeping prices low. What he fails to realize is that big companies reduce their prices only temporarily to destroy their competitors, but later raise them sharply to reap unseemly profits and incomes for their executives. No wonder, with Greenomics pervading the American economy in recent years, Exxon and Mobil merged again in 1996, followed by other mergers in the oil industry. And gasoline prices were the highest ever in the nation in 2004. Other factors may also matter here, but the failure of antitrust enforcement was arguably a major factor.

What is really appalling to me is that Greenspan bashes the government for generating monopolistic control in some markets by prohibiting prostitution and narcotics. He is against the minimum-wage and maximum-hour laws. This belief reflects the influence of classical writings, especially Jeremy Bentham, who maintained that only hunger prods people to work. If it were up to Greenspan, it appears he would do away with all regulations. He sees little value in the social good done by the Food and Drug Administration (FDA), the Securities and Exchange Commission (SEC), and anything else that impedes greed and profits but protects the consumer. Such agencies hurt productive efficiency and are unnecessary, because, says Greenspan, "it is precisely the 'greed' of the businessman or, more appropriately, his profit-seeking, which is the unexcelled protector of the consumer."[13]

Clearly, Greenomics puts business greed on a higher pedestal than did Adam Smith. The greed sanctioned by Smith is not without limits, which are set by the presence of numerous firms that divide industry profits among themselves. But with Greenspan, given free capital markets, monopolies may generate competitive outcomes of output levels, prices, and efficiency, provided the government creates no entry barriers. Even then the entire industry's profits will accrue to just one producer, or a few behemoths, and not to a large number of businesspeople. Profits for one or a few firms will be exorbitant, but that is fine with the maestro, because efficiency will stay high. However, as argued above, efficiency soon vanishes once the dominant firms are able to pay off the politicians and obtain laws in their favor, or gobble up the emerging competitors with their enormous profits.

Greenspan rails against the government agencies established to protect the worker and the consumer, because "capitalism is based on self-interest and self-esteem; it holds integrity and trustworthiness as cardinal virtues."[14] He obviously disregards Robber Barons and all those businessmen who in the past exploited women and children, making them work for up to 12 hours per day for subsistence. Today, in the absence of regulations, multinational firms are doing the same things in the third world.

In Greenspan's world, it appears to me, corporate scandals and those associated with them—the likes of Ken Lay, Andrew Fastow, Martha Stewart, Henry Blodget, the Rigas family, and Jeff Skilling, to name a few—do little harm to society and warrant no government interference. Corporate shenanigans of the past and present, to him, are purely innocuous; all that stock manipulation that occurred in the 1920s and even victimized his father in the form of the stock market crash of 1929 was just a concoction of welfare lunatics, like Keynes, who were later obsessed with the New Deal. A businessman is just making an honest buck, and no amount of government interference is justified in his unbounded pursuit of riches. This is Greenspan's ideology, or Greedomics.

As a counterargument Greenspan might say, "the possibility of individual dishonesty applies to government employees fully as much as to any other group of men."[15] This is a valid point, but politicians have to face voters every two or four years, and abusive incumbents can be voted out of office. Today, government practices are perhaps just as dishonest as business practices, but the public can hold politicians responsible for what they do, whereas businesses can go on cheating for decades with impunity. It took 40 years before Alcoa lost its monopoly to rivals; Standard Oil dominated its industry for 25 years, and was broken up not by its rivals but by antitrust action in 1911.

Classical Economic Policies

It is clear that Adam Smith's rehabilitation of greed and the profit motive had a deep influence on Greenspan; but the maestro had gone a step further in exalting avarice and the corporate pursuit of profits. Actually, Greenomics evolved as a product of classical economic thought and the views of an influential libertarian scholar, Ayn Rand, whom Greenspan met in 1952.

Let's first explore the classical economic policy, which was originally expounded by Smith and later by economists such as Irving Fisher, who is well known for his remark, made a week before the crash of 1929, that stock prices had reached a permanently high plateau.

The classical model began with what is known as Say's law, named after Jean-Baptiste Say, a French economist. Let's see what Monsieur Say had to say. Actually, not much. He argued that supply creates its own demand so that there is never any possibility of excess supply or overproduction. This is because everything produced in the economy is mostly distributed among households in the form of wages, rents, interest income, and dividends. The rest goes to the government as sales tax or remains with corporations as the depreciation expense of capital goods such as machines and office buildings.

The households receiving national output in turn spend money out of their incomes, and that creates demand for goods and services. Since the market value of aggregate output, called the gross domestic product (GDP), always equals the distributed incomes, supply automatically creates demand.

Picture yourself owning a store, or a small business. Suppose you manage a china shop; then your net sales are a miniature version of the GDP. What remains after you pay for your inventory is net revenue. Out of that you pay your own salary and that of your employees, rent for the store, interest for any money you may have borrowed from a bank, sales tax to the government, and depreciation for your equipment. What remains is your profit. GDP accounting works in much the same way. Total output or net revenue in the economy automatically equals the sum of various incomes.

Incomes, however, need not be spent completely. Some households and businesses save a part of their earnings. Clearly, then, supply will exceed spending or demand at least by the amount of savings. Classical economists solved this problem by arguing that savings eventually find their way into the hands of investors through the medium of commercial banks. So long as companies spend that money for investment, supply matches demand. Business investment or capital spending is thus the key to the validity of Say's law. It is also the key to affluence.

The simple statement of Say's law that supply creates its own demand has profound implications for us all. It implies that the economy can never suffer from over-production. At most the excess supply of goods is temporary and vanishes within a few months, because in their self-interest banks transfer savings to the companies for investment. This is how the lenders make money. Thus savings don't sit idle at banks, but are injected into the economy.

In the labor market also there is no possibility of excess supply or unemployment in the long run. Joblessness occurs if labor demand is short of labor supply, or when businesses lay off workers. However, no one likes to remain without work for long. Unemployment induces a fall in wages, so employers find it profitable to increase their hiring. In other words, falling wages eliminate joblessness.

This way, free markets solve their problems without government interference. No regulations are needed for a smooth operation of the economy. In fact, according to the classicists, government intervention such as the minimum wage legislation creates more trouble than it solves. On the face of it the classical logic is simple and appealing. Why would anyone champion state interference with markets? However, there is one tiny hurdle. The reality eluded classical eloquence.

Classical thought began to rule economic policy soon after the appearance of *The Wealth of Nations*, especially in the United States, where the classical ideal of small government appealed to the individual-istic spirit of the freedom fighters. Many assumptions of the theory were satisfied with the advent of manufacturing in the new republic. The country had started out as an agrarian stronghold, but, after the passage of the Tariff Act of 1816 that protected industries, had embarked upon rapid industrialization.

As start-up firms, American companies were small but numerous. They easily fit into Smith's assumption of keen competition. Workers had few rights, and their wages were set by the pressures of labor demand and supply, at least partly. Prices were also flexible, up and down. Thus classical assumptions seemed to be realistic. The classical framework has been denounced time and again, especially after the 1930s. Many have chided it for its faulty assumptions, but at least in nineteenth-century America, classical requirements were more than met by industries. How did the model perform in its ideal setting? Miserably.

Oscar Wilde, the celebrated playwright, once said, "The well-bred contradict other people. The wise contradict themselves." You will now discover that the classical economists were extremely wise. In the classical world recessions and joblessness, if they ever come about, are short-lived, lasting no more than one or two years. Of course, depressions, where business activity and employment remain depressed for a long time, say three years or more, are simply out of the question. Yet even a cursory look at nineteenth-century America reveals something else.

There were two recessions during the 1820s, and one around 1835, which was followed by a seven-year long depression in the 1840s. The 1850s saw only one recession, as did the 1860s, but the 1870s suffered another seven-year depression. While the 1880s experienced a deep recession, the 1890s suffered a deep depression.

Thus, even though for much of the nineteenth century the classical assumptions were aptly fulfilled by the U.S. economy, there were long periods of falling output and rising unemployment. Evidently, there was something amiss with the classical logic, not with its assumptions. To be sure, years of calamity gave way to longer expansions and the economy grew at an extraordinary pace in the nineteenth century. But that is not the issue. Classical economists focused on prosperous decades and ignored those of poverty and starvation. In their theories there was no room for mass suffering.

Why? Why were the classicists blind to the reality of long periods of unemployment? The reason is good old self-interest. I have argued elsewhere that from the beginning the United States has been in the age of acquisitors, where money dominates politics and inspires the ideas of intellectuals.[16] Throughout history the majority of intellectuals have championed those ideas that justify the needs of the dominant group in society. Therefore when money rules politics, popular theories reflect the concerns of the affluent.

During the nineteenth century money was in the hands of the newly emerging capitalists. Their interests were pitted against the concerns of wage earners and farmers. Since businessmen hated government intervention, the classical economists also hated government intervention. Corporate tycoons financed the activity of many think tanks, which in turn advised the government to keep its hands off banks and companies even as the public agonized over mass unemployment. Then, as now, it was not in the self-interest of the economist to focus on the agony of the destitute.

The classical illogic mainly afflicted the analysis of credit markets. The classicists had argued that when an excess of savings leads to overproduction, then banks are stuck with idle funds, because, after all, people park their savings with the banking system. These idle funds induce banks to lower the rate of interest, so that business investment rises to absorb all the excess saving, and overproduction disappears.

But the classical economist forgot that few idle funds exist in the case of overproduction, because the banks then have to finance the excess inventory that piles up on store shelves. If some goods remain unsold, businesses have little revenue coming, so they have to borrow money just to continue their truncated operations. In the absence of these idle funds, banks have no reason to trim their interest rates. So the classical logic breaks down.

Another problem with the logic is that overproduction generates a recession, and who would want to increase investment in a slump? Who would like to expand their business when unsold goods are piling up on their shelves? For these two reasons, overproduction does not vanish in a hurry, and recessions can last longer than one or two years.

KEYNESIAN ECONOMICS

When an illogical idea reigns for long, the end result is a catastrophe. That's what happened in 1929 when the lofty stock market crashed and spawned the Great Depression. This slump was the granddaddy of all, and even economists could not ignore its impact. This time the explosion was heard around the world, and the think tanks confronted the sort of shame they had never faced before.

Moved by mass suffering, a brilliant economist named John Maynard Keynes offered an alternative to the classical paradigm. His masterpiece, *The General Theory of Employment, Interest and Money*, appeared in 1936. Turning Say's law around, Keynes argued that demand creates its own supply. This made far more sense than the thesis that supply creates its own demand, at least in an advanced economy, where the engines of production already exist, because if there is adequate spending or demand, companies come forward to match that demand through supply to earn a profit. It is in their self-interest to do so.

However, if demand is insufficient, businesses are stuck with unsold goods. There is overproduction, and workers are fired. Under these circumstances, according to classical economists, the interest rate falls and employers expand their investment until excess supply disappears in both the product and the labor market.

Keynes, however, saw it differently. If the producers have already over-invested, they are in no position to expand capital spending; they may also be reluctant to do so in the wake of inadequate product demand. In this case overproduction will remain a problem for a long time to come. Therefore, because of insufficient demand, the economy will be trapped in a downward spiral of unemployment, poverty, and mass starvation.

Here then is a rationale for government interference. When the system, by itself, is unable to move out of the poverty trap, someone from outside has to give it a nudge. Keynesian medicine reflected his diagnosis. The government must artificially expand aggregate demand by increasing its spending or cutting taxes, which in turn induces the public to increase its spending. Thus expenditures have to rise, either by the government or the people or both. All this to Keynes was expansionary fiscal policy.

The State could also help by inducing the banks to lend more money to businesses in order to stimulate investment. Keynes called this expansionary monetary policy. But with business aversion to investment so high during the Depression, he preferred fiscal expansion to monetary ease.

Keynes offered very general ideas, even those that tackle inflation, which was far from anyone's mind in the 1930s. His prescriptions for what he called true inflation were just the opposite of those for fighting unemployment. Inflation could be cured with the help of surplus budgets and/or restrictive monetary policy. The idea was to dampen aggregate demand or spending to bring prices under control.

Keynesian logic made a lot of sense at the time. But intellectuals, in general, have another problem. In addition to kowtowing to the rich, they also usually have massive egos, which keep them from new ideas. Most experts seek to offer their own theories to win recognition and perks. It is only in the last resort that men and women of letters discard their outdated dogmas. That is why throughout history intellectuals as a class have been the last to adopt new ideas. Nonintellectuals, inspired by a rebellious intellectual, are always in the vanguard of progressive philosophies.

Under the influence of orthodox economists, FDR largely disregarded earnest pleas from Keynes to launch a massive public works program. Classical experts had always favored balanced budgets to avoid market intervention and inflation. Keynes's advocacy of budget deficits to stimulate demand was something new and irritating to them.

President Herbert Hoover had already ignored Keynes by more than doubling the income tax in 1932. FDR added another insult by raising the tax in 1934 and then by lifting taxes frequently till the end of the decade. The results were predictably disastrous. The Depression lasted all through the decade with the rate of unemployment as high as 17 percent in 1939. See what happens when irrationality shapes policy? People suffered because the leaders trusted the self-serving ideas of economists, most of whom were engaged in pleasing their affluent patrons.

Keynesian economics replaced the classical model after World War II, which forced the Western world to adopt deficit budgets. Europe and the United States had no choice except to spend massively on armament. Soon unemployment vanished and gave way to spot shortages of workers. Keynes was right after all; demand was creating its own supply.

Greenspan devoured Keynes's writings as he had those of the classicists, but he did not accept Keynesian ideas wholeheartedly. Deficit budgets through higher government spending would never appeal to him, but Keynesian monetary policy held its charm; he practiced it frequently after becoming the Fed chairman in 1987, not just to fight unemployment or inflation but also to protect the profits of businessmen from their own mistakes. Keynesian economics infused a dose of pragmatism in Greenspan when he joined the government and had to deal with politicians as well as crises.

Ayn Rand

Just about the time Keynesian thought took hold among economists, Greenspan graduated summa cum laude with a B.S. in economics from New York University (NYU) in 1948. Two years later, he earned his master's degree, and two years after that he met Ayn Rand, who would influence him like no one else. Rand was a Russian novelist and philosopher, who had emigrated to the United States. She had made her mark through a best-seller, *The Fountainhead*, which offered libertarian philosophy disguised as a novel. The book was made into a popular film, starring two Hollywood celebrities, Patricia Neal and Gary Cooper, and turned Rand into a celebrity herself. By the early 1950s, she had become the center of her own movement, which championed what is known as objectivism and exalted rational selfishness à la Adam Smith and Jeremy Bentham. In *The Virtue of Selfishness: A New Concept of Egoism*, she explained why the pursuit of self-interest is a person's highest moral obligation.

Rand denounced pre-capitalistic thought as altruistic: altruism to her was an idea that calls upon men and women to make sacrifices for the sake of the common good. This was not rational, because it is self-interest, not the public benefit, that is natural to people. Thus all pre-capitalist societies were based on unnatural ideas and therefore suffered from poverty and tyranny. Rand believed in individualism as opposed to state collectivism and welfare states that uphold tribal or communal values. Needless to say, she opposed socialism, communism, and any form of government intervention in the economy.

She regarded JFK as a fascist dictator because he had the gall to say: "Ask not what your country can do for you. Ask what you can do for your country." President Kennedy may be acclaimed by millions for making this statement, but to Rand it was the height of altruistic betrayal, because it amounted to sacrificing the individual good at the altar of the social good. Her contempt for JFK was no less than that for Mussolini and Hitler. Alan Greenspan and his co-disciples were Rand's ardent supporters. They cheered her lustily when at a speech delivered in Boston she called JFK's program "The Fascist New Frontier."[17] With Kennedy's election, writes Jerome Tuccille, "Alan [Greenspan] and his cohorts were convinced that the Brave New World of Fascism had taken root in America."[18]

Ayn Rand had a profound and lasting influence on Greenspan. He told *Newsweek* in 1974: "When I met Ayn Rand, I was a free-enterpriser in the Adam Smith sense—impressed with the theoretical structure and efficiency of markets. What she did—through long discussions and lots of arguments into the night—was to make me think why capitalism is not only efficient and practical, but also moral."[19] However, this is one case in which the flow of ideas was not just a one-way street between the teacher and the pupil. Greenspan's biographer, Tuccille, suggests that "Rand, *taking a cue from Alan*, referred to big business as 'America's persecuted minority' "[20] (my italics). While Rand taught him about JFK's fascism and about the moral superiority of capitalism, Greenspan shaped her views about the "utter nonsense" of antitrust laws and the American persecution of big business.[21]

Stagflation

Keynesian economics helped Greenspan in an unexpected way. Most of the prominent economists in the early 1960s were Keynesian while Greenspan held conservative and libertarian views. He was frequently sought out by the media to offer the alternative point of view. This way he gained prominence as a conservative economist and captured the attention of influential Republicans. In 1968, he became a part-time adviser to President Nixon, and later offered him advice on various economic issues. But he never got close to the president. In 1974, however, Greenspan became a full-fledged government official when President Gerald Ford appointed him as the chairman of the Council of Economic Advisers.

Greenspan had finally arrived, but it was not the best of times for an economist. The United States and the rest of the world faced intractable challenges that included joblessness and inflation at the same time.

Such a state of affairs is known as stagflation, i.e., inflation in a stagnant economy.

One reason for stagflation was the enormous rise in the international price of oil engineered by OPEC, the oil cartel. The cartel had jacked up the price of crude oil fourfold, and created a global recession along with some inflation. Keynesian economics was not particularly suited to this problem; nor were the economists who were mostly Keynesian.

Another reason was the degeneration of Keynesian economics itself. Unfortunately, every rational idea falls into the hands of pundits who abuse it with abandon and ultimately bring discredit to its originator. Keynes had favored deficit spending to combat depressions, not to fight low levels of unemployment. He had also counseled creating surplus budgets to retire government debt in times of prosperity. But his followers, known as Neo-Keynesians and Post-Keynesians, argued for monetary and fiscal ease whenever joblessness rose in the economy, while politicians failed to adopt budget surpluses even in good times.

A new problem now arose. While employment remained high, prices began to rise, never to fall back to their old levels again. Keynesians argued that high inflation was the evil that society had to endure to escape the greater evil of layoffs. Persistent inflation, in other words, was a small price that the developed economies had to pay to avoid the recessions that had afflicted workers in the past. And all that was needed were high levels of money growth to finance the persistent budget shortfalls. Thus was born the dogma that deficit financing can permanently lower the rate of unemployment.

On the surface this was a myopic thesis. If it is so simple to eradicate unemployment and hence poverty, all a country has to do is to print money to finance its budget deficits. This is another version of the economics of "free lunch." You don't need a copious brain to see the dubious nature of the dogma of deficit financing. Yet the economists persisted with it and eventually hurled the world into another major crisis—this time stagflation.

JFK was the first president to adopt budget deficits for the sole purpose of stimulating economic growth. He followed Keynes by trimming taxes mainly for middle-income individuals and small corporations. Tragically, he was assassinated a year before his tax cuts went into effect in 1964. What followed was a long period of expansion during which joblessness fell from 6 percent to about 3.5 percent of the labor force. However, the rate of inflation, which climbed from 1 percent in 1964 to 5 percent in 1969, became a major headache.

After 1969 both unemployment and inflation began to rise, and the world faced a new menace. Those who seemed to have discovered a permanent cure for unemployment were now on the defensive. They had viewed inflation as a small price for high employment. But now joblessness and inflation rose together, for the first time since 1920. No longer was there a tradeoff between soaring prices and layoffs.

The worst was yet to come. In 1973, OPEC raised the price of oil from $2.59 per barrel to $10. The result was a traumatic shock to the world economy. Supply and demand are like two feathers of a bird, which cannot fly on one wing alone. If the Great Depression resulted from plummeting demand, the stagflation of the 1970s arose from tumbling supply. Soaring oil and energy prices sent production costs into an upward spiral, forcing employers to trim their output of goods and services. When supply falls relative to demand, Keynesian strategy becomes self-destructive.

Deficit financing had already generated higher inflation; the supply shock pushed prices into the stratosphere. As production fell, the employers needed fewer employees, forcing further layoffs. Stagflation became worse in 1975, a year after Greenspan arrived.

Despite the maestro's objections, a Democratic Congress piled more deficit financing on the nation. The Fed chairman, Arthur Burns, even though worried about inflation, printed enough money to finance the budget deficit, so that inflation remained stubborn even in 1976. But unemployment began to fall, aided by a temporary income-tax cut that had the reluctant blessings of Greenspan. This reflected the Keynesian streak of deficit budgeting in the CEA chairman, but it relied on a cut in the income tax, not a rise in government spending. Greenspan had also sought a cut in federal spending to match the fall in income-tax receipts, but the lawmakers did not go along. So while the income tax was trimmed, government expenditure was not, and the budget deficit only went up.

The economic recovery was too tepid to help Ford in the presidential election of 1976, and he lost to Jimmy Carter in a close election. Greenspan along with other Republican officials now had to resign. But deficit financing and stagflation continued and become worse with yet another jump in the price of oil in 1979. Inflation was now out of control. It had persisted for so long that it generated inflationary expectations, which led to rising interest rates and wages. In 1980, the rate of inflation jumped to 13.5 percent, coupled with a jobless rate of 7 percent. It was clear that President Carter's days were numbered. He was defeated in a landslide by

Reagan, who, as you already know, brought Greenspan back into the government with an offer to chair the Social Security commission in 1981.

Greenspan, along with other economists, learned an important lesson from the experience of the 1970s: don't let inflation persist and get out of control, because it then spawns inflationary expectations that feed on themselves. Wages rise, lead to a rise in production costs for businesses, and further fuel the price spiral. Don't let money growth run amok, because, when too many dollars chase too few goods, prices swell at a torrid pace. Finally, keep the budget deficits under control, so the Fed does not have to print money to finance them. The experience of the 1970s reinforced Greenspan's belief in balanced budgets and low money growth.

Supply-Side Economics

A new school of economic thought came into prominence when Reagan became president in 1981. During the election campaign he had assured the electorate that he would cut income and corporate taxes, raise defense spending, and still balance the federal budget. So incongruous was this plan that during the heat of the primaries in 1980, his own vice-president to be, Bush Sr., had denounced it in the strongest possible terms, and called it "voodoo economics." Voodoo or not, Reagan's program was enacted in mid-1981, and its theoretical underpinnings, known as supply-side economics, then came into the limelight.

Although the supply-side theory is philosophically aligned with classical economics, it is principally associated with two individuals—one economist, Arthur Laffer, and one politician, Jack Kemp. It has been taken seriously for more than two decades, even though it blatantly peddles the interests of the affluent.

Supply-siders argue that low income and capital gains taxes on the rich stimulate savings, investment, and economic growth. This was the gospel of Republicans and conservative economists throughout the twentieth century, and in that respect it differs little from classical economics. To many people this viewpoint sounds self-serving, but it was implemented in the 1980s, and again between 2001 and 2004. Former HUD (Housing and Urban Development) Secretary Jack Kemp was and remains a vocal supporter of this idea. In his view, "all proposals to expand the economy by lowering taxes on work, saving and entrepreneurship . . . deserve to be discussed and debated, without being dismissed as a boon to the rich."[22]

Never before has the argument about cuts in the income tax been presented in a straightforward, candid way. It has always been cloaked in the masquerade of the public benefit. The income tax should be trimmed not for the welfare of the well-to-do, but for social welfare. Such has been the persistent refrain of Republican politicians and their supportive think tanks, although both groups are usually on the payroll of multimillionaires.

As Mr. Kemp argues, low taxes are not just a nice gift of the U.S. Treasury to the rich, but also stimulate economic growth by promoting work effort, savings, and investment. The behavior of the economy in the 1980s is often cited in support of supply-side economics. In the Reagan–Greenspan tax cut of 1981, Congress enacted the president's program, in which the average income tax rates were reduced by 25 percent over three years. This was an across-the-board cut that replaced the 14 to 70 percent tax range of the 1970s with an 11 to 50 percent range.

Supply-siders argue that such incentive-oriented cuts in taxes expand national output more than national demand. So when supply runs ahead of demand, prices fall and inflation comes under control. With rising supply, new jobs are created to trim the rate of unemployment. So the supply-side prescription seems to be the best antidote for stagflation; it claims that falling joblessness can go along with falling inflation, provided the government unleashes the productive and innovative energies of the rich through tax handouts and incentives. The government budget deficit also turns into balance, because incentives generate so much economic growth and income that tax receipts soar because of dwindling taxes. Thus the Laffer–Kemp theory truly offers a free lunch. People get tax benefits, new jobs, and a declining rate of inflation—without any sacrifice.

Free lunch always fascinates the public. It also fascinated Mr. Reagan, who campaigned on this platform and then quickly had it passed once he became the president. In the background of the disastrous economy that Jimmy Carter had left behind, people were desperate for hope, which the new president supplied in abundance, and they supported him even in a voodoo-oriented experiment. We shall explore the efficacy of various economic ideas in the pages to come, but here you may recall how desperate the lawmakers had become for new revenues after the Reagan program was adopted, so much so that they raised payroll and excise taxes sharply. The supply-side plan was truly rational selfishness, because it really offered free lunch—to the wealthy, while everyone else got the shaft.

Paul Volcker

If Ayn Rand initiated Greenspan into the virtues of selfishness and the moral excellence of capitalism, Paul Volcker showed him how important it was to tame the monster of inflation. Volcker became the Fed chairman in 1979, in the background of roaring inflation and surging interest rates and unemployment. At first, the new chairman persevered with the policies adopted by his precursor, Arthur Burns, who had frequently printed the greenback to finance government deficits; but soon the worsening stagflation convinced him that something new had to be tried. Deficit financing could not tackle the mess caused by rising oil prices.

Volcker had to take on the Neo-Keynesians who believed in a tradeoff between inflation and unemployment. The reality appeared to be very different: instead of curing joblessness, rising inflation accentuated the specter of unemployment. Thus the price spiral had to be tamed first, if only to suppress inflationary expectations, so workers, bankers, and businesses could plan their future with less uncertainty. This would then trim demands for wage increases, lower the rate of interest, and spur investment.

But taming inflation first was politically unpopular, because it would initially worsen the problem of unemployment, a risk Volcker felt he had to take to restore the long-term health of the economy. He restrained the money pump and trimmed the growth of money supply below the growth of prices. Initial results were catastrophic—a further rise in interest rates, from 1980 to 1982, followed by plummeting spending and the worst recession since the 1930s.

But as aggregate spending fell, inflation began to sink, blunting the inflationary expectations. Interest rates also declined, enough to enable Volcker to change the course by the end of 1982. As he opened the money pump, interest rates fell further, and a virtuous cycle began. The end result was a long period of recovery and business expansion, lasting up to 1989, with both inflation and unemployment shrinking gingerly.

Greenspan, along with other economists, learned a precious lesson from Volcker. Never print so much money that inflation gets out of control, because then joblessness grows, not falls. Tame the inflation monster the moment it shows up and strikes, even if politicians frown. So today any inflation rate persisting above 3 percent causes alarm among economists and policymakers, especially Greenspan.

GREENOMICS: AN OVERVIEW

It should be clear by now that Greenomics has been influenced by a variety of writers and circumstances. It's a complex brew of classical, Keynesian, and Randian ideas. Let's summarize its various prescriptions as they had developed by 1987, the year Greenspan became the Fed chairman:

1. As much as possible, the government should leave the economy alone.
2. There should be no legislation setting a minimum wage.
3. Income tax rates on individuals and corporations should be low.
4. The government budget should be in balance, and lower income taxes should be followed by lower government spending or higher non-income levies.
5. There should be few, if any, regulations inhibiting businessmen and bankers.
6. Money growth should be kept low to keep inflation under control.
7. Antitrust laws should be abolished or enforced sporadically.

All these measures, except number 7, reflect the ethos of classical laissez-faire economics, which requires antitrust laws to preserve competition and thus ensure production efficiency and high growth. However, Greenspan maintains that such laws may hurt productivity and profit, and thus inhibit growth. Exuberant profits or after-tax income of business executives play a supreme role in Greenomics, which, in this regard, resembles supply-side economics.

But unlike a supply-sider, who is at best indifferent to budget shortfalls, Greenspan exalts balanced budgets. For both of them, unfettered profits, or super greed, define free markets. To Greenspan, once any measure restrains profits, markets cease to be free and give way to a mixed or regulated economy.[23] This much has been argued here, and will become even clearer in the pages to come. Greenomics is Greedomics, pure and simple.

Greenomics is a caricature of supply-side economics, which would rather have the government borrow money from credit markets than balance its books, and let the future generations face the hammer of debt. Greenomics oppresses the poor of today, supply-side economics those of tomorrow. Which is worse? They are both cowardly and nefarious, because they shift the tax burden from the haves to the have-nots. They both reward the opulent and trample the destitute. Contrary to popular belief, it's Greenomics, not supply-side economics, that has largely shaped government policy since 1981, because the tax rises of 1982, 1983, 1990, and 1993 infuriated the supply-siders, but had Greenspan's blessings.

Greenomics has been followed in the United States ever since 1981. At first, its rewards made people dizzy with joy as they tasted free lunch for many years, but then disaster struck in the form of the share market crash from 2000 to 2002. The Nasdaq stock index was especially hit hard, sinking by as much as 78 percent. Scandal after scandal engulfed corporations, forcing even the maestro to denounce, of all things, greed. The man who had once acclaimed business greed as "the unexcelled protector of the consumer," railed against corporate excesses that occurred in the 1990s because of "an outsized increase in the opportunities for avarice. An infectious greed seemed to grip much of our business community. . . . It is not that humans have become any more greedy than in generations past. It is that the avenues to express greed had grown so enormously."[24] You wonder whose ideas and actions germinated all those avenues and opportunities for avarice.

4

GREENSPAN'S
INTELLECTUAL FRAUD

G reenspan is a household name, not just in the United States but also around the world. Even a brief statement or unintentional nod from him can send ripples in financial markets across the globe, up and down. Some consider him to be the best economist in the world, far and above the Nobel laureates. Whenever and wherever he talks, people, especially stock analysts and brokers, take notes and listen. "If commerce rules the world, then Alan Greenspan is its king," said an editorial in *The San Francisco Chronicle* in September 1998.[1] Bob Novak, the columnist of *The Chicago Sun-Times* and a regular presence on CNN, called him the "Master of the Universe" in 1999.[2]

But that was then. Following the stock market crash in 2000–2002, the sluggish job market, and his latest assault on Social Security benefits, Greenspan's gloss has dimmed considerably, and some have gone to the extent of declaring his actions a scam, a con job, or worse. Here's what William Greider, a best-selling author and an expert on the workings of the Federal Reserve, thinks of him:

> It is not exactly that he lies, but Alan Greenspan certainly ranks among the most duplicitous figures to serve in modern American government. Using his exalted status as economic wizard, the Federal Reserve chairman regularly corrupts the political dialogue by sowing outrageously false impressions among gullible members of Congress and adoring financial reporters.[3]

So who is Greenspan—the intellectual genius or maestro of adoring biographers and executives managing giant Wall Street firms, or one of the most duplicitous government officials in recent years? You have already observed the relentless Social Security fraud that he has inflicted on tens of millions of Americans for over two decades. Now we will explore his major contributions as Fed chairman, for which he has mostly received acclaim. The picture that emerges below is one of an intelligent man centered on the self. More than anything else, Alan Greenspan seems to take care of Alan Greenspan. His life and accomplishments turn out to be a fitting monument to Ayn Rand's philosophy of rational selfishness.

I will show that Greenspan repeatedly used his genius to alter his arguments, theories, and opinions to rise to the seat of power and remain there as long as possible. This amounts to intellectual fraud on a grand scale. Some exalt his changing views as pragmatism, but if you carefully examine his background, beliefs, mentors, and, above all, actions, it becomes clear that Mr. Greenspan has tailored his positions time and again to remain at the helm of the Federal Reserve and be adored as possibly the most powerful person in the world, towering at times over the president. An honest scholar sticks to his logic and theories and alters them only when faced with new, compelling evidence. But Greenspan usually changed his views when there was a changing of the guard at the White House.

WHAT IS INTELLECTUAL FRAUD?

Normally intellectual fraud implies grave misconduct on the part of a researcher with an intent to deceive the reader or audience, using fake or selective data, plagiarism, or some gross falsification. This type of deception occasionally occurs at universities or research-oriented institutions. The culprit commits the act intentionally or recklessly for personal benefit in the form of monetary gain, self-promotion, or both.[4]

This is not the notion adopted here. Intellectual fraud does not have to be based on faulty research. It can also appear when someone doggedly pursues self-interest to foster theories that have no historical basis at all, or that repeatedly contradict themselves. This type of deception usually involves preconceived ideas, ideological agendas, or illogical notions that a person tailors to fit with changing circumstances, mostly for personal gain.

Usually such fraud has little impact on society, but it can be disastrous to people if the perpetrator is a man of influence. The spate of corporate scandals reported from 2001 to 2004, aided by highly literate men and women, is a case in point. The scandals bankrupted companies, and destroyed the lives of millions of workers and investors associated with them. People lost billions in the stock market tumble linked partly to corporate malfeasance.

This was financial fraud that could not have been perpetrated without the active participation of some bankers, Wall Street analysts, attorneys, and accountants. These hucksters were well-educated people, mostly with postgraduate degrees, who used their superior intellect to write or endorse false reports about the financial strength of corporations they studied. They earned millions for themselves, while inflicting pain on millions of people around the globe. They had committed an intellectual trickery that culminated in a financial scam. In an informative book, *Origins of the Crash*, financial writer Roger Lowenstein details the culture of corruption that plagued corporate America in the 1990s.[5] He describes the stuff of which intellectual fraud is really made.

Intellectual fraud involves the misuse of intellect to fool others or offer baseless theses for personal gain. The perpetrators of fraud generally contradict themselves, often changing their views with changing circumstances. It is their intelligence that helps them con others. They have no core convictions; they profit by cooking up theories or insisting on something that is false. The main point is that intellectual fraud involves the abuse of one's superior intellect to generate contradictory ideas or theories mainly for personal benefit.

It is well known that Wall Street analysts frequently deceived their clients during the 1990s. They inflated company earnings, knowingly recommended worthless stocks to investors, and almost always asked people to buy, not sell, shares. Most of them worked for large brokerage houses. But for the relentless pursuit of New York Attorney General Eliot Spitzer, their fraudulent activities would still be unknown. His diligence forced five big Wall Street firms—Morgan Stanley, UBS Warburg, Salomon Smith Barney (a unit of Citigroup), Credit Suisse of First Boston, and Bear Stearns—to pay more than half a billion dollars in fines for their role in the research scam. They either hired analysts who falsified stock research or paid money to obtain research beneficial to their client companies.[6]

Securities fraud by Wall Streeters is the latest, and perhaps the most blatant, example of intellectual fraud. But there are some not so obvious types as well. Supply-side economics is a theory where fraud is not so obvious, but where scholarship is so self-serving that it verges on fraud. Its ideas defy common sense, and not surprisingly all its forecasts have repeatedly turned out to be wrong.

In 1980–1981, supply-side acolytes predicted that sharply lower income and corporate taxes would increase national supply much more than national demand, so that inflation and unemployment would quickly fall and the government budget deficit would vanish, definitely by 1984, when President Reagan would be up for reelection.

They had inherited a jobless rate of 7 percent, an inflation rate of 13.5 percent, and a deficit rate of 2 percent from Jimmy Carter. Then unemployment jumped to 10 percent by December 1982, and did not come down to the 1980 rate until 1986. For six long years the public paid a price for the dogma of supply-siders. The budget deficit also jumped to 6 percent of output in 1983, and remained above its 1980 level even at the end of the decade. Inflation did tumble, but most economists credit that achievement to Fed Chairman Volcker's policy of monetary restraint, which, in fact, was resisted by supply-siders.

In 1993, President Clinton engineered an economic package that included spending restraint coupled with a rise in the income tax on the top 2 percent of earners. Supply-siders vehemently opposed this policy, which they claimed would destroy the economy. Not a single Republican senator voted for this program.

Eventually all the rosy forecasts that supply-siders had made in the early 1980s came to pass in the late 1990s, not from their plan but from Clinton's plan. Joblessness, inflation, and the deficit all plummeted. So what did the supply-siders claim? The Clinton economic boom sprang from Reagan's program. This is intellectual fraud. The boom occurred after 1995, whereas the Reagan plan was adopted between 1981 and 1983. So, how is Reagan responsible for the Clinton boom?[7]

Greenspan's intellectual fraud loosely fits with the cases mentioned above. It is not a perfect fit, as few examples are for each other, but it has elements of the scams we have just explored. We will examine the illogical nature of Greenomics in chapters to come. Here we will explore Greenspan's actions and views that led up to his appointment as the chairman of the Federal Reserve, and his subsequent policies.

GREENSPAN'S UPBRINGING AND CAREER

Greenspan was born on March 6, 1926 in New York City, and spent his early childhood in a small, unassuming apartment in upper Manhattan. He lived in poverty in a household broken by divorce. He was a child prodigy, a math wizard, and even early on displayed a love for numbers and classical music. As a young boy, he was idealistic and capable of displaying moral courage. "From the time he was very young," writes Justin Martin, an author and biographer, "Greenspan showed an idiosyncratic but highly developed sense of morality."[8]

Greenspan displayed unusual versatility in his youth and excelled in many areas. A precocious student from childhood, he became good at playing clarinet and saxophone. Also, he almost made it onto his school's baseball team.

Later, after graduating from high school at age 17, he would lose interest in music and turn to classical economics and philosophy, but the love of sports would continue. He also became a reasonable tennis player. Another man of great fame in the future, Secretary of State Henry Kissinger, attended the same school as Greenspan, but the two did not become friends until much later, in the 1960s.

A big problem that Greenspan faced as a teenager was not poverty, but his social life, which, like that of many youngsters, was lackluster. He wanted to go out with several girls, but few were interested in him.[9] His math wizardry and a sharp mind seemed to be of no help in the matter. Perhaps his shyness and quiet demeanor had something to do with it. Such lack of social life would later play a role in his career.

When Greenspan turned 20, he attended New York University (NYU). By that time he had read, and perhaps mastered, the works of Adam Smith as well as Jeremy Bentham, the duo that exerted major influence on the classical economic thought explored in chapter 2. Bentham appears to sway the maestro even more than Smith. Bentham's well-known principle of hedonic calculus left a lasting imprint on Greenspan, because, as we shall see later, many of his variegated activities seemed to be guided by this principle.

Hedonic calculus begins with the idea that the pursuit of happiness is the fundamental purpose of human life. All actions offer pleasure or pain, utility or disutility, both of which can be measured and entered into an equation that shapes one's actions. A person does something only if the sum total of pleasure from the act exceeds its potential pain. Otherwise, the person turns to some other act and then applies the same principle. This way all actions are determined by hedonic calculations. Thus, employment, friendship, relationships, asceticism, liberty, altruism, duty, faith, law abidance, etc., are all reducible to the considerations of pain and pleasure.

Bentham's hedonic calculus is closely linked to his view of human nature. Motivated by pleasure and pain, people value self-interest above social interest. They act to maximize their utility regardless of the consequences for the rest of society and are primarily concerned with their own welfare. Thus all individuals are egoists and coldly calculating in attaining their goals, and little else than rationality determines their activities.

Bentham's thought has a lot in common with that of Ayn Rand, the philosopher, who as we saw in the last chapter, strongly influenced Greenspan's views in the 1950s and the 1960s. Both Bentham and Rand believe that human beings are rational and act primarily in self-interest. They both suggest that man's rationality involves using the faculty of reason in order to be happy or to survive.

Bentham believes that people are egoists, forever engaged in hedonic calculus, whereas Rand argues that if people act egoistically and selfishly, society prospers. Bentham's system is usually called psychological egoism, Rand's ethical egoism. Both Bentham and Rand exalt the individual over family and society; they both argue that the individual precedes society, which is simply the sum total of all individuals; thus personal interest dwarfs the social interest.

Of course, Rand and Bentham have serious differences, altruism being one of them. Rand categorically rejects it, Bentham embraces it. Similarly, while Bentham believes people act selfishly, Rand advises that people should act selfishly in order to enhance social well-being. However, Rand's concept of selfishness does not include dishonesty and lethargy, and it is easy to see why Greenspan was attracted to her when he met her in the early 1950s. Their common attraction to Bentham's views made it natural for them to mingle.

From Bentham Greenspan learned that one acts in a calculating way to maximize one's happiness; from Rand, he learned that one should act selfishly, so social welfare is maximized, and they both taught him that individual interests are primary, while social interests are secondary.[10] Add to all this the judgement by classical economists that people don't like to work unless forced by hunger, and you have the bulk of the thought process that underlies Greenspan's modus operandi and ideas, culminating in Greenomics.

Classical economics is often said to derive from the abstract philosophy of classical liberalism that viewed the poor as undeserving of anything more than subsistence living. (Classical liberalism should not be confused with the modern liberal creed that relies more on Keynesian thought.)

The most popular idea prior to the psychological egoism postulated by the eighteenth century liberals, was known as the Christian paternalistic ethic, which held that the family, not the individual, was the fundamental or dominant organ of society. So the family had to take care of its indigent members, a view that had spawned a variety of laws in England to deal with poverty. Everyone was entitled to a minimum, subsistence lifestyle, and the State offered welfare to the sick, the destitute, and the handicapped. Such laws had existed since 1601, originating in the days of Queen Elizabeth.

However, the paternalistic ethic gave way to the doctrine of individualism in nineteenth-century England. Classical liberalism maintained that everyone was responsible for his own welfare; everyone had to learn to stand on his own feet. The practical impact of the new view was the repeal of laws that tended to keep people from hunger and abject poverty. The classical view that wages should be as low as possible was also an extension of the prevailing belief that laborers labor only when goaded by hunger.

Greenspan knew classical economics almost by heart. Adam Smith and other classicists were his real teachers at NYU, which in the 1940s was a bastion of conservatism and tended to slight Keynesian economics. But Keynes was the talk of the whole world at that time, and Greenspan could not but be infected by the emerging revolution in economic thinking. On balance, Greenspan persisted with his tilt toward free-market ideas, although the novelty of Keynesian economics fascinated him.

After graduating in 1948, Greenspan took a job with the Conference Board, a non-profit think tank that conducted research on individual industries and the economy. He earned $4,000 a year, a respectable salary at the time. The money enabled him to take night classes at NYU to pursue his master's, which he obtained in 1950. The same year he switched to Columbia University to do his doctorate in economics. There he met a prominent conservative economist, Arthur Burns, who also championed free-market capitalism. Naturally, Greenspan and his mentor became good friends, and remained so for life. But two years later, Greenspan had to drop out of the university for lack of time and sufficient funds. His full-time job kept him busy and left him with little energy and time to continue with his Ph.D.

In 1952, Greenspan married, but the marriage failed and dissolved ten months later. This must have been a traumatic and lonely period in his life. Perhaps for this reason, from 1953 on, he began to frequent the Objectivist club that had been founded by Ayn Rand. The club not only offered heated and extensive debates on economics but also a familial atmosphere, along with like-minded women for socializing.[11] Soon he became a part of Rand's inner circle. He was charmed by Rand's exaltation of capitalism as a moral system, and quickly discarded whatever sympathies he had developed for Keynesian ideas.

On her part, Rand respected Greenspan for his sharp mind and business acumen, but occasionally doubted his commitment to her cause. She thought "Alan might basically be a social climber," an "undertaker," and an opportunist interested mainly in advancing his career.[12] Over time, however, they grew closer, especially after she began writing her new novel, *Atlas Shrugged*, for which Greenspan provided extensive research assistance. The novel, notes author Justin Martin, was "a twist on the old Robin Hood tale. Danneskjold [a character in the novel] steals from the poor and gives to the rich."[13]

The novel, written in 1957, received less than complimentary reviews. A critic described it as a lousy piece of fiction; another deemed it preposterous. The worst came from Granville Hicks, who wrote for *The New York Times:* "loudly as Miss Rand proclaims her love of life, it seems clear that the book is written out of hate."[14] Rand was shocked; so was Greenspan. He sent an angry retort to the *Times*, claiming that "*Atlas Shrugged* is a celebration of life and happiness. Justice is unrelenting."[15]

Now we can surmise what motivated Greenspan when he later became the chairman of the National Commission on Social Security Reform. In view of his background, his recommendations about Social Security were also a twist on the Robin Hood tale, just as in *Atlas Shrugged*. In 1981, Greenspan advocated a massive cut in the income tax, in 1983 a massive rise in the payroll tax. So, "Justice is unrelenting": rob the poor via high payroll taxes and reward the rich in the form of income-tax cuts. This was not Robin Hood but Robber Baron taxation.

In 1954, Greenspan quit his job with the Conference Board and formed a partnership with a businessman named William Townsend. Their firm, called Townsend-Greenspan & Company, offered consulting services about the economy, something similar to the work that Greenspan had done at his previous job. Greenspan's scholarship and math aptitude now found full expression and brought him monetary rewards. He began to win acclaim as a forecaster, bringing the firm an increasing number of clients. For the first time in his life, Greenspan was becoming rich.

His partner died in 1958, and Greenspan took over the company, turning it into a highly profitable operation that offered consulting services to some of the biggest banks in the nation. He would soon become a millionaire, which was quite an accomplishment for someone deprived of money all his life.

During the 1960s, Greenspan would learn firsthand about the difficulties of forecasting. He purchased a computer (about the size of a small office), programmed it, and fed it data. He was sure that the new contraption would enhance his forecasting accuracy. But it did not. As he was to recall much later, at a party in 1995, "we thought we could really pin down the business cycle" with the help of the computer. Computers have become very sophisticated since, but "our ability to forecast has not improved," Greenspan observed. This is because "that crazy economy out there doesn't stand still long enough for us to get a fix on it."[16]

Even though his firm kept him busy, Greenspan found time to write for Rand's newsletter, *The Objectivist*, through which he vented his conservative and iconoclastic views. That is where he aired his tirade against American antitrust laws, FDR's New Deal, and some popular social programs, which he claimed were turning the United States into a welfare state. He had become a committed Randian. But his opinions gained him friendship with high-placed Republicans.

In 1968 Greenspan's life took a new turn. With encouragement from Rand, he entered the arena of politics, and volunteered to join Nixon's presidential campaign. His growing reputation as a conservative economist and forecaster got him a spot on Nixon's team of advisers. But he returned to private practice in early 1969, soon after Nixon was sworn in as the president.

Greenspan was now fascinated with politics, but he remained preoccupied with his consulting firm, offering only informal and part-time economic advice to the new president. For some reason, he was not comfortable working with Nixon. But his old friend and professor, Arthur Burns, who was the Fed chairman under Nixon, prevailed upon him and asked him to join the administration.

However, Nixon resigned in the Watergate scandal in 1974 and was replaced by Gerald Ford, who nominated Greenspan to become the chairman of the Council of Economic Advisers (CEA). This was another coup in Greenspan's meteoric career. He did not have a Ph.D. yet, and had written no seminal article in economics, none that appeared in a major economic journal, but his connections had landed him one of the most prestigious jobs for an economist. Was Rand's reading of him as a social climber right after all?

During the Senate hearing on his confirmation, the Democrats were uneasy about Greenspan's radical views, not his mediocre credentials. Senator William Proxmire remarked: "I have great, great difficulty with the fact that you are a free enterprise man who does not believe in antitrust, does not believe in consumer protection, does not believe in progressive income tax. The latter may be consistent with a laissez faire position, but you seem to be opposed to many of the social programs that we have been able to achieve."[17]

Neither Greenspan nor his backers believed he would be confirmed, but in that electrified air tainted by the Watergate scandal, credentials and beliefs did not seem to matter. What mattered was that Greenspan had stayed aloof from Nixon. He was easily confirmed.

Greenspan had already learned what connections could do for a person, so now he became chummy with the new president. He advised the president not only about economics but also about politics as well as public relations. Ford was an accomplished football player in his youth; so Greenspan developed an instantaneous interest in football, and attended some games with the president. Ford also had an avid interest in golf, so Greenspan hired a golf instructor to learn the game.

Greenspan's sporting interests were baseball and tennis, not football and golf. But football and golf provided avenues to get close to the president, so Greenspan developed a taste for both sports. William Seidman, a Ford adviser in 1974, when interviewed by biographer John Cassidy, said: "He [Greenspan] has the best bedside manner I've ever seen."[18]

Greenspan handed the management of his firm to senior employees, mostly women, of whom some had remained with him since the mid-1950s. According to his biographer, Jerome Tuccille, he enjoyed working with ladies and "was romantically involved with women he hired."[19] There was a reason why Greenspan preferred young female workers to males—lower wages. He confirmed it during an interview in 1983 with *The New York Times:* "I always valued men and women equally, and I found that because others did not, good women economists were cheaper than men. Hiring women does two things: It gives us better quality work for less money, and it raises the market value of women."[20]

Such remarks by the maestro appear to reflect Bentham's hedonic calculations. Greenspan hired qualified women, took better quality work from them, possibly with romantic involvement, paid them lower wages, and still believed that he treated men and women equally. How did paying them lower salaries raise the market value of women? Such glaring contradictions were not lost on the *Times* readers, and some of them said so in their letters to the editor. Letters came from Marsha Levick, the legal director of a New York–based education fund; Mary Ellen Reilly of Pennsylvania; and E. S. Goldman of Massachusetts. They pinpointed the inherent contradictions in Greenspan's words. "How smart can Alan Greenspan be?" Goldman wondered; similarly, Levick opined: "His persistent wage disparity is particularly shameful now . . . 20 years after the passage of the Equal Pay Act."[21]

More than his adviser, Greenspan became Ford's confidant. They developed a natural affinity for each other. But Greenspan's cold calculating nature would shine through once in a while, even though he was a man of reserve and spoke as little as possible. Ford's tenure was marred by surging inflation, combined with high unemployment. These were the days of soaring oil prices along with the torrid money growth that Fed Chairman Arthur Burns, despite his free-market predilection, had engineered. The resulting stagflation created misery in the nation.

The consumer price index rose faster than 10 percent, and joblessness approached 8 percent. Homelessness, hunger, and unemployment stalked the country, while the stock market nosedived. Most people suffered, some far more than others. But a calculating head like that of Greenspan could not fathom the different degrees of suffering. At a summit conference on inflation in 1974, Greenspan said:

> . . . we all have an interest in this economy. If someone believes that there is some way that someone is not hurt by inflation, we are obviously all hurt by inflation. If you really wanted to examine who percentage-wise is hurt the most in their incomes, it is the Wall Street brokers. I mean their incomes have gone down the most. So if you want to get statistical, I mean let's look at what the facts are.[22]

Greenspan's biographers have dismissed these remarks as a "gaffe." But they are far more than a gaffe. They reveal the man's true character. How can anyone who believes big business is America's persecuted minority, or thinks there is unrelenting justice in *Atlas Shrugged*, fathom the difference between the agony of the poverty-stricken hungry and that of the rich Wall Street broker, who may have lost millions from the share market but still has plenty left to eat and drink well?

But you see Greenspan is correct technically, or in terms of Bentham's hedonic calculus—the broker's percentage loss dwarfs that of the destitute.

If the poor and the elderly cannot afford medicines because of soaring prices, the broker may be unable to afford vacations. So what is this mumbo-jumbo about inflation afflicting the poor more than the rich? Such was the refrain of a heartless mind that failed to understand the difference between the pangs of hunger and the discomfort of lost brokerage commissions.

What is so surprising is that Greenspan himself was raised in poverty. He, more than others, should have known how it feels to face galloping prices along with low earnings. But materialistic ideas, especially those that make a virtue of selfishness, can change the makeup of any man. Anyway, Greenspan, ever the pragmatist, was quick to show remorse. "Obviously the poor are suffering more," he declared before an aroused Congress. Of course, the remorse did not last long, because the Social Security provisions of the Greenspan commission in 1983 reveal the same coldness toward the poor that Greenspan displayed in 1974.

Under the tutelage of Burns and Rand, Greenspan had come to deride both deficits and inflation. In Washington's jargon, he was a deficit hawk as well as an inflation hawk. He despised high government spending as well as high money growth. Both, he thought, generated inflation, which he regarded as a bigger evil than unemployment. Ever since World War II taxes had stayed high, even after the ballyhooed tax cut engineered by JFK. Many wanted to trim them during the 1970s, especially because rising inflation and money incomes pushed more and more families into higher tax brackets. But Greenspan resisted the idea of big tax cuts because of their potential to raise the budget deficit, and thus worsen the price spiral.

1975 was a year of crippling stagflation, with inflation at 9 percent and unemployment at 8.5 percent. The situation befuddled economists and lawmakers alike; the roaring price of oil made it all but impossible to devise a proper economic strategy. Some economists wanted to lick inflation first by controlling government spending and money growth; others placed a priority on tackling unemployment by raising the federal deficit through a combination of tax cuts and increases in spending. There were few clear-cut choices.

Greenspan faced an unprecedented dilemma. He was caught between the pull of free-market economics and the Keynesian call for government intervention. The policy choice was complicated by the fact that Ford faced an election the following year, and no president wants to confront the electorate with high joblessness.

After initial reluctance and hand-wringing, Greenspan and Ford opted for a tax cut, despite the objections by other advisers. Greenspan had made a flip-flop; a free-market conservative had tilted toward government intervention called forth by the deficit rise that was now inevitable. Yet the flip-flop was minor, not a major departure from his core conviction. For one thing, the tax cut was just 1.4 percent of the nation's GDP; for another it was temporary, and did not touch the tax rates per se. It centered around tax rebates and a slight increase in the standard deduction. However, this was a harbinger of things to come: Greenspan's flip-flops, and major ones, would become common in the future.

The economy recovered in 1976, and both inflation and unemployment declined, with the miniscule tax stimulus playing a tiny role. Greenspan, the unabashed free-marketer, had now become the pragmatic free-marketer. As he told economists Erwin Hargrove and Samuel Morley in 1984: "I often come out almost ad nauseam with free market solutions not because I have an ideology, but because I believe it works. Where it doesn't, I recognize that it doesn't. There are others that presume that unless you prod it all the time, it will never function."[23] And 1975 was the first time the maestro realized that the free-market solution wouldn't work, at least not in time to bring about Ford's election.

However, Greenspan fell a little short of his goal, and Ford was defeated by Jimmy Carter in a close contest. The economy had recovered, but only tepidly, not fast enough to ensure Ford's return. Greenspan went back to New York and took charge of his old firm. But he had been bitten by the bug of politics. It seems he missed his authoritative position and the limelight surrounding it. In order to endear himself to the Republican Party, he frequently criticized the Carter administration. He also made himself available to the media and influential politicians, even the Democrats including, of all people, Senator Ted Kennedy, the brother of JFK, who, to Greenspan and Rand, had fostered that odious altruism.[24] Greenspan knew how to advance socially and politically.

Under Carter, joblessness began a slow decline, but inflation picked up steam, providing ample ammunition to critics like Greenspan, who denounced the president for his excessive spending and budget shortfalls. Greenspan became a deficit hawk again and accused the president of putting the economy "on a track of inflationary deficits."[25]

In December 1977, he wrote an article for *The New York Times*, in which he explained his position regarding tax reductions. He argued that in general all types of tax cuts were inflationary, especially during the price spiral of the 1970s, because they tended to aggravate the budget deficit; but if you must have a tax cut then the corporate tax relief was preferable to one aimed at individual incomes, because only a large tax cut for corporations would spur investment and the economy: "To the extent that one opts for a tax cut at all, the risks of failure are far greater with a heavy emphasis on individual income tax cuts than a very large corporate tax cut."[26]

Again and again Greenspan railed against government spending, which he thought would lead the nation into a severe crisis. On NBC's *Meet the Press* in April 1978 he expressed his worries: "I'm very concerned about a resignation [revival] of inflationary forces in a fundamental way, late in 1979 and 1980. The type of inflation I'm envisioning in that period is clearly a function of federal deficit spending and the expansionary monetary policies required to finance it."[27] He went on to propose sharp cuts in federal spending to control inflation.

In August 1979, Greenspan proposed trimming the corporate income tax from 46 percent to 40 percent to stimulate business investment. This way he kept himself in the headlines and emerged as the chief proponent of business-oriented incentives, favoring tax relief for corporations, not individuals.

Among Republican bigwigs who replaced Gerald Ford and came to dominate their party were George H. W. Bush and Ronald Reagan. They were neck and neck in polls and primaries in early 1980. By then a sea change had already occurred in the nation's thinking. Persistent inflation and the resultant bracket creep had raised the income tax bite for most Americans; the Social Security levy had also risen since 1977, and more than anything else, people wanted tax relief—while still retaining social programs. Few recognized this sea change faster than Reagan, who began advocating a major overhaul of the tax system to bring about a steep reduction in tax rates. He proposed a 30 percent reduction in the income tax collection over three years.

Bush derided Reagan's program as voodoo economics, but its promised tax cut won over the Republican electorate, who chose Reagan to represent their party. 1980 was a year of major flip-flops. First, Bush agreed to join the Republican ticket as its vice-presidential candidate and began campaigning for voodoo economics. Then Greenspan emerged as a front runner in Reagan's economic team, offering an influential voice behind the tax-cut argument. Gone was his concern about inflationary deficits; gone was his worry over rising inflation generating high unemployment; gone was his aversion to high deficits generating high interest rates.

At a meeting of the American Economic Association in September 1980, Greenspan said, "a balanced budget is not an end in itself." "Mr. Greenspan was vague but reassuring about the compatibility of tax cuts, higher defense expenditures and balanced budgets," wrote economist and columnist Leonard Silk.[28] Reagan wanted income tax cuts, so Greenspan—and Bush—wanted income tax cuts as well. Reagan favored higher defense spending to fight the Soviet menace, so Greenspan no longer worried about higher deficits. Opportunism had prevailed over sanity again. Now Reagan, Bush, and Greenspan, the trio of influential Republicans, endorsed the voodoo miracle.

But the Republican self-delusion had just begun. Following Reagan's election in early November 1980, Greenspan's vague support for Reagan's program turned into full-fledged support. On November 8, just four days after Carter's defeat, columnist Philip Shabecoff wrote this: "He [Greenspan] said, 'it was the increasingly common belief among economists that a significant reduction in unemployment would occur only when the long-term inflationary trend was reversed.' That would happen, he added, only when long-term interest rates came down. Mr. Greenspan . . . said that passage of the tax cut sought by Mr. Reagan would be vital in giving credibility to the anti-inflation effort."[29]

In the same interview, Greenspan urged the departing Congress to pass the tax cut even before President-elect Reagan took office next January. Greenspan said this was the "best case" that would convince markets about Reagan's seriousness in tackling inflation and would lead to "a fairly dramatic decline of long-term interest rates. . . . The response of interest rates could be very quick—a matter of weeks." A few months later, on February 18, 1981, he predicted that "enactment of the Reagan program would touch off a substantial decline in such long-term rates as those on home mortgages."[30]

The famous Bush flip-flop is nothing compared to Greenspan's. His remarks to Shabecoff contradicted his prior harangues about Carter's policies and his own article in *The New York Times:* Carter's deficits were inflationary, because they required high money growth to finance them, leading to galloping inflation and interest rates, and hence soaring unemployment. This was Greenspan's prognosis of the Carter program, and it made sense.

But as Reagan's economic adviser, he needed arguments to rationalize what Reagan had promised to win the election. So now the major tax cut would reflect Reagan's seriousness to fight inflation, and convince markets to lower long-term interest rates, even though it might exacerbate the federal deficit. Now the deficit was no longer inflationary. With one wave of the voodoo magic wand, Reagan's deficits would choke inflation and lower interest rates. So argued Greenspan. He essentially asserted that a Republican deficit works opposite to a Democratic deficit.

In his defense, it may be noted that Greenspan also recommended major spending reduction to accompany the tax cut and thus keep the deficit under control. But Greenspan knew from his experience as the CEA chairman that spending cuts were simply impossible, especially in an inflationary environment, because with soaring prices the same level of funding bought substantially less in terms of government services. The most you could hope for was a cut in spending growth below the level of inflation, and that meant a definite rise in the federal deficit. In fact, the budget deficit had jumped sharply from 1975 to 1976 after the Ford-Greenspan tax cut—tiny relative to the Reagan-Greenspan cut of 1981—went into effect.

Greenspan's flip-flop in November 1980 was his first intellectual fraud, and its ramifications could not but have been disastrous. Until then he had backed Reagan's plan vaguely, but now he provided a serious economic argument for its validity. He contradicted his earlier convictions and used his intellect to generate a fraudulent logic, which did not portend well for the economy. Greenspan's belated conversion to tax cuts even made the supply-siders uneasy. "The *newness* of his support," wrote Steven Rattner, "for a 30 percent tax cut over three years has led the supply-siders, who backed that cut, to view him with suspicion"[31] (my italics).

You have already seen how Reagan's program was enacted in 1981; how it resulted in a vast rise in the budget deficit; how the interest rate climbed to its highest level in U.S. history, and then induced Greenspan to recommend a gargantuan rise in the Social Security tax. But the deficit, in spite of a reduction in the growth of federal spending, kept swelling, and the long-term interest rate, which was supposed to fall in a matter of weeks, remained sky-high for three long years. Consequently, the nation suffered the worst recession since the 1930s.

When someone commits one intellectual fraud, he may have to commit another to nullify its ill effects. Greenspan urged Congress to pass the payroll tax rise in 1983 ostensibly to create a Social Security surplus and save the retirement program. So this tax hike was another flip-flop to his long-held view that the government has a tendency to overspend.

All his life he had viewed state authority with suspicion, but now he convinced himself and others that the government could be counted on to do something it had never done before, namely to preserve its surplus. In his Senate confirmation hearing in August 1974, Greenspan had lamented: "In the last ten or fifteen years, there has been an extraordinary buildup of special interests in our society who have ongoing commitments from the federal budget running in excess of the revenue-raising capacity of our tax system."[32] In August 1983, just three months after the passage of the Social Security law, he told *The New York Times* that the government has "a regrettable tendency to spend revenues when we have them."[33]

Greenspan knew or should have known from prior experience that the government would spend all it received, including the revenues of the Social Security Trust Fund. Yet he crafted a plan that relied on Congressional commitment to do just the opposite. Thus the Social Security fraud was not just a financial fraud, it was an intellectual fraud as well, because it contradicted his earlier views and experience and relied on recent forecasts that, incidentally, had already proved to be grievously wrong.

He had overestimated inflation and predicted that Reagan's tax cuts would be followed by a sharp decline in interest rates in a matter of weeks. Even his short-term predictions had been off the mark. Yet he relied on innately dubious long-range forecasts about the giant Social Security deficit to bring about a rise in the payroll tax.

Even after the passage of the Social Security tax hike in April 1983, in October, Greenspan advocated a value-added tax, which is equivalent to a national sales tax. His proposal was designed to raise as much as $50 billion, or a quarter of the budget deficit.[34] Also, in December 1981 he had suggested a tax rise to slash the deficit increase resulting from the just-enacted tax cut. In the previous month he had predicted that the combination of the tax cut and the recession would lead to a large deficit in 1983 amounting to "a whopping $109 billion."[35] The actual 1983 deficit turned out to be over $200 billion.

The point is that after the voodoo cuts of 1981, Greenspan and company, along with Reagan, were caught off guard by the size of the deficit, and scrambled to undo the budgetary damage done by that legislation. In 1982, they raised excise and gasoline taxes; in 1983 payroll taxes; and when all that failed to trim the deficit, Greenspan proposed a brand new levy, i.e. the valued-added tax, in fall 1983. The one thing that Greenspan could not bring to his lips was the income tax: it was fine to increase myriad other taxes, but his theory, ideology, or the self-interest to stay in Reagan's good graces, would not let him consider raising the tax primarily paid by the wealthy people like himself—all in the name of social welfare. If this is not intellectual fraud, what is!

Reagan did not perpetrate intellectual chicanery, because he was not an economist. His deception amounted to what is usually expected from a politician—promise all sorts of goodies in a crisis to win an election, and later blame the opposition for failure. But Greenspan was an intelligent economist who could easily foresee the budgetary impact of the 1981 tax cuts. He himself had faced the music in 1976, when his tiny tax relief raised the deficit sharply to $73 billion from $53 billion the year before, or by nearly 40 percent. Those days he openly worried about what high deficits can do to inflation and the rate of interest. But with Reagan as his patron, he changed his tune.

Of course, there were other culprits in the budget mess, especially the supply-siders, but at least they were ignorant of what could happen. They had made obviously ridiculous claims for their prescription that no serious thinker including Greenspan and others, like Nobel laureates Milton Friedman and Paul Samuelson, took seriously.

Supply-siders had committed intellectual fraud as well, but theirs paled before what Greenspan had wrought. True to their tax-bashing convictions, they rarely opted for a tax rise even after the budget fiasco that followed their suggestions. But Greenspan was instrumental in transferring the tax burden from the rich onto the feeble backs of the poor and the middle class. So were Reagan and Congress, but career politicians cannot be blamed for misunderstanding economics. Greenspan's fraud had a wider impact on tens of millions of Americans than the supply-siders'.

A PATTERN OF FLIP-FLOPS

Greenspan was just warming up. With the help of all those connections he had developed over the years, he would grow to become Fed chairman in 1987. Merely as an outsider and Reagan's unofficial adviser, he had picked the pockets of the public; just imagine what he could do once he was in charge of the Federal Reserve, the most powerful central bank in the world. His appointment as the Fed's head was ominous for the American economy and society. The haves would prosper as never before, but the have-nots would take a beating.

Reagan nominated Greenspan to replace Paul Volcker in the summer of 1987. Once again, Greenspan faced his old nemesis, Senator Proxmire, who now headed the Senate Banking Committee. In the confirmation hearing, the senator wondered about Greenspan's dismal record about forecasting inflation, his opposition to antitrust laws (because the Fed oversees certain mergers), and about his independence from Reagan's influence. From columnist Louis Uchitelle's viewpoint, Greenspan's "estimates of future economic growth have been as close to the mark as most forecasters get, but his inflation predictions have been below par. And as a government official in the mid-70's, the forecasts for which Mr. Greenspan was responsible were often far off."[36]

Greenspan had already learned the art of politics, and had attended many hearings. He knew what answers to give, especially to a largely friendly crowd that he had faced a few times before. Eventually, the full Senate confirmed him resoundingly in the month of August, with a vote of 91 to 2.

A few weeks into his new job, Greenspan faced the biggest challenge of his life. On October 19, 1987, now known as Black Monday, share markets collapsed in the United States. In a single-day record, the Dow Jones Index (the Dow in short) sank 507 points or 22.6 percent, wiping out nearly $500 billion of shareholder wealth in a matter of hours. In both absolute and percentage terms, this was the largest drop since 1929. The Tokyo market plummeted 15 percent the next day; other parts of the world followed dutifully. Financial markets in Hong Kong, Italy, Australia, England, France, and elsewhere shook violently. The world trembled and presented Reagan and Greenspan with a question that President Herbert Hoover had faced in 1929. How do you douse a wild fire before it consumes the neighborhood? How do you keep it from spreading?

Reagan responded with a Hooveresque remark that the underlying economy was sound. That only compounded public anxiety. But Greenspan rose to the challenge, even though ironically on Black Monday itself *Fortune* appeared with a cover story about him: "Why Greenspan Is Bullish?"[37] The Fed chairman flooded share markets with liquidity, which is a euphemism for new debt. In the aftermath of the 1929 crash, credit was virtually unavailable, as banks, operating under an indecisive Fed, faced so much uncertainty that they stopped lending to shareholders. But this time, the Fed acted with alacrity, lowering interest rates by buying a few billion dollars' worth of government bonds.

When a central bank purchases such bonds from securities dealers, it pays them with checks that are deposited with commercial banks, which in turn find themselves with new cash. The banks then have more money to lend to their clients. This way the stock market crash of 1987 did not develop into the full-blooded credit crunch that had followed the debacle of 1929. A few opulent shareholders—Warren Buffett, Bill Gates, etc.—suffered mega losses, but the rest of the economy escaped pain. Within a few months, the worst crash in history was all but forgotten, and the Dow ended the year with a slight gain.

This was perhaps Greenspan's greatest accomplishment, which occurred within weeks of his appointment to chair the Fed. *Forbes* and many other media sources declared this to be Greenspan's finest hour. The chairman emerged as the darling of Wall Street brokers. Those who percentage-wise had suffered the most from inflation in the early 1970s had now been saved by someone who always cared about their welfare. Wall Street would cheer him again and again as the American economy evolved under the thickening shadow of Greenomics.

Greenspan learned a new lesson form the entire episode—debt creation can solve problems and keep the system afloat, as long as it is timed properly. In the immediate aftermath of the 1987 crash, he swiftly reduced the interest rates, but once the danger had passed, he raised them back to scoop up excess liquidity and thus keep inflation under check.

This was smart central banking and would also help him navigate crises yet to come. But it made a mockery of his core belief that the economy should be left to itself. In fact, as we shall see now and in subsequent chapters, Greenomics left him with no choice except to interfere with the markets time and again. Greenspan had learned the art of fine-tuning the system, and would use it with near perfection in years to come. He would become a Keynesian of sorts, while claiming to be a free-marketer for the consumption of his followers.

In 1988, Greenspan's fellow flip-flopper, George Bush Sr., was elected as president. He also had made a promise to the electorate—"Read my lips. No new taxes"—a promise that he would end up breaking toward the end of his term. Bush and Greenspan had a lot in common: they both were opportunists, had abandoned their core beliefs to endorse voodoo economics and endear themselves to Reagan, had been good students, and were smart. They should have gotten along well, but for some reasons they did not. Politics creates strange bedfellows, but these two became more strangers than fellows. Their interests clashed.

Both Bush and Greenspan wanted to remain in power for as long as they could. For Bush it meant getting reelected for another term, for Greenspan getting nominated to Fed chair, again and again. Even in his childhood and youth, Greenspan had shown a remarkable knack for authority and power. He was sociable with boys in his high school, and was president of his class for a year. At NYU, he had become president of the Symphonic Society, and later of the Economics Society. His social skills would bring him close to CEOs and political bigwigs later.

Greenspan's proclivity for power was well known long before he became Fed chairman. Even as the CEA head from 1974 to 1976, he had clashed with fellow economists, because he reserved choice projects for himself and controlled access to President Ford. "It's worth noting," writes Justin Martin, "that throughout Greenspan's career, he has fostered a collegial environment—provided, of course, there is no argument that he is the one in charge."[38]

The appointment of a Fed chairman usually requires great care. It's not a job for loquacious souls or the faint at heart. The chairman has to deal with both the president and Congress, and they may all have diverse, at times irreconcilable, interests. Aloofness, not mingling—reserve, not loquacity—are needed for the Fed to maintain a dialogue with conflicting groups. The central bank must also stand up to politicians or lose the confidence of financial markets, especially Wall Street brokers. The Fed can make or break political careers through its control over interest rates that sway the economy, at least in the short run. For this reason, Fed chairmen prize their independence from political hacks.

By instinct, Wall Streeters—the executives of big brokerages, big banks, big mutual funds, and insurance companies—despise inflation, whereas incumbent politicians, especially those up for reelection, detest high unemployment. Inflation tends to raise interest rates or bond yields that directly compete with share markets from which much of Wall Street makes money. High joblessness, by contrast, has shortened the careers of many presidents and Congressmen.

Given enough time, low inflation is good for low unemployment. In the short run, however, the two may clash with each other. In order to control inflation, interest rates must be raised. As credit becomes expensive, people buy fewer homes and cars, so national demand as well as inflationary pressures decline. But lower demand also means lower production and greater layoffs, at least initially. Once inflation sinks, and inflationary expectations cool, interest rates can be lowered to stimulate demand and the economy to eliminate those layoffs. But for all this to materialize, the policy-maker needs sufficient time.

In American democracy, with elections occurring every two or four years, incumbents may not have enough time or patience to see the salutary effects of initially higher interest rates. That is why lawmakers and presidents usually decry interest rate hikes, which are also despised by shareholders, but the latter will tolerate them as bitter but necessary medicine in an environment of high inflation. Wall Street firms have a slightly longer time horizon than politicians, and usually regard inflation as a meaner evil than unemployment.

There is also the matter of the time lag. If the Fed lowers interest rates, the stimulus to employment usually arrives a year or two later, but share prices jump immediately. The timing of monetary ease or restraint can make all the difference to the state of the economy in an election year. From the president's viewpoint, the bitter medicine should be applied early in his term so that its tasty fruit is available to voters when he faces reelection.

When Bush Sr. campaigned for the presidency in 1988, the economy was in mediocre health—neither too weak nor roaring. Thanks to Volcker and Greenspan, the inflation monster had been tamed, but people still had fresh memories of high inflation. Inflationary expectations had eased but not vanished. Greenspan had expanded money growth and lowered the interest rate sharply to combat the 1987 stock market crash. Fearing the onset of inflation, he began to trim money growth and raise the interest rate in 1988.

The Fed sways interest rates by influencing what is known as the federal funds rate. At times a private bank falls short of cash and borrows money from other banks, and the interest that it pays in the process is called the federal funds rate. This rate moves up or down as the Fed sells or buys government securities in the bond market. Short-term interest rates that usually apply to loans maturing over one to five years move in direct proportion to the federal funds rate. People undertake such loans to buy cars, furniture, and appliances.

Fearing the onset of inflation, Greenspan began to sell government bonds and gradually raised the federal funds rate in 1988, a move that collided with the immediate goals of the Republican presidential candidate—Vice President George Bush. Bush Sr. feared that high interest rates would raise joblessness, which was the last thing he needed at the time. He howled; so did his advisers, but this only stiffened

Greenspan's resolve to display independence from his fellow Republicans. The chairman kept raising the federal funds rate all through the year. His policy had no imminent effect on the economy, because monetary measures usually act with a lag. Bush Sr. won easily, but his relationship with Greenspan would be strained forever.

By February 1989, the federal funds rate hit a peak of 9.75 percent. Greenspan felt he had done enough to slow the economy and tame inflation. By June, he opened the money pump, and the funds rate began to fall; yet growth remained anemic. By July 1990, a year later, the funds rate was down to 5.75 percent, but the economy was already in recession, with mounting layoffs. Greenspan, however, was in a state of denial. Even with rising joblessness, he would not use the "R" word. This was definitely a low point in his career.

In August 1990, Iraq invaded Kuwait, and the international price of oil almost doubled in two months, hitting $40 per barrel by October. The recession deepened as a result, and Greenspan responded with further cuts in the funds rate, but the inflationary potential of expensive oil kept his cuts gradual and small. Slowly the funds rate came down to 4 percent, not enough to suit most Republicans, who faced a mid-term election that year.

By early 1991, rumors flew high that Greenspan might not be renominated as Fed chairman, something he could do little about.[39] He lowered the funds rate to 3.75 percent in April and then cut it sharply in one swing to 3.25 percent by July 2. This is all he could do to retain his post, because the funds rate was now at its 30-year low. The rest was up to Bush Sr. and his cabinet. Or was it?

There was a more influential constituency backing Greenspan—big Wall Street firms. The Gulf War started in January 1991 and was over within three weeks, liberating Kuwait and its oil in the process. Oil prices plummeted; this along with the falling funds rate provided a powerful stimulus to share prices, which simply took off.

Up and up the stock market went, lifting Greenspan's spirits and his reappointment chances with it. In July, a week after the latest cut in the funds rate, Bush renominated Greenspan against the backdrop of 2 million lost jobs and swelling Republican angst with the chairman. In view of Wall Street's growing infatuation with the maestro, there was nothing that Bush could do in the matter. He could not afford a rift with big business and risk losing their millions in campaign funds, which would be sorely needed in the election the following year.

His reappointment became an important milestone in Greenspan's evolution as Fed chairman. He learned yet another lesson. Wall Street support had proved decisive in his retention of the Fed post. Neither higher inflation nor higher joblessness, both running at 6 percent in 1991, had been able to derail his reappointment, which went through in spite of the hostility of the president and some senators. None of that mattered. What made a difference was big business, especially that enshrined on Wall Street.

From now on Greenspan would pursue his ideology with gusto. He had regarded major corporations as "America's persecuted minority." He would now strive to enhance their well-being. Free and unfettered profits of the tycoons, their unencumbered salaries, their friendly or hostile takeovers of other businesses would now define free markets for him. The minority had to be saved from government interference and labor unions, especially their wage demands. Henceforth he would use his monetary policy to restrain wages and inflation, but that would effectively raise the minority's profits. Wall Street firms and Greenspan would form a sinister partnership, as it were, to further each other's goals. Greenspan would help them prosper exponentially, and they would help him keep a grip on power. This way businesses would flourish, but ethics and laborers would take a beating.

The Bush administration's fears were not entirely groundless. The 1992 election occurred against the backdrop of a weak economy, and that was enough to hand Bush Sr. a stinging defeat. Just a year before, in the after-glow of easy American victory in Gulf War, his popularity rating had climbed above 80 percent. But joblessness has been the graveyard of many American presidencies, and Commander-in-Chief George Bush also succumbed to it. Wall Street alone could not do for George what it had done for its pal, Alan.

In came the new president, a Democrat, Bill Clinton. This was uncharted territory for Chairman Greenspan. Never before did he have to contend with a Democratic head of state. The two met prior to Clinton's inauguration. Much to Greenspan's surprise, they hit it off right away. Clinton was a quick learner. Unlike Bush, the new president wanted to make friends with the Fed chairman. He knew there was no point in picking a fight with someone who held a grip on the nation's supply of money and interest rates.

On his part, Greenspan gave Clinton a lecture in the art of macroeco-nomics. The chairman emphasized the need to trim the federal deficit to keep inflationary expectations at bay, because otherwise high deficits tend to generate high interest rates, especially those dealing with long-maturity loans. In 1992, the 30-year home mortgage, where the loan lasts for three decades, still commanded an interest rate of 9 percent as compared to 13 percent in 1980. The inflation rate had declined by almost 11 points (from 14 percent to 3 percent) but the mortgage rate by only 4 points. Greenspan blamed this anomaly on the federal deficit, which had swollen to a record $290 billion in 1992, some 5 percent of the nation's output.

Greenspan hammered the point again and again that government spending and the deficit had to come down to trim the high long-term interest rate, which tended to keep economic growth mediocre and joblessness high. GDP growth hovered around 2.5 percent those days. Greenspan made it clear that he had no power over the long-term interest rate, which remained high because financial markets feared the onslaught of inflation from the gargantuan budget deficit.

This was a throwback to his Jimmy Carter days. He had come full circle—again. This was another flip-flop, a move away from Greenomics, and a refutation of what he had said in 1980 to rationalize Reagan's economic program. This was a return to sanity, because he no longer needed Reagan but Wall Street, which backed the same views that Greenspan had used to assail Carter's policies.

In parting, Greenspan again stressed the need to trim the federal deficit, especially by pruning those programs that ate up gobs of money.[40] Clinton gave the maestro a long hearing and seemed to agree with him. A few months later, the president offered a plan to cut the deficit in half by the end of his term. The plan aimed to raise the top-bracket income tax rate from 31 percent to 39.6 percent, increase the Social Security fees by another $30 billion, and trim spending cosmetically. The package focused primarily on tax increases rather than spending cuts, but Greenspan offered it his support. For the first time in his life, he had backed a substantial rise in the income tax rate, although he had endorsed a similar but modest plan offered by Bush Sr. in 1990. This was further confirmation that he no longer needed the supply-siders and Republicans who vehemently opposed the Clinton plan.

The president's package went through a churning in the House, but the plan that eventually emerged was credible. It sought to trim the deficit by nearly $500 billion over five years, half through a rise in taxes and the rest through spending cuts. The Senate voted 50–50 on the House program, with Democratic Vice President Al Gore breaking the tie. The Clinton deficit reduction plan had been basically adopted, much to the chagrin of the supply-siders. Not a single Republican senator voted in its favor.

Long-term bond yields fell immediately, which showed how myopic Greenomics, a caricature of supply-side economics, had been all these years. The drastic tax changes that had occurred each year from 1981 to 1983—the main planks of Greenomics—had basically decimated the living standard of working Americans. True, Wall Street was dizzy, but tens of millions of Americans had seen their after-tax wages lag behind the rise in prices.

The recession of 1990 was one of the shallowest on record, and ended in spring 1991 as output began to rise, with unemployment budging barely from 5.5 percent to 6.4 percent. But people were smitten with despair, because joblessness continued to increase even with improving business conditions. Unemployment would peak in 1992 at 7.4 percent. In a cover story that appeared shortly after Greenspan's reappointment to the Fed, *Time* was moved to ask:

> Well why are Americans so gloomy, fearful and even panicked about the current economic slump? . . . In one of history's most painful para-doxes, U.S. consumers suddenly seem disillusioned with the American dream of rising prosperity even as capitalism and democracy have con-signed the Soviet Union to history's trash heap.[41]

Even American victories in the Gulf War and against the Soviet Union were not enough to undo the damage done to the American psyche by the lethal combination of rising payroll taxes and wages trailing inflation. Even after the passage of the Clinton plan the public gloom did not lift for many months. Bond yields had surely declined and the economy began to pick up, but the pickup was too slow to make a dent in sluggish wages. Nevertheless the economy continued to expand and GDP growth in Clinton's first term averaged 3.25 percent, more than double the average of 1.5 percent under Bush Sr.; unemployment also fell steadily though grudgingly, but family incomes remained stagnant.

Meanwhile, stock markets broke records year after year. With slug-gish wages, profits took off, even in a slow-growth economy, and so did share prices. Mergers also heated up, so share prices rose even faster. For Wall Street this was a Goldilocks economy—neither humming nor standing still but yielding oodles of profit. Greenspan was instrumental in arranging this economic nirvana. He raised the federal funds rate a few times in 1994, because it had sunk to a 30-year low of 3 percent. His policy was also designed to cool surging growth, with potential implications for inflation. The funds rate doubled to 6 percent by February 1995. This time it was the Democrats' turn to howl, but to no avail.

Wall Street greeted the chairman's policy with approval, but the ruling incumbents cried foul with little effect. This way, Greenspan, the ever-vigilant inflation hawk, was able to engineer the Goldilocks economy, which sent share markets to dizzying heights. Greenspan did not personally profit from this euphoria, because his assets were mostly in bonds. But he was well satisfied with his performance, because giddy brokers meant that his nomination for a third term was assured. This was a low-growth, low-inflation, low-unemployment economy in a milieu of low-paid workers. Clinton was furious with the Fed's monetary policy, but it would actually assure him another term in the ensuing election, even though his opponent Bob Dole promised a 15 percent tax cut à la Reagan.

As with Bush Sr., Clinton also had second thoughts about reappointing Greenspan. He too had looked for someone more congenial to his goals and waited almost to the end of Greenspan's term before announcing his choice. But once again Wall Street backing proved decisive. In January 1996, inflation stood at 3 percent, unemployment at 5.5 percent, and the Dow above 5,300, up 40 percent from the previous January. There was no way the president could ignore the movers and shakers on Wall Street and ditch the maestro. Greenspan was renominated in February 1996, about a month before the appearance of *Fortune*'s memorable cover story: "In Greenspan We Trust." The Senate, however, was engaged in partisan politics over other matters and took four months to reconfirm him—resoundingly—on June 20.

Toward the end of the year, the president won reelection in a landslide. Greenspan's star shone brighter than ever, even though the Republicans had taken a beating in the election. Share prices had been rising since the early 1980s, with seemingly a minor glitch in 1987. The Dow hit a low of 777 in August 1982, only to go past 6,000 by the end of 1996, almost an eightfold rise in a matter of 14 years. The Nasdaq composite index also matched the giddy pace of the Dow. Roaring share markets had lured millions into their domain, and shareholder population broke annual records.

Free lunch is rare, but when it comes, it makes us dance with joy. The country was euphoric, and Wall Street simply could not contain its adulation for the maestro. Greenspan had every reason to be ecstatic. This is why he had worked so hard in his youth and in his middle age. In mid-1996, with Greenspan turning 70, a grateful nation and the Senate had crowned him with a third term to head the Federal Reserve.

Greenspan was not done yet. At the end of 1996, just when the country wanted to keep the celebration going, he chided the American investor for "irrational exuberance." No one at the Fed, not even the elderly maestro, had ever seen the kind of euphoria that gripped the nation in the 1990s. True, Greenspan had been born during the Roaring Twenties, but he was only three years old when the market crashed in 1929 and spent his childhood in the midst of the Great Depression. Perhaps it was the memory of that depression or of the devastating stock market crash in Japan in 1990 that moved him to warn the shareowners that American stock assets were overvalued; so it was time to pause.

Greenspan was afraid that the share-price party in America could end the way it had in 1987; he was concerned about the investor getting drunk overnight and waking up one morning with a terrible hangover. He acted like a master bartender worried about the intoxicated state of his drinking customers. But he didn't know what he had let loose. The genie was now out of the bottle and demanded ever-new delicacies.

Financial markets responded to the chairman's remarks with alacrity and sank around the world. Greenspan faced the wrath of investors immediately. For the first time, Wall Streeters jumped on him en masse. Those who had cheered him before now threw verbal darts at him.

The lure of free lunch is so powerful that it clouds our vision. For once Greenspan had offered words of wisdom, but in so doing he lost his audience. The master bartender wanted his customers to sober up, but they were in no mood to listen. They wanted more; whiskey, champagne, rum, just bring it on. Even politicians ganged up on Greenspan for a variety of reasons. They feared he was about to raise short-term interest rates to curb excessive stock valuations, which could raise unemployment even in a low-inflation environment.

Greenspan was stung. No longer did he have the confidence of his true believers. In fact, no one—neither Wall Street nor Congress nor the public—wanted to see an end to the party. So it was time for a flip-flop—once again. Instead of instructing the public into common sense, Greenspan made an about-face and became a cheerleader for Wall Street.

As Fed chairman, he had defied a lot of influential people of various political hues—Congressmen, presidents, cabinet officers. He had raised interest rates even as elected officials swore at him. He had been in constant conflict with Bush Sr.'s administration, and occasionally with Clinton's as well. He had done all this to create an aura of independence around him. But when the shareholder world turned against him, he quickly gave in. This was his core constituency, his key to renomination; how could he alienate it for long? The shareholders had elevated him to a cult figure, and he could not disappoint the faithful again.

Greenspan turned into an apostle of what is known as the "new economy." He had heard about the phrase before but seldom mentioned it in his speeches and testimonies. Briefly, the new economy is an arena in which information technology plays a crucial role and enables companies to compete efficiently in international markets. Among its leading sectors are computers, the Internet, telecommunications, and biochemicals—in short, the high-tech industries. In the 1990s, the likes of Microsoft, Dell Computers, Amazon.com, MCI, AOL, and Enron were among its brightest stars.

The new economy was supposed to be highly productive because of its proclivity for innovation and new technologies. Its hallmarks were said to be low inflation, high growth, growing global trade and investment, and, above all, rocketing profits. In short, it offered a paradise to the stock investor; not surprisingly, it served to rationalize the public's obsession with share markets.

Within a year of his fateful remarks about irrational exuberance, the maestro made another flip-flop and became a patron of the new paradigm. In a cover story on July 14, 1997, *Business Week* described Greenspan as an "avant-garde advocate of the new economy." A few days later, the *Ottawa Citizen* wrote about his semi-annual testimony to Congress: "Federal Reserve Chairman Alan Greenspan . . . didn't specifically use the words 'new economy.' But he could have, for the belief is growing that American financial policy makers, led by Mr. Greenspan, are becoming devotees of the 'new economy' theory."[42] The *Business Week* story also cited President Clinton in agreement with the maestro: "I believe it's possible to have more sustained and higher growth without inflation than we previously thought."[43]

The media anointed Greenspan, because he did not touch the federal funds rate for more than a year, from 1996 to 1997, even though the economy grew faster and the jobless rate continued to fall. Under similar circumstances in 1994 and early 1995, he had engineered a series of rate increases. But now shrinking unemployment in a galloping economy did not seem to bother his anti-inflationary genes.

The absence of price pressures in the high-employment economy of 1996, in fact, stirred up the staid world of economists. Until then they had believed in something called NAIRU (nonaccelerating inflationary rate of unemployment), a rather abstruse idea with serious practical applications. It implied that in modern capitalist economies inflation would speed up if the jobless rate fell below a certain level. NAIRU provided an unemployment threshold, approximating 6 percent for the United States, that should not be breached to keep inflation dormant. The threshold was smaller for Japan (2 percent), but larger for much of Europe (8 percent), especially for countries like Germany and France that offered generous welfare and unemployment benefits.

It is not altogether clear if Greenspan relied on NAIRU, but some of his colleagues at the Fed did.[44] In any case, he raised the federal funds rate in 1994 and 1995 as the jobless rate approached 6 percent. The idea was that at a lower unemployment rate, business demand for workers is so strong that wages shoot up, forcing companies to raise prices sharply. Greenspan's interest rate hikes at the time were considered a preemptive strike against inflation. When credit becomes expensive people spend less on goods for which they borrow money. Consequently, both national demand and inflation decline, but so does the real wage, which is the purchasing power of a person's salary. On July 22, 1997, with inflation under the leash, Greenspan told the House Banking Committee:

> We have as close to stable prices as I have seen, certainly since the 1960s. . . . We do not now know, nor do I suspect can anyone know, whether current developments are part of a once or twice in a century phenomenon that will carry productivity trends nationally and globally to a new higher track.[45]

Once Greenspan came to patronize the new economy, stock markets around the world defied gravity and flew into space. The sky was the limit now. Greenspan's pronouncements about a new era in which innovative technologies nourished ever-increasing productivity and profits seemed to assure investors worldwide that a new age had dawned for share values. Old and stodgy criteria like price/earnings ratios, dividend rates, industry's competition, etc., no longer applied to stock valuations. So financial markets kept testing new highs.

By fall 1997, just three months after his mid-year Congressional testimony, Greenspan began worrying anew about a lofty stock market that seemed to be unsustainable in the long run. He sent a warning that even the new economy could not grow recklessly without igniting inflation, which would then require proper treatment from the Fed. His skepticism cooled the market mania somewhat, but before long the public reverted to its euphoria, as did the maestro. In May 1998, Greenspan told Clinton, "This is the best economy I've seen in 50 years," and reiterated the view in Congressional testimony two months later.[46]

Actually Greenspan couldn't make up his mind. He himself alternated between euphoria and sanity. Finally, he offered his own summation of the new economy in a speech delivered at the University of California at Berkeley in September 1998: "Hence, as the first cut at the question 'Is there a new economy?' the answer in a more profound sense is no. . . . But having said that, important technological changes have been emerging in recent years that are altering, in ways with few precedents, the manner in which we organize production, trade across countries, and deliver value to consumers."[47] Such remarks reflected his ambivalent attitude toward the new paradigm. In a profound sense there was no new economy, yet technologies and free trade were unprecedented and altered the way production was organized. He went on to explain and defend why share prices had hit the sky:

> Coupled with the quickened pace of productivity growth, wage and benefit moderation has kept growth in unit labor costs subdued in the current expansion. This has both damped inflation and allowed profit margins to reach high levels. That, in turn, apparently was the driving force beginning in early 1995 in security analysts' significant upward revision of their company-by-company long-term earnings projections. These upward revisions, coupled with falling interest rates, point to two key underlying forces that impelled investors to produce one of history's most notable bull stock markets.[48]

For share markets it was enough that Greenspan understood the forces that were driving productivity, profits, and hence share prices. It was the profit, not the label of the new economy, that mattered, and so long as the maestro was on top of things, nothing could go wrong in the go-go land of investors. In 1992, Clinton had campaigned on the slogan, "It's the economy, stupid." The Wall Street slogan, as always, was "It's the profit, stupid."

Greenspan had come to accept the view, relentlessly vented by big business, that, because of impressive productivity gains, profits and shares would stay high. How and why these profits climbed did not seem to matter to him. As we shall see in chapter 6, *it is simply impossible for productivity alone to generate high profits in a low-wage economy. It needs the helping hand of something old-fashioned—new debt, gobs of it.* Blinded by his faith in low wages and unfettered profits, Greenspan could not fathom this simple logic, and would eventually preside over another stock market crash.

In spite of his initial ambivalence, the new economy, confusing and mysterious, continued to fascinate Greenspan. In 1999, for the first time in history, the Dow roared past 10,000. The U.S. market mania seemed to dwarf even the share market bubble of Japan in the 1980s. However, with declining joblessness, torrid growth, and soaring imports, the maestro grew nervous about the onset of inflation. He had eased monetary policy to combat a series of crises in 1998. Once he felt reassured about the state of the world economy, it was time to apply the usual antidote.[49]

June 1999 marks a turning point of the stock market bubble, as Greenspan began taking preemptive action against the threat of inflation. He raised the federal funds rate on June 30, and then kept raising it till the middle of the next year. Growth slowed somewhat, as bond yields that directly compete with share prices rose sharply. Still the share markets continued to soar, peaking in early 2000. The Dow reached its zenith on January 14 at 11,723, and the broader index, the S&P 500, at 1,550 in March. The Nasdaq Composite also peaked the same month—at 5,049. But by the end of the year, it was clear that the party was all but over.

Greenspan's preemptive strike in 1999 against the menace of inflation no longer alarmed Clinton and his cohorts. Everybody, including Wall Street, was nonchalant. Greenspan was a demigod by now, and duly expected his appointment for yet another term. The president did not disappoint him by dragging the matter out this time. Clinton quipped: "I bet he'll stay there until they carry him out," and went on to renominate him for the fourth term in January 2000—just ten days before the Dow peaked. He told Greenspan: "After doing so well, no one would blame you for wanting to go out on top." "Oh, no," Greenspan hastened to say, "this is the greatest job in the world. It's like eating peanuts. You keep doing it, and you never get tired."[50]

Thanks to the market mania and resulting revenue from the capital gains tax, the federal budget showed a small but growing surplus in

1999 and 2000. Excluding the Social Security fund, the surplus was a miniscule $87 billion at the end of the millennium out of an outlay of $1.6 trillion; but the grandiose talk of the politicians—including the Republican presidential candidate George W. Bush—made it appear that the surplus would last through another millennium.

They began to build castles in the air. Bush wanted to reserve half of the projected ten-year surplus for a mega cut in the income tax; Al Gore, the Democratic candidate, wanted it to retire the federal debt. But the maestro knew better. Testifying before the Senate on January 28, 1999, he said, "How can we ignore the fact that virtually all forecasts of the budget balance have been wide of the mark in recent years?" Greenspan was even more skeptical in a speech to the Cato Institute on October 19, 2000: "But I believe most of us harbor doubts about whether the dynamics of the political process, some of which have been on display in the current budgetary deliberations, will allow the surpluses to continue to grow."[51]

The rocketing stock market, which had a big role in creating the small surplus in 2000, was already beginning to tank. Yet few intellectuals, especially those backing their candidates, would heed this minor glitch, even after Bush was elected president in November.

THE STOCK MARKET CRASH: 2000-2002

Greenspan's monetary tightening had some effect in March and April 2000, especially for technology stocks bulking large in the Nasdaq index, which fell sharply. This was a harbinger of things to come, yet no one panicked. The March hiccup was soon forgotten, but share markets only moved sideways, leading some to believe that a healthy correction had occurred. In fact, in May the chairman responded by raising the Federal funds rate by a full half point to 6.5 percent. However, a bloodbath started in September, and the Nasdaq index fell nearly in a straight line thereafter. The Dow's fall was not so steep, although on September 17 it suffered the largest ever single-day drop of 685 points.

Clearly the financial markets were in agony, but Greenspan failed to respond. He was worried about the inflationary potential of the recent rise in oil prices and did not want to ease up on the money pump to spur demand. Signs of a slowdown appeared clearer in October and November. Company sales and profits were beginning to decline—something that heralded a softer economy. However, Greenspan, ever the inflation hawk, took no preemptive action against a possible downturn. The economy had been expanding for 9 straight years—the longest expansion ever. A minor slowdown did not seem to be worrisome.

The continuing bloodbath in the Nasdaq market, however, made some financial experts jittery. They wanted the Fed to at least abandon its inflation bias, if not cut the funds rate outright, to thwart a possible recession. But, in the middle of Wall Street's spreading gloom, Greenspan delivered an unusually upbeat speech in New York about the state of corporate earnings on December 5, basing his optimism, of all things, on "security analysts' long-term earnings projections." Later, some of the security analysts were found to be great swindlers. See how Princeton University Professor Burton Malkiel described their abuses: "While Henry Blodgett and other analysts at Merrill Lynch were officially recommending some internet stocks, the same analysts were referring to the stocks in e-mail messages as 'junk,' 'dogs,' or less attractive epithets."[52] Apparently, the new technology revolution had clouded the maestro's vision, enhancing the analysts' credibility.

> Moreover, despite recent short-term earnings disappointments, many corporate managers appear not to have measurably altered their long-standing optimism on the future state of technology. At least this is the impression one gets from the persistent upward revision through most of this year of security analysts' long-term earnings projections. Analysts, one must presume, obtain most of their insights from corporate managers, who are most intimately aware of the potential gains from technological synergies and networking economies.[53]

Not surprisingly, the markets responded joyfully on December 5, the Nasdaq surging a record-breaking 9 percent. But what a difference two weeks make. On December 19, 2000, the Fed reiterated its continued concern for inflation, prompting a retort from London's *Daily Telegraph*:

> With US economic growth more than halving to 2.4pc in the third quarter of this year and nearly a quarter of the companies in the Dow Jones index warning about profits, the Fed was widely expected to drop its warning that inflation poses the biggest risk to the US economy. However, it stunned Wall Street by eschewing a neutral bias in favour of a position that the economy's biggest danger is that the current slowdown will lead to a recession.[54]

Greenspan's studied indifference to slump premonitions stunned Wall Street; markets sank around the world, and kept sinking, and sinking, and sinking. The year ended with the Nasdaq Composite down 50 percent from its March peak, and the S&P down 10 percent. Greenspan proved to be the Grinch who stole Christmas at the end of the old millennium.

As the new economy crawled into the new year, shares tumbled again on the first trading day. Greenspan now panicked and scrambled to cut the federal funds rate by half a point on January 3, 2001, and then by another half point at the end of the month. But the market bubble had burst, and it was impossible to put the air back into it. By midyear, the Dow hovered around where it had started the year, but the Nasdaq was down to 2,000, nearly 60 percent below its peak.

By year's end the funds rate was at a pitiful 1.75 percent as compared to 6.5 percent the previous year. But share prices had not responded; nor would they until almost the end of 2002, when the Nasdaq was down by a whopping 78 percent, the S&P by 50 percent and the Dow by 40 percent. From anyone's reckoning this had been a stock market debacle. In all, American shareholders had lost $7 trillion of wealth at the worst point of the crash.[55]

FLIP-FLOPS AGAIN: 2000-2004

After March 2000, when the Nasdaq index first plunged below its peak, some financial experts began to grumble, at first in a whisper, and then in hushed tones. The chairman had already raised the federal funds rate five times since 1999. True, the speculators had been unmindful, because the stock index had kept rising. But the plunge in March and April was unnerving, and investors began to take notice. The Nasdaq Composite tumbled more than 30 percent within five weeks of its peak. The market volatility also frightened the investors. A *Wall Street Journal*/NBC News poll, reported on May 5, 2000, found a 51 percent positive rating for Greenspan, while 45 percent of respondents complained about higher interest rates.

This was a rather lukewarm and unexpected reception for the maestro, who had just been confirmed by a resounding vote by the Senate. In fact, publications from both left and right joined hands in denouncing Fed actions to raise the interest rate. John Ryding, a senior economist with Bear Stearns, told CNNfn on May 16 that the nine-year-long economic expansion might not survive another Fed tightening. Before the end of the year, Ryding would issue a call for rate cuts that went unnoticed by the Fed. In October, John Crudele of the *New York Post*, who has a following on Wall Street, pleaded with the maestro to "save the market." He even sought the chairman's resignation.[56] But Greenspan did not act for all of 2000. This came as a great blow to shell-shocked investors, and the number-crunching maestro could not but recognize their despair.

Even after the chairman scrambled to cut rates in 2001, the markets kept falling, and some of those who had silently grumbled against him before now complained openly. Lisa Singhania, an Associated Press business writer, noted on March 3, 2001, that "the Federal Reserve chairman's refusal to lower interest rates immediately ignited a sell-off in stocks and complaints from many market pundits about Wall Street's suffering."[57] CNBC, the business news channel, also received numerous complaints. As Bill Bonner reported on March 16: "CNBC says it is already getting emails calling for Greenspan's resignation. He kept rates too high for too long."[58]

For Greenspan this was a sudden reversal of fortunes. Still revered in many circles, he had lost the adoration of his core constituency. Perhaps the grumblers were few and far between, and over time he might regain their loyalty, but he couldn't be sure. The 50 percent plunge in the Nasdaq index in just nine months from its peak was unprecedented, and wiped out the meager savings and fortunes of millions of people. The loss amounted to over $2 trillion in 2000 alone.

The Senate had reconfirmed the maestro in February 2000, and he could remain in the Fed post until June 2004, when George Bush would still be president. Wall Street no longer seemed a sure bet to the chairman. So why not switch loyalty—again. "Power, and the proximity to people of power, was the primary aphrodisiac in his life," observes his biographer, Jerome Tuccille in colorful words.[59] No longer could Greenspan face down the politicians, yet he wished to retain his post as long as possible. True to his form, he went back into the same kowtowing mode as in 1980, when the Republican candidate Reagan invited him to be his economic adviser.

Of course, Greenspan would have to change his views again, but that had not stopped him before. As regards fiscal policy, Bush seemed to be a mirror image of Reagan: just cut the income and corporate tax, enrich the rich, and the budget would take care of itself. For 13 years, ever since his first term as Fed chairman, Greenspan had lectured Congress and presidents on the virtues of balancing the budget. In 1993, to pursue this goal, he had even supported Clinton's deficit package that included a large income tax hike, which did not suit his ideology. This was contrary to what he had advised Reagan as his adviser for seven years, but then who remembered that blatant flip-flop?.

President-elect Bush invited Greenspan to his suite at the Madison Hotel on the morning of December 18, 2000, just around the time the Nasdaq market was tanking. Bush sought the chairman's support for the tax cut he had promised during the campaign. The media had offered conflicting reports on where Greenspan stood on that issue, because in his various testimonies Greenspan had advised Congress to use the projected budget surplus mainly to pay off the national debt.

But in his breakfast meeting he told the president-elect flat out that he also favored the idea of tax relief.[60] Their courtship was mutual. Bush wooed Greenspan, who, having lost the adulation of shareholders, was eager to join Bush's bandwagon. Greenspan needed a new anchor and found it in a Reaganesque Republican. The maestro, already 74 years old, was planning way ahead, because he had tasted the forbidden fruit and wanted to remain atop the world of power and acclaim. Power, if you recall, was his primary aphrodisiac.

On January 25, 2001, Greenspan offered an intriguing testimony to the Senate budget committee. He cited the threat of an impending economic downturn and politicians' predilection for wasteful spending as reasons for trimming the projected budget surplus, which could be as high as $800 billion in fiscal 2011. $800 billion surplus in one year? Was he dreaming? Perhaps he was, because he completely forgot that the Nasdaq index had already crashed and others were sinking; so the main source of the projected surplus—namely exploding capital gains—had already vanished and turned into capital losses, which would then drain the Treasury.

But Greenspan persisted in his chase of the mirage. An intellectual, after all, can invent artifacts to justify anything, and who was going to defy the mighty maestro? Unless taxes were trimmed, he argued, the government would be so awash in money that it would have to pay off the national debt quickly and then be forced to acquire the assets (stocks and bonds) of private companies. This, he claimed, would diminish economic efficiency and should be avoided. Otherwise, the living standard would be lower than it had to be.

So what was the remedy against the impending calamity of surplus budgets? "It is far better, in my judgment," he declared, "that the surpluses be lowered by tax reductions than by spending increases." Barely a year later, his words would prove hollow as the projected surplus evaporated in a hurry. The government had not balanced its books since 1969, and here the maestro worried about retiring the $5 trillion national debt prematurely.

In the Senate hearing, Senator Ernest Hollings challenged Greenspan's numbers, which derived primarily from the surplus in the Social Security Trust Fund. In fact, in 2001 itself, the federal budget was in the red without the Trust Fund. "Where, Mr. Chairman," he exclaimed, "do you find a surplus? I find a deficit."[61] Greenspan, of course, was relying on forecasts that included the Trust Fund's cash in the federal budget.

To his credit, Greenspan counseled that the legislation should have a provision to suspend the tax cut in case the projected surplus vanished. In other words, there should be a trigger mechanism to limit or eliminate the tax relief in the event of mistaken budget forecasts. But Bush did not accept the idea of a trigger, nor did Greenspan withdraw his backing from the tax proposal. So, with Greenspan's enthusiastic support, a $1.35 trillion tax cut was passed in June 2001 without any defenses against the return of deficits.

The main provision of the act was to lower the top-bracket income tax rate to 35 percent from 39.6 percent over ten years, and the bottom rate from 15 to 10 percent. Since this tax is paid primarily by the affluent, it offered modest relief to the poor and the middle class, with the bulk going to the richest taxpayers, but it was temporary and its provisions would expire on the last day of 2010.

Over his long public career, Greenspan has supported all sorts of fiscal legislation, some designed to lower taxes and some tending to raise them. Regardless of his ideology or private agenda, he was not permanently committed to the idea of tax cuts. What was permanent was his penchant for power. This was his prime mover, dwarfing even his passion for balanced budgets.

As recently as August 1999, President Clinton, with Greenspan's support, had vetoed a big tax cut passed by the Republican-controlled Congress. In fact, at the time Jack Kemp had accused the chairman of immeasurably damaging the Republican cause.[62] That bill also aimed at trimming taxes for the wealthy, but Greenspan had opposed it for its budget-busting potential. So what had changed in less than 18 months?

Greenspan could no longer count on unflinching support from Wall Street. He courted Bush for the same reason he had Reagan. They were his keys to authority in government. They were his insurance policies to official rewards. Once he became Fed chairman, he knew the plum post could last a long time, because he did not have to face the electorate. All he needed was an ardent backing from some powerful constituency. It did not matter if he had to contradict himself in the process, or devise novel artifacts to achieve his overriding goal.

He had seen firsthand how Wall Street's insistence had ensured a second term for Volcker, who could have long remained in his post if he had not resigned. Once Greenspan became Fed chairman, he no longer regarded Reagan and fellow Republicans as crucial to his goal. He then sought independence from their influence, because Wall Street valued such a posture.

His economics also changed. He fought inflationary pressures and deficit budgets with gusto to please his patron—the macho Wall Street. He tailored his monetary policy to do its bidding; he embraced the new economy, because the rich shareholders endorsed it. He intervened numerous times in financial markets to protect the profits of big banks and financiers, who faced losses from their speculation linked to Mexico, Asian Tigers, Russia, and a hedge fund called Long Term Capital Management. (This is a story that will be detailed in the next chapter.) He defied the political machine, and at times public opinion, because Wall Street revered him.

Unfortunately for Greenspan, his inflation aversion amid a stock market bubble unexpectedly routed the same entity that had come to adore him. Wall Street fervor for him cooled when shareholders suffered terrible losses resulting from rising interest rates in 1999 and 2000. He scrambled to undo the damage with rate cuts, but it was too late. He could not reinflate the bubble. Nor has any one ever done so. Once the bubble pops, it stays popped for years. For instance, the Dow crashed in 1929 and then took more than two decades to regain its footing.

When some Wall Streeters turned against Greenspan, he did another intellectual somersault and reverted to courting the man who would control his destiny in the future. All that he repeatedly did was to take care of number one—himself. Why else would an intellectual, especially a cult figure intensely aware of his reputation, repeatedly contradict himself? He changed his theories, arguments, opinions, and testimonies with perhaps one goal in mind—ensuring his job as the chairman of the Federal Reserve.

He was savvy enough to make about-turns and occasionally invent peculiar arguments to suit his own needs. He contradicted himself again and again to pursue his self-interest, and in the process hurt millions of gullible investors and taxpayers. This is nothing but massive intellectual fraud, which occurs when someone contradicts his ideas repeatedly to feather his own nest, regardless of what happens to others. It was not partisanship or ideology that made him support Clinton's tax rise and Bush's tax cuts. It was his love for reappointment as Fed chairman.

In 2001 Greenspan forfeited his deficit-pruning credentials, and needed to restore his credibility with the public. It was a common practice with him to revert to his core convictions once his pet project had been enacted, and the law could not be changed any more. This way he could offer something to many sides of an issue and don the mantle of a moderate or a compromiser.

For instance, after the budget-busting tax cut was passed in 1981, he became a deficit hawk again and called for increases in anything but the income and corporate tax. This way he could have it both ways. By holding out against the income-tax hike, he could placate Reagan on one side and still show the world that he cared for the budget deficit. More examples of such opportunistic fence sitting—have your cake and eat it too—will be presented in subsequent chapters.

Once the 2001 tax proposal was enacted, it was time for Greenspan to start worrying about its potential for the deficit. In fact, he didn't have to wait long because even with the Social Security surplus, the federal deficit returned by year's end and continued to get worse. So when George Bush offered a new tax-cutting proposal in 2002, Greenspan insisted that it should be subject to the so-called pay-go (pay as you go) rules that had been enacted in 1990 and were about to expire. Pay-go required that any tax cuts must be matched by an equal rise in other taxes or a cut in spending, so that the immediate deficit level would stay constant. Despite Greenspan's opposition, the new bill passed in March 2002, primarily offering relief to corporations.

Toward the end of 2002, the president introduced yet another tax bill. By then the projected surplus was just a cherished memory; it had turned into a mega deficit, as far as the eye could see. Greenspan again redeemed himself by opposing the new proposals. Testifying before the Senate banking committee on February 12, 2003, he saw no need for a new round of tax reduction, and even hedged on his previous support to make the 2001 tax cut permanent. He did endorse the president's plan to eliminate the tax on dividends, but said that any such change should be deficit-neutral, which meant that it had to be offset by spending cuts or a rise in some other tax.[63]

Later, on April 30, he reiterated his opposition and said, "you will be undercutting the benefits that would be achieved from the tax cuts."[64] Congress, however, ignored Greenspan's pleas again and passed a watered-down version, which became the law in May 2003. Its main provision was to cut the tax on dividends sharply to 15 percent over the next five years and give a bit more relief to corporations. Thus the tax cuts of 2001 and 2003 applied mostly to individuals, and that of 2002 mainly to corporations, with almost all changes expiring by 2011.

Ever since the carnage in share markets starting in early 2000, Greenspan's star had dimmed. In spite of his aggressive cuts in interest rates, a recession had started in 2001, leading to persistent questions about the maestro's legacy to posterity. As Richard Stevenson, a financial writer, put it: "It has been a common line on Wall Street and in Washington: Alan Greenspan, the chairman of the Federal Reserve, should have gotten out while on top last year, when the economy was still booming and his legacy as the embodiment of prosperity was secure."[65] Even after the 9/11 massacre, which literally shook Wall Street and led Greenspan's detractors to cool their criticism, there was a steady drumbeat that questioned his zeal for the new economy. This was not a pleasant time for him.

On April 22, 2003, the chairman went to a hospital to undergo minor surgery. He must have noticed that there was no market rout around the world; stock exchanges no longer cared if he was ill or healthy, something that was unthinkable three years ago, when a single nod from him would send share prices into frenzy. As London's *Guardian* described it: "News latest: 'Fed chairman rushed to hospital; shares unchanged.' Perhaps this is a callous point, but until recently, reports that Alan Greenspan was being admitted to hospital with prostate trouble would have been cause for a possible stock market rout. Indeed, during the heady days of the boom, just a rumour of his untimely demise was enough to send asset prices reeling."[66]

His renomination did not seem to be a sure thing. Greenspan still had good relations with the Bush administration, but Wall Street was divided over his contributions. Even some Bush advisers felt sore with the maestro for his failure to back the 2003 tax cut, and privately urged against his reappointment.[67] Robert Novak wrote a column on February 24, headlined as "Is it Goodbye for Greenspan?"[68] On the whole, though, the chairman had zealously backed Bush's program, but that had not quelled rumors about his departure.

On April 23, while replying to a reporter's question, the president laid these rumors to rest, and said that he would nominate Greenspan for another term. The chairman felt relieved and the same day responded positively to Bush's announcement. Just the day before he had undergone prostate surgery, and instead of a get-well card the president gave him a plum gift to help with recovery.

The maestro's support for the pivotal 2001 tax cut, along with his aggressive reduction in interest rates, had finally proved fruitful. Greenspan's astute planning about his career had paid dividends. It was now a matter of time before the president would follow through. But he seemed to be in no hurry. Greenspan waited, and waited, and waited. Almost a year passed, but Bush failed to make good on his word about the renomination.

Meanwhile, the job market remained soft long after the recession's end, and the maestro's handling of the economy appeared increasingly questionable. What more could Greenspan do to escape his uncertainty? What more could he do to please the president and secure his reappointment? Were the president and his advisers upset because Greenspan had repeatedly opposed the 2003 tax cut?

In January 2004, a startling book, *The Price of Loyalty*, came out, and added turbulence to Greenspan's world. Authored by Ron Suskind, this was a tome of sensational revelations about the Bush presidency based on the recollections and private papers of former Treasury Secretary Paul O'Neill, who had been sacked by the president in December 2002 for insubordination.

The book made certain accusations that were unflattering and embarrassing to both the maestro and the White House. O'Neill was Greenspan's buddy from the Ford and Nixon years. In fact, his closeness with the maestro was one reason why the administration had offered him the plum job. It turned out that O'Neill had given his private files, all 19,000 pages, to Mr. Suskind to help with the book, which offered a terrible portrait of the Bush White House. The treasury secretary described the president as incurious and disengaged—"a blind man in a room full of deaf people," who valued loyalty more than anything else, his cabinet's dialogue an exercise in "incestuous amplification." O'Neill showed no compassion for the compassionately conservative man.

From Greenspan's viewpoint, what mattered most was that the maestro appeared to be a "partner in crime throughout the book," as

Caroline Baum, a reviewer, put it.[69] In 2001, according to the book, O'Neill had held frequent discussions with the maestro about Bush's first tax proposal, agreeing upon the trigger mechanism to undo the tax cut should the projected surplus disappear. Apparently Greenspan had told him, "Without the triggers, that tax cut is irresponsible fiscal policy";[70] but that was fine with Vice President Dick Cheney, who said, "Reagan proved deficits don't matter."[71]

The book unleashed a firestorm in the media and Washington. A week after its publication, Greenspan reacted with predictability, and said he had different recollections of events at the White House. However, it did not matter if O'Neill was telling the truth, or if he had sour grapes for his firing by the president. What must have mattered to Greenspan was the president's reaction to O'Neill's revelations, especially the one that the administration placed a premium on loyalty. O'Neill had been ousted for his opposition to the tax proposal enacted in June 2003. Greenspan had also been disloyal and opposed that bill. Could he be next? Greenspan, of course, like any Fed chairman, was sack-proof, but the president could certainly deny him his coveted reappointment.

Greenspan couldn't be sure. The book's damaging revelations and the resulting maelstrom seemed to undercut his chances for another term. The White House retort to O'Neill was swift and forceful. One top aide said: "We didn't listen to him when he was there, why should we now?"[72] The Treasury Department even launched an investigation to see if O'Neill had provided classified materials to Suskind. The Republican angst against Greenspan resurfaced, leading his old nemesis, John Crudele, to wonder: "Who's going to be the next one to hear the immortal words, 'you're fired'? It just might be Alan Greenspan."[73]

What was worse, some reviewers believed that Greenspan had personally egged O'Neill on to assist Suskind. See what Michael Lewis, a financial writer with Bloomberg News, wrote: "The character in this drama with interesting motives isn't O'Neill, but his more shadowy friend, Alan Greenspan. It's evident that Greenspan helped with the book; his fingerprints are all over it."[74] Lewis's comments on February 5, 2004, must have unnerved the chairman, because in Congressional hearings a week later he strived to repair the damage that the commotion over the trigger mechanism had done to his standing with the president.

On his part, Bush faced reelection in the near future and had been seeking to make his tax cuts permanent for some time. This would be part of his economic agenda for the forthcoming campaign. However, the

Democrats were dead opposed to his proposal, because the estimated federal budget, including the Social Security surplus, was already in the red by as much as half a trillion dollars.

Budget projections could no longer help the president. In one of history's fastest somersaults, the trillion-dollar projected surpluses had turned into trillion-dollar projected deficits. In a Senate hearing on February 12, 2004, in spite of the new projections, Greenspan advised Congress to make all of the Bush tax cuts—including those he had initially opposed—permanent, and cut entitlement programs, all in order to promote economic growth. His testimony was a throwback to his Robber Baron ideas from 1980 to 1987:

> I am still in favor of pay-go and discretionary caps as a critical issue in budgetary processing. . . . And if that is indeed the case . . . you would have to have a pay-go evaluation for any change in the tax structure. *So I am in favor, as I have indicated in the past, for continuing the tax cuts that are in dispute at this particular stage.* But I would argue strenuously that it should be taken out on the expenditure side. . . . we have constructed a good deal of the benefit structure over the last quarter-century without a real, firm look at whether or not the real resources were there to meet those benefits. . . .
>
> My real concern is that when the time comes to start to pay these benefits, we're going to find that we are in very serious fiscal difficulty.[75] (My italics)

These excerpts from Greenspan's testimony offer a clear, though disturbing, window to the maestro's priorities. Remember that under pay-go rules any tax cut had to be offset by equal spending reductions or a rise in other taxes. Let's look at the tax side first. There are four major sources of federal revenue—individual income taxes, corporate levies, payroll taxes, and excise taxes. Greenspan sought to retain the corporate and individual tax cuts, which meant that the other two taxes had to be increased enough to provide a full offset for Bush's reductions. Isn't this precisely the potion that Reagan and Greenspan had fed to Americans between 1981 and 1983? So we're back to face the virus of Greenomics, which was partially suspended during the Clinton administration.

If you recall, Greenomics means raising taxes on the poor and the middle class, while lowering them for the opulent. This is essentially what the maestro championed when he asked Congress to make all of the Bush tax cuts permanent and apply pay-go rules to other taxes. We're back to

Greenspan's version of "unrelenting justice" in *Atlas Shrugged*, where someone robs the poor and rewards the rich.

Since, historically, excise tax collection has been miniscule—and is not likely to rise greatly above 3 or 4 percent of total outlays—the tax side of pay-go rules implies that Greenspan's proposal, amounting to $1 trillion over ten years, involves almost an equal rise in payroll taxes. On the other hand, if the Social Security tax cannot be touched—and because of its relentless assault on the poor since 1984 it will be sheer insanity to raise it further—then spending cuts would require entitlement programs to be reduced by nearly a trillion.

Thus perpetuating Bush's tax cuts under pay-go rules required that almost all the sacrifices would have to come from retirement programs including Social Security. This is the kind of snake oil that the maestro offered to Americans—once again. He had not changed one bit. As Reagan's adviser or as Fed chairman under Bush, he practiced Robber Baron economics.

In fact, this is the way many newspapers saw it. One of them remarked on February 18, six days after the maestro's testimony: "The Federal Reserve chairman . . . told the House Financial Services Committee last week that Congress should make President Bush's tax cuts permanent and . . . pay the $1 trillion cost by cutting Social Security and other entitlement programs."[76]

Another newspaper was even clearer: "Alan Greenspan said yesterday Congress should reinstate budget rules that would force lawmakers to cover the estimated $1 trillion (U.S.) that it will cost to make President George W. Bush's tax cuts permanent. Greenspan said he favoured reductions in government spending to pay for making the tax cuts permanent and suggested that one place to look should be in reducing the social security benefits."[77]

No wonder during the February 12 Senate hearing mentioned above there was a sharp exchange between the chairman and Democratic Senator Paul Sarbanes of Maryland, who saw through the maestro's machinations. The senator addressed Greenspan brusquely, "It's difficult for me to understand why you can't state very simply that one way of addressing the budget deficit is to show restraint on both spending and tax cuts, since they both make up the combination that determines the budget deficit." To this, Greenspan replied, "Oh, I'm certainly willing to say that, because I believe that."

However, in his subtle way, the maestro had informed the world that his top priority was to make Bush's tax cuts permanent, even while conceding to Senator Sarbanes that there should be restraint on the tax side as well. Everyone could see that such restraint meant a rise in taxes paid by the poor and the middle class, leaving the income and corporate taxes unscathed. How did the maestro justify retaining all of Bush's tax cuts? Take a further look at his words in the Senate hearing on February 12:

> I think that the budget deficit problem needs to be resolved primarily or fully on the expenditure side . . . we ought to be looking at all the possible changes, reductions we can make in expenditures before we find we have no other alternative but to add taxation to fill in the gap. . . . We do not know the extent to which increased taxes will inhibit the growth of the GDP and hence the revenue base . . . because it's very obvious that if you put very substantial tax rate increases in, you could slow the rate of growth enough so that the revenue base does not increase anywhere near the amount of expectations when you raise taxes.

On February 25, Greenspan reiterated his support for the president's tax cuts, leaving out any reference to triggers in his prepared remarks, and advised lawmakers to "close the fiscal gap primarily, if not wholly, from the outlay side," while trimming entitlement programs such as Social Security and Medicare (see chapter 1).

Greenspan had made several flip-flops in his testimonies in the month of February 2004. First he had reverted to the Robber Baron economics of Reagan's days—i.e., rob the poor and reward the rich with tax cuts—after discarding it under Clinton. Second, he had fully accepted the supply-side argument, which he had rejected many times before. During the 1980s he had convinced himself that lower income taxes promote GDP growth, but doubted if they could raise the tax revenue enough to close the budget gap. But now his words implied that a tax rise could even endanger the revenue base and possibly increase the budget deficit. Thus he performed two intellectual somersaults just to please the president, who is an ardent supply-sider himself.

In 2001, the chairman had asked lawmakers to cut taxes to trim the projected budget surplus; three years later, he asked them to keep the tax cuts to trim the projected budget deficit. If you see another blatant contradiction here, you're not alone. Many others see it too.

There was no compelling reason for Greenspan to endorse Bush's campaign agenda, go back on his views on the 2002 and 2003 tax cuts, and risk the fury of the elderly, who surely wouldn't take kindly to his proposed benefit cuts. Why make the public scowl even prior to his reappointment? There must be some reason for it. And the likeliest explanation is that Greenspan wanted to do another favor to the president to seal his own renomination, which was endangered by O'Neill's startling revelations; he backed all of Bush's tax cuts in his testimonies, coaxing the poor and the middle class to foot the massive bill.

His top priority was now crystal clear—his own reappointment. It is worth noting that in 2001 Representative Carolyn McCarthy had directly asked the maestro about the impact of the proposed tax cut on Social Security programs, especially after the big surge in retiring baby boomers beyond 2010. In a hearing on March 2, he had assured her that

> the receipts for Social Security . . . would be enough, under existing benefit formulas, to essentially maintain a continued gap between receipts and benefits . . . so that . . . the effect of this acceleration in productivity is such that it just turns out that the receipts, especially including interest, are more than adequate to meet that big surge through a goodly part of the decade subsequent to 2010.[78]

Greenspan's assurance to lawmakers is clear from these remarks that the tax cut would not require a benefit cut to meet baby boomers' retirement needs even after 2010. Then why did he renege on his word three years later? You already know the answer. To perpetuate all the tax cuts, please President Bush, and secure his reappointment.

Finally, on May 18, 2004, Bush rewarded Greenspan with nomination for a fifth term, and the Senate confirmed the maestro a month later. Within two weeks of the Senate action, the chairman turned to the urgent task of fighting inflation, which had been heating up since the start of the year. To avoid riling the president, he had delayed such action until after his reconfirmation, but on June 30 he raised the federal funds rate a notch— 0.25 percent. Greenspan's intellectual trickery is captured in a nutshell in Table 4.1, where you get a bird's eye view of the maestro's self-contradicting statements and positions over three decades.

Over three decades, from 1975 to 2004, Greenspan reluctantly supported an income-tax cut under Ford, opposed it in 1977 during Carter's presidency, and endorsed it in 1981 under Reagan. In 1991 and 1993, he favored raising the income tax first under Bush Sr. and then under Clinton. In 1999, he opposed the income-tax cut again, and then reversed his position in 2001 and 2004. How many flip-flops are

Table 4.1. Greenspan's Intellectual Fraud Over Three Decades: 1974–2004

1974–1976: As the CEA chairman, Greenspan reluctantly endorses a temporary income tax cut, because it could worsen the budget deficit and hence inflation.

1977–1979: Greenspan advises against an income tax cut for its inflationary potential, but supports a corporate tax cut to spur investment. He decries President Carter's budget deficits, because they raise inflation and interest rates.

1980–1981: As Reagan's economic adviser, Greenspan backs income tax cuts to lower inflation even though they will raise the budget deficit. So the income tax cut and deficit are no longer inflationary, and in fact will lower the interest rate, argues Greenspan.

1982–1983: With the deficit breaking records, Greenspan backs a gasoline tax rise in 1982, and a Social Security tax rise in 1983 to lower the deficit and the interest rate. So now again the deficit is inflationary and raises the interest rate.

1990: Greenspan opposes the Moynihan plan to cut the payroll tax, because it will erode the public confidence in the Social Security system, even though he knows the system's surplus is zero, because its extra cash is being used completely for government's operating expenses.

1991–1999: Greenspan argues that budget deficits are inflationary and generate high interest rates, so spending should be cut substantially. He backs Bush Sr.'s modest income tax increase as well as Clinton's larger income tax rise to trim the deficit, thus contradicting his earlier support for Reagan's program.

2000–2004: Greenspan backs Bush's income tax cut in 2001 to lower the projected budget surplus. In 2004, he backs all of Bush's tax cuts to lower the projected budget deficit. He also supports pay-as-you-go rules, which effectively would require a big rise in Social Security taxes or a cut in retirement programs. This is precisely what he had done from 1982 to 1987, while advising Reagan.

Oscar Wilde once said, "The well-bred contradict other people. The wise contradict themselves." Greenspan has been exceptionally wise over roughly three decades of government service.

---

these? Perhaps half a dozen. In February 2004, *The Nation* business writer Ian Williams also noted some somersaults by Greenspan, especially those done under the Bush administration: "The lifelong critic of budget deficits has been mysteriously silent on the Bush administration's fiscal policies. Guess whose term runs out this year. . . . All the signs are that Wall Street's favorite icon is unlikely to rediscover his principles until after November. Greenspan's four-year term as chairman will end in six months. And he probably wants to anoint his place in history by being reappointed, making him the longest serving Fed Chair ever."[79]

At times he reversed himself even though economic conditions had changed little. Stagflation, a combination of high unemployment as well as inflation, was the scourge of the 1970s. It plagued the United States and the world from 1974 to 1981. Yet, during that span he altered his views about the income-tax three times under three presidents, even though the economic climate was more or less unchanged.

Economic dilemmas of the 1980s and the 1990s were very different from those in the 1970s. Inflation had cooled after 1982, while jobless-ness fell gradually, but the budget deficit had constantly nagged the nation. The unemployment rate did fluctuate, up and down, but not by much. Fiscal discipline was the need of the hour, which Greenspan, to his credit, had repeatedly emphasized for 18 long years from 1982 to 2000. After 1981, he had essentially abandoned Reaganomics, as had Reagan himself, when regressive taxes were raised repeatedly. But as soon as George Bush was elected in November 2000, the maestro reverted to Reagan-style income tax cuts, brushing aside the need for fiscal austerity and relying on dubious forecasts of surplus budgets.

Who would back a trillion dollar tax cut, using projections of a budget surplus, when the government had not balanced its books in the past 27 out of 30 years? Who would completely reverse his position regarding fiscal discipline held for the past 18 years? Only someone centered on the self; someone who could profit by altering his views. This is what compels me to make the strong claim that Greenspan has committed intellectual fraud.

Intellectual fraud occurs when someone uses his/her superior intellect to contradict his/her ideas, theories and opinions to further his/her self-interest. As the table indicates, Greenspan contradicts himself repeatedly in his political career over three decades. Thus Greenspan has committed intellectual fraud on a grand scale.

5

GREENSPAN AND THE GLOBE

The United States is the largest economy in the world, generating about a quarter of planetary output, for a people that constitute less than 5 percent of global population. In terms of consumption of the globe's goods and resources, the U.S. share even exceeds 25 percent. What transpires within American borders cannot but move the earth. Greenspan's long career as a political economist who has swayed America could not but influence the global economy. Footprints of the maestro's ideas and policies are embedded all over the world. Europe, Japan, China, India, Russia, North and South America, and Australia, one way or the other, have been nourished, or malnourished, by them. If Greenomics spawned myriad economic imbalances inside America, it did the same for the world.

Greenspan's short stint as the CEA chairman in the mid-1970s left few imprints in the United States, or other countries. Stagflation then stalked the globe and the maestro couldn't do anything about it, partly because he had little control over the Federal Reserve. But his policy-making role since 1981, both inside and outside the government, has shaped global policies and the living standard.

You may recall that following the tax cut of 1981, both short-term and long-term interest rates soared in the United States, hurtling the nation into a steep recession. There is an old saw that when America catches cold, the world catches pneumonia. With the United States in a serious slump in the early 1980s, Europe wobbled into high unemployment, while some other nations, especially in the developing world, faced the specter of hunger, soaring joblessness, and destitution. Many highly indebted countries (HICs) like Brazil, Mexico, and Argentina all but defaulted on their foreign obligations. Latin America in particular saw major declines in employment, production, and wage rates.

They were doubly hurt. The American slump slashed their exports to the United States and other countries, whereas high global interest rates magnified their debt burden. Their export prices also sank, while their import bills jumped because of the recent rise in the price of oil. The trade deficits of HICs doubled in just two years, from 1979 to 1981.[1] The debt crisis broke loose in August 1982, when Mexico, beset by a foreign exchange drain, announced its inability to meet the interest payment due on its international debt. Within a year another 20 nations joined the country in its plight.

The crisis would have passed with little notice, except that many big Western banks—Citibank, Bank of America, Chase Manhattan Bank, Barclays Bank, and Lloyds Bank among others—were entangled in its web. They had loaned their surplus cash with abandon to the HICs, earned vast amounts of interest and fees in the 1970s, but now faced disaster. They and their governments could not just walk away from the crisis.

The Western financial community, spearheaded by the Reagan administration, acted swiftly. With the stability of international global finance at stake, its first priority was to eschew major losses for creditor banks. Global financial institutions such as the International Monetary Fund (IMF), the World Bank, and the Bank for International Settlements were called upon to join the fray and assist with the cure. They helped restructure the HIC debt, slashed the immediate debt-service burden, and provided fresh loans so debtors could partly meet their obligations to commercial banks. In return, the indebted countries had to trim their budget deficits and wasteful government spending. This way the world avoided the dreaded financial meltdown.

While the HICs hemorrhaged because of high interest rates spawned by the huge American budget deficit, some countries, especially Japan and the Asian Tigers—Taiwan, Hong Kong, South Korea, and Singapore— actually benefited from their U.S. trade. Rocketing interest rates lured gobs of foreign money to America. International investors sold their holdings of other currencies and bought the U.S. dollar to purchase dollar-denominated bonds and shares. Foreign demand for the dollar soared, and when demand increases for something, its price has to rise. So the dollar appreciated in terms of foreign currencies. The greenback rose against the Japanese yen, the French franc, the German mark, the British pound, and so on. It also jumped relative to the currencies of the Tiger economies.

The dollar climb meant that foreign goods became less expensive to Americans, whereas U.S. goods became pricey abroad. Since the prices of a nation's goods are expressed in terms of national currency, a rise in its foreign exchange value makes home products expensive relative to foreign goods. Japan and the Tigers were the biggest beneficiaries of this development, because their goods became cheaper to Americans and because they were more focused on the American market than on Europe and other countries. Japan's trade surplus jumped the most, followed by Taiwan's and that of the other Tigers.

Europe, Australia, and Canada also enjoyed an improvement in their trade position with the United States, as did most other countries. But the Soviet Union and China, for lack of efficient industries, did not. For the United States, something unprecedented happened. The country began to suffer a perennial deficit in its foreign trade. This was a reversal of almost a century-long trend and had wide-ranging repercussions, especially in U.S. labor markets, which we will explore in ensuing chapters.

When the 1980s started, the United States had a minor surplus in its trade, defined by what is called the balance on current account, but in 1983 a deficit began, continued to rise, and reached as much as 3.6 percent of GDP in 1987. The trade shortfall alarmed U.S. Treasury officials, because it showed no signs of reversing itself. The deficit had been rising at an unprecedented rate since 1983, prompting the G-7 nations to act in unison in 1985, leading to the so-called Plaza Accord. Besides the United States, the G-7 includes Canada, the United Kingdom, France, Germany, Italy, and Japan. The Plaza Accord called on the G-7 to intervene in the foreign exchange market and bring down the global value of the greenback by selling dollars in international markets in exchange for their own currencies.

For the first two years, the U.S. trade deficit failed to respond, but then began a dramatic fall because of a ceaseless decline in the value of the dollar. By 1991, the deficit was close to zero; but the very next year, the trend reversed itself, as the dollar's value turned around.

The fall of the Berlin Wall at the end of 1989 followed by America's quick victory in the Gulf War that liberated Kuwait left the United States as the only military and economic superpower in the world. Japan had already suffered a rupture in its stock-market bubble; Germany was beset with problems resulting from its unification with East Germany in 1991; as a result, the dollar had little competition from other international currencies. Foreign money poured into America again, and the dollar resumed its climb. So did the U.S. trade deficit, never to reverse its course.

In fact, since 1991, the trade deficit seems to be immune to the value of the dollar. The dollar goes up, and the deficit gets worse; the dollar goes down, and the deficit worsens. In 2004, the U.S. shortfall on the current account was the worst in history—almost 6 percent of output—with no sign of a turnaround.

During the 1980s, Japan was the biggest beneficiary of the American penchant for imports, followed by Taiwan and other Asian Tigers. In fact, the trade surplus of Japan partly fueled its boom as well as the share-price mania. But by the end of the millennium, China had replaced its neighbors and become the largest net exporter to the United States. Net exports are the difference between exports and imports. China-based companies sent as many goods as possible to America but bought little in return. By 2004 China accounted for almost 30 percent of the U.S. trade deficit with the world, followed by Japan, which had a 12 percent share.

The Chinese boom, as with that of its northeastern neighbor, thrived because of its American connection. Japan had stagnated since its stock market crash of 1990, but without its U.S. trade, its economy would have shrunk significantly. Asia in general, including India, prospered from America's profligacy in world markets. India emerged as a software giant with the help of some U.S.-based companies that opened subsidiaries in the developing nation.

Europe, too, benefited from its own American connection, although its benefit paled relative to Asian gains. The point is that by 2004 the United States and the world were interlocked in a bottomless pit of trade imbalances generated by the U.S.-inspired policy of globalization, which had the blessings of Greenspan. In fact, as with taxation and money supply, America's trade liberalization had the maestro's fingerprints all over it. And all his policies proved infectious for the world.

THE GLOBAL BUBBLE

You have already seen how the 1987 crash of the Dow spawned stock market crashes around the world, which was increasingly interconnected because of new technology and globalization. Computers, the Internet, and telecommunications, along with goods and capital crisscrossing the oceans, had knit the countries into a global village. Greenspan's swift action to slash the federal funds rate following the market debacle restored confidence around the world. He won praise from investors and speculators all over the earth. It was clear that share markets worldwide were now almost totally integrated with the Dow. Local economic conditions still mattered, but American markets seemed to matter more.

Although financial markets recovered quickly after 1987, share prices in America remained subdued for a variety of reasons. For one thing, Greenspan began raising the funds rate in 1988 and did not stop until early 1989. For another, Saddam Hussein invaded Kuwait in 1990, raising the international price of oil, which always generates inflation and hurts stocks. Global share markets also moved slowly, reflecting the crawl of the Dow and the Nasdaq Composite from 1988 to 1990. But following American victory in the Gulf War in early 1991, the Dow and the Nasdaq took off; so did share prices in most countries, except Japan, where the bubble had burst the year before.

Greenspan had something to do with the rise of markets, as he continued slashing the federal funds rate from its level in 1990. By September 1992, the rate hit a three-decade low of 3 percent, and while American GDP did not surge, share prices did, and the rest of the world dutifully followed. Except for Japan's Nikkei, other indexes—Britain's FTSE, Germany's Dax, France's CAC, Italy's Mibtel, Canada's TSE, Australia's All Ordinaries—all began to break records. Consequently, while Greenspan's star glowed in the U.S. sky, it sparkled elsewhere. In America he occasionally faced critics for his mishaps, but elsewhere he was adored without question. And why not? People were raking in money left and right with little effort, and the man who was responsible must be the god of wealth.

Annualized stock market returns exceeding 25 percent were common around the world, compared to paltry historic levels around 10 percent. Not that the economies were roaring. In fact, following the 1987 crash, high joblessness afflicted much of Europe, with rates in excess of 9 percent dotting several European lands. But, with Greenspan in charge of the Federal Reserve, share markets didn't care. With his deft handling of the 1987 crash, he had demonstrated that, given enough time, even a crash could not tame the markets for long, a belief that withstood the "*shoku*" (shock) of the Nikkei carnage in Japan. Japan, after all, did not have a Greenspan.

THE MEXICAN CRISIS

Much went to the liking of the global investor until the end of 1994, when the Mexican currency, the peso, veered toward collapse. Early that year three neighbors, Canada, America, and Mexico, had knotted their economies in terms of a treaty called NAFTA, or the North American Free Trade Agreement. This was not much of a change for Canada and the United States, both of which already had similar economies and cultures, but for Mexico it was a coup that no other Latin American country had been able to accomplish.

The Mexicans, especially the elite, were euphoric. Their economy was now tied with the richest nations in the world. They expected to export much to the north and attract prominent U.S. companies to their soil. The likes of General Motors, IBM, Ford, Citibank, Chase Manhattan, Chrysler, and countless others had already opened their subsidiaries in Mexico and many more were expected to follow.

However, within a year of NAFTA's inauguration in January 1994, the Mexican economy tottered. Believing the official euphoria and propaganda about NAFTA's glories, the Mexicans went on a buying spree on their northern border, leading to an unprecedented trade deficit of $30 billion. At the same time, bankers and investors from North America poured money into short-term Mexican bonds that paid extraordinary interest rates. Such flow of capital financed the Mexican deficit. But then came an armed rebellion from the army of the unemployed in Chiapas, and with it an unstable political climate. Meanwhile, Greenspan had raised short-term interest rates in America, blunting the lure of Mexican bonds.

Investors fled the Mexican financial markets, and the peso collapsed in December 1994. Poor Mexico. It hadn't learned a lesson from its American connections in the early 1980s, when its living standard plummeted from the HIC debt crisis. It trusted the same banks that had ditched it in its hour of need in 1982. The result was nearly fatal this time. Greenspan, unlike in the 1980s, was now directly entangled with the peso crisis.

In 1993, NAFTA had aroused fears and opposition from many circles in the United States; it was backed mainly by big business, which saw the next-door neighbor as a haven for cheap labor, working for pennies per hour as compared to American labor that on average demanded

$10 for similar work. Labor unions and a populist billionaire, Ross Perot, bitterly resisted the proposed pact, but the Clinton administration, backed by economists, the media, the financial community, and, above all, Greenspan, supported NAFTA with gusto.

On March 26, 1993, the *Buffalo News* described the maestro's response to Perot's critique in this way: "Greenspan Thursday rushed to the defense of the North American Free Trade Agreement, a day after Ross Perot attacked the deal as a sure-fire way to send American jobs to Mexico. . . . 'The presumption that this would cause a major disruption in our economy doesn't make sense to me,' Greenspan said."[2] Eventually, after long debates and recriminations, Congress enacted the agreement in a close vote.

With the Mexican economy teetering from the peso crisis, both Clinton and Greenspan faced a major challenge to their credibility. The Mexican imbroglio had emerged within a year after NAFTA went into effect, so the memories of the brawl over the passage of that agreement were still fresh. Sensitive to the polls, both chambers of Congress now washed their hands of the crisis. But the maestro and the Clinton administration were too entangled with the mess to ignore it. So the president, Treasury Secretary Bob Rubin, and Greenspan mounted a rescue effort to bail Mexico and themselves out of their dilemma.

On January 17, 1995, *The New York Times* described Greenspan's involvement in the effort in this way: "Officials at the notoriously reticent Federal Reserve say they have seldom seen anything like it. Not only did Mr. Greenspan join President Clinton at the White House to persuade Congressional leaders to accept the plan, he also went on to plead to a large gathering of senators and representatives to pass the necessary legislation quickly."[3]

Congress, however, refused to budge. Finally, the trio of Clinton, Rubin, and Greenspan devised another plan. Using Treasury funds along with IMF cash, they offered Mexico a $40-to-$50 billion package of loans in three installments. As with the 1987 crash, the timely creation of new debt worked its magic. Soon the peso stabilized, along with Clinton's chances for reelection and Greenspan's chances for reappointment.

During the months leading up to the rescue effort, Greenspan worried about the dangers of what is known as "moral hazard," an idea that once you rescue investors from their mistakes, they expect to be helped again in the future and so indulge even more in risky ventures. The Mexican bailout also clashed with his free-market principles.[4] But once again, his self-interest took over his core convictions, and he sided with expediency. Mexico's collapse could have meant the collapse of financial markets, along with his hopes for renomination.

But Mexico needed hundreds of billions of dollars in aid. The paltry $50 billion package could not prevent the Mexican calamity. GDP in Mexico fell 7 percent in 1995. The Mexican free-traders and bankers tried to put a positive spin on the disaster, but Jose Luis Mastretta, an officer at Monterrey's National Chamber of Commerce, knew better: "In reality these numbers are not good news. How can you be happy or even encouraged when you have an annual contraction of 6.9 percent? These numbers prove what we have been saying all along, and that is that thousands of businesses and factories are failing and many people have lost their jobs."[5]

Following the devaluation in late 1994, the peso lost half of its value, the annual inflation rate jumped to 52 percent and more than a million people were laid off. Thousands lost their cars and homes because of soaring interest rates. Taxes went up sharply, gasoline prices skyrocketed and real wages plummeted by 34 percent. But few officials in America and Mexico called it a failure of NAFTA, not even for the land south of the Rio Grande.

Wall Street, that bastion of free enterprise, also insisted on the rescue package—and then how could its lackeys, the government servants, disappoint it? Billions were at stake for speculative ventures of the financial giants, which had to be protected from their mistakes after they had pocketed millions for their risky investments.

Did American banks lose in the Mexican fiasco? No. The administration and its free-market savants bailed out everyone with a stake in NAFTA's success. In a year when the poorest Mexicans lost their shirts and homes, Citibank managed to earn $81 million from its Mexican operations. J. P. Morgan came up with a profit of $40 million, Bank America with $10 million, and Chase Manhattan with $7 million.[6] In the final analysis, NAFTA was of the bankers, by the bankers, for the bankers. How could they, including the Federal Reserve Bank chairman, possibly lose?

As was common with the maestro, soon after an intervention package had been adopted with his blessings, he returned to touting his free-market beliefs as well as the excellence of free-market economies. This time, following the Mexican bailout in 1995, it took him about a year before he showered effusive praise on free enterprise. On July 18, 1996, he announced:

The good performance of the American economy in the most fundamental sense rests on the actions of millions of people who have been given the scope to express themselves in free and open markets. In this we are a model for the rest of the world, which has come to appreciate the power of market economies to provide for the public's long-term welfare.[7]

He conveniently forgot that the Mexican bailout just a year before blatantly conflicted with the tenets of laissez-faire.

THE ASIAN CRISIS

Greenomics was unleashed on America and the world in the early 1980s, and, besides its immediate carnage for the HICs in 1982 and another for global stock markets in 1987, its variegated fruits would not show up until the 1990s. More moral-hazard dilemmas were about to emerge. Greenspan himself was worried enough to make his famous remark about "irrational exuberance" in December 1996. Within seven months, a global currency crisis, mimicking the recent peso disaster, developed in the Tiger economies of Asia.

There are two types of Tigers—Little Tigers and Baby Tigers. The first four included Hong Kong, Singapore, Taiwan, and South Korea, although Hong Kong is now part of China; the second batch includes Indonesia, Malaysia, Thailand, and the Philippines. The eight were called Tigers because of their superlative growth performance from the 1960s to the 1980s.

The new currency crisis started in Thailand in the month of July, in much the same way it had in Mexico. As before, the culprits were international speculators, global capital movements, and good old debt nourishing the new economy of the eight Tigers. With the help of foreign money Thailand had exhibited spectacular GDP growth, surpassing 8 percent annually in the 1990s. High growth attracted even more foreign funds into its high-yield bonds. Its currency, the *baht*, was linked to the dollar, so that international speculators from Europe, Japan, and the United States worried little about the negative effects of the Thai currency's depreciation on their interest earnings.

Thailand was actually one of the star performers among the Baby Tigers. In 1989, it had a tiny foreign debt of $12 billion. Thanks to the Greenspan-sponsored policy of financial deregulation along with globalization, which eased restrictions on inter-country transfer of funds, Thai foreign debt grew by leaps and bounds and jumped almost seven-fold to

$95 billion by 1997. Other Tigers were also burdened with debt. Their superb GDP performance had endeared them to global speculators.

As with Mexico three years earlier, in 1997, Thailand experienced a huge shortfall in foreign trade, which made it impossible for its currency to stay linked with the dollar. Fearful of its impending depreciation, currency speculators began to sell the baht in the foreign exchange market. When the demand for something falls, its price has to fall. So the baht lost considerable ground in July 1997.

Overseas investors were stunned, even though the latest episode was simply a replica of events in Mexico—which, of course, had been bailed out, leaving speculators with no bitter memories. Thai devaluation spread with lightning speed to other Tigers, because they were all in the same boat, their debt problems compounded by giant trade deficits. Foreign money fled as fast as it had moved in; East Asia's currencies sank like dominoes. As *Time* magazine described it in its November 3 issue:

> On July 2 the baht plunged more than 12% in value against the green-back. Then it crashed into the Philippines, Malaysia and Indonesia, where government officials were forced to devalue their currencies. That triggered a region-wide crisis, in which stock markets gave up as much as 35% of their value, inflated real estate prices fell through the floor, banks collapsed, and hundreds of thousands of Southeast Asians, rich and poor, lost their jobs and fortunes.[8]

This is what *Time* wrote in November 1997. By then, several bailouts had been arranged by the IMF and the government of Japan, which worried about the spread of economic infection from its neighbors. The latest rescue packages were far larger than the Mexican package—$17 billion for Thailand, $40 billion for Indonesia, $60 billion for Korea. There seemed to be no end to the spreading contagion of currency devaluations.[9]

In October 1997, share prices began to crash in the Asian Tigers and quickly afflicted other nations. The New York Stock Exchange made history on October 27, 1997, when trading was halted twice, with the Dow sinking a record 554 points. In percentage terms, the Dow lost only 7 percent, and recouped much of the loss the very next day. Nevertheless, U.S. share markets were jolted, with those in Asia and Latin America in a free fall.

Investors had been afraid that a 1987-style crash could happen in the month of October, as the Asian conflagration continued to rage. The Dow had soared past 8,000 in the summer, for the first time in history, and the market was extremely vulnerable to bad news. It sank sharply that month, as expected, but recovered very quickly. Once again, the maestro faced the moral-hazard dilemma. The choice as usual was between intervention or nonintervention in financial markets. Discarding his free-market formula, he sided with intervention and chose to bail out Wall Street and global speculators, who had suffered losses in Tiger economies as well as at home.

Together with the Clinton administration, he called on Western and Japanese banks to restructure and increase their loans to indebted nations. By now the IMF cash horde was all but depleted, so in January 1998, Greenspan urged Congress to offer the international agency a multi-billion-dollar package of financial aid. The maestro's support for the rescue efforts was sweet music to markets, and the Dow roared past 8,000 by the end of the year. Yet while the United States seemed to remain an oasis of prosperity amid the world's whirlpool, the Asian contagion kept on spreading. Mexico and Brazil were expected to be the next dominoes to fall, but the IMF offered them loan packages in advance and kept the speculators at bay.

August 17, 1998 turned out to be a memorable day for two totally unrelated events. First, Russia devalued its ruble and defaulted on its foreign debt; then, in a speech before the nation, Bill Clinton devalued his credibility by admitting his romantic affair with former intern Monica Lewinsky. Russia's debacle routed the global bond market, Clinton's led to his impeachment by year's end. Both episodes, for different reasons, caused temporary declines in American share markets, but the impact of the Russian carnage was swift and decisive, with long tentacles.

When Russia defaulted on its bonds, global bond markets virtually became comatose. Bond-trading in risky ventures especially ground to a halt. Highly leveraged investors and institutions that had borrowed funds at low interest rates and then purchased high-yield but risky assets faced traumatic market conditions. They scrambled to unload their risky bonds, but could find no takers. As a result, their bond portfolios verged on collapse.

One of the riskiest ventures went by the name of Long Term Capital Management (LTCM). It had borrowed almost $100 billion from banks and investment companies such as Goldman Sachs and Merrill Lynch, on an equity base of just $3.5 billion. It was more than 95 percent leveraged. Its officers included the likes of former Fed Vice Chairman David Mullins and two Nobel laureates in economics, known, of all things, for risk management. Its influential executives enabled it to obtain all those loans.

With that borrowed money LTCM was heavily invested in short- and long-term bonds as well as stock options. It was a hedge fund; that is, it played on both sides of investments in a market. It sometimes made simultaneous bets on an asset's upside as well as downside potential. It would buy put options and sell call options at the same time. In other words, it was a highly risky fund. With that $100 billion of borrowed money, it had placed option bets on as much as $1.25 trillion of Treasury bonds.

Following the Russian default, the hedge fund suffered heavy losses that wiped out its equity overnight—almost $4 billion. It was left with no money to service its own debt, which meant that it would have to unload its portfolio in bond markets at further losses, causing another round of falling bond prices. LTCM was about to go down, along with many of its lenders, and possibly the U.S. financial system. $1.25 trillion is no pocket change after all.

The fortunes of as many as 16 banks and Wall Street firms were directly tied to LTCM. Either someone had to buy the hedge fund or lend it money. In other words, the fund, like many indebted countries, needed a bailout. But who would want to throw good money after bad? That is where Greenspan and the Federal Reserve came in. With his consent, the New York branch of the Fed arranged a $3.6 billion bailout of LTCM, coaxing its creditors to put up the cash. The lenders had no choice—who was going to defy the Fed?

On October 1, 1998, Greenspan defended the Fed action before the House Banking Committee:

> Financial market participants were already unsettled by the recent global events. Had the failure of LTCM triggered the seizing up of markets, substantial damage could have been inflicted on many market participants, including some not directly involved with the firm, and could have potentially impaired the economies of many nations, including our own. . . .
>
> The plight of LTCM might scarcely have caused a ripple in financial markets or among federal regulators 18 months ago. But in current circumstances, it was judged to warrant attention.[10]

Ironically, the true story about LTCM became known six years later. In 2004, a federal judge ruled that the hedge fund was more than just an investment vehicle. It was actually an abusive tax shelter and owed millions of dollars in taxes to the IRS. The judge also questioned whether LTCM was about to go bankrupt at the time of the bank bailout.[11] But how quick were Greenspan and company in arranging that bailout? It showed that the maestro was single-minded in protecting his rich friends, who had won him over when they faced no real trouble.

Again, Greenspan chose expediency over his laissez-faire philosophy and forgot about moral hazard. This time, however, he continued to tout his free-market beliefs, while intervening relentlessly in the world markets to stabilize them. Ever since the Thai currency devaluation in July 1997, the globe had been in financial turmoil. Share and currency markets had been rocked and routed. Greenspan himself encouraged the IMF bailouts of nations on the verge of debt default. But that didn't stop him from singing the glories of free markets, even though none existed. For one thing, markets were monopolistic, forever manipulated by a few large players. For another, he himself had made a mockery of laissez-faire and free enterprise through his perennial interventions.

Since international capital movements were mainly responsible for the currency turmoil, some nations wanted to control short-term capital flows in and out of their porous borders, while retaining free trade in goods and services. Malaysia in fact took a lead in this matter. But Greenspan was critical of such moves, blaming the crisis on insufficient regulation in afflicted countries. On September 23, 1998, he testified:

> Much of today's crisis stems from emerging nations' failure to couple capital account and financial liberalization with sufficient regulatory oversight. Such international advice will allow them to prosper in the global marketplace and realize the large benefits inherent in free and unrestricted commerce. Indeed, it would be a tragedy if nations renounce free market policies due to recent financial turbulence. We must help them to see that long-run economic wellbeing does not stem from capital controls and other market interventions.[12]

In pleading the interests of international speculators, who favored unlimited access to the high-yield bonds offered by Asian and Latin American countries, Greenspan seemed to forget that he had decried regulations all his life. It was a classic case of sour grapes. The lack of "sufficient regulatory oversight" was his scapegoat for the birth of the Asian debacle. What an irony; the man who had derided regulations time and again now blamed

the Asian crisis on their absence. Of all people, he was the least qualified
to argue for increased regulation of financial institutions.

It was difficult to believe that he exalted free markets soon after
arranging the bailout of a private corporation like the LTCM. Greenspan
also defended the lending practices of the IMF and the stiff conditions
that the institution imposed on borrowing countries for its loans. What
really galled some critics was that he wanted to solve the problems of
highly indebted countries by creating even more debt. There was a growing
chasm between Greenspan's actions and words. His actions bespoke
intervention; his words nonintervention.

For almost 18 months, the maestro and global speculators had been
locked in an endless duel. The speculators sought to rattle currencies and
share prices, and Greenspan fought back by generating new debt. Finally,
the chairman started to fling his ultimate weapon, which usually fostered
optimism. On September 29, 1998, after a pause of a year and a half, he
cut the federal funds rate by a quarter point, and followed suit with
another cut on October 15. The potion worked, and the Dow soared
331 points to 8,229 that day.[13] He cut the rate another notch in November
to drive a stake through the monster of the Asian contagion. At 4.75 percent,
the funds rate was the lowest in four years.

Soon share markets around the world resumed their upward march.
About half of the world was in recession, but the other half, especially
North America, was thriving. Although European stocks had been bat-
tered by the Russian default, they had stabilized by September. Greenspan's
three rate cuts in the fall were followed by easy money policy in Europe as
well. As a result, share prices in the Euro Zone ended the year with a
slight gain.

Greenspan's relentless zeal to generate new debt when nothing else
worked had finally paid dividends—once again. The Asian monster had
been repulsed. The maestro had done a masterful job in restoring calm to
the landscape of global finance. Soon the highest honors would pour
from abroad.

In 2000, at the end of the millennium, France decorated Greenspan
with the French Legion of Honor. Two years later, Queen Elizabeth II
knighted him "in recognition of his outstanding contribution to global
economic stability and the benefit that the UK has received from the
wisdom and skill with which he has led the US Federal Reserve Board."[14]
Could he now call himself Sir Alan Greenspan? No, because he was not
a British citizen; but he became a K.B.E.—in short, a Knight of the

British Empire. The title was an exact fit, because he was in reality a Knight of the Bubble Economy that was already unraveling around the world.

THE BUBBLE OF THE MILLENNIUM

From mid-1997 to the end of 1998, Greenspan had acted as a financial generalissimo crushing his market-devouring enemies, the speculators, to smithereens. It was time for his soldiers—that motley throng of share-holders, options buyers, day traders, investment bankers, IPO peddlers, financial analysts—to celebrate and get drunk, again. Get drunk they did—like nothing before. The market hoopla that followed in 1999 had no prior parallel in the entire millennium.[15] The maestro had become the god of wealth all over the world. The greenback bears the words—"In God We Trust." But the greenback and Greenspan became synonymous in the minds of shareowners. Money poured into American stock and bond markets in unprecedented amounts. Investors were now fearless—all over the globe. Who could touch them, shielded as they were by Greenspan's impenetrable armor?

Risk-takers were now the brave, venturesome soldiers. They mortgaged their homes, closed their saving accounts and CDs, sold their properties, cashed their bonds, restructured their pensions, all for the sake of making a killing in stocks. Those who preached caution were scorned. From students to professors, workers to CEOs, youths to grannies, all were dazzled by the Nasdaq and the Dow. Money could grow on trees after all.

Following Greenspan's three rate cuts in fall 1998, the market action shifted from the Dow to the Nasdaq. Who cared for 25-plus percent annual returns anymore? The Dow now became a stodgy old behemoth that only knew how to crawl. The Nasdaq was the place to be, where the new economy shares abounded and thrived. "Give me the Internet and its links, the Dot.com stars," declared the investor. Amazon.com, Theglobe.com, Marketwatch.com, Priceline.com—Anything.com. So what if the stars showed only grandiose names and schemes, but no profit? It was enough that they were peddled by Wall Street, which was chummy with the mighty Greenspan. "His actions," argues John Cassidy, "added to the growing belief that the Fed would always bail out investors if anything went wrong, and this made investors more willing to take risks."[16]

On February 11, 1999, Greenspan made positive comments about the economy. Up went the Nasdaq Composite, by 96 points from

2,310 to 2,406, its strongest single-day gain till that time. In addition to the public frenzy, money was cheaply available in the aftermath of the Russian debacle, so stock prices had to jump. Too many dollars chasing too few stocks. It was as simple as that. This time the stock inflation astonished the world. In just 13 months, the Nasdaq index would peak at 5,049—a jump of more than 119 percent, or roughly 9 percent per month. The Dow rise of barely 30 percent for the period was hardly noticeable.

Global stock indexes tried but could not match the dizzy pace of the Nasdaq. Still the British, the French, the Germans, the Italians, and the Canadians were well rewarded for their painstaking investment work. Their gains ranged from 18 to 30 percent for the year of 1999—miniscule relative to the Nasdaq, but nothing to grieve about.

Canada's TSE 300 started the year from 6,554, but ended at 8,473—a climb of 29 percent; Britain's FTSE 100 jumped from 5,879 to its peak of 6,930 in the same period for a gain of 18 percent; the German Dax rose 30 percent for the year; the French and Dutch stock gains also approximated the German rise. Italy's Mibtel, however, was a laggard with a gain of just 5 percent.

Euro Zone stocks were subject to two complementary pulls. First, the successful launch of the euro started 1999 on a positive note that persisted through the year; the second factor was the locomotive effect of the Nasdaq mania, and to some extent the momentum of the Dow. Britain, however, did not do so well, because it refused to give up its own currency and be part of the Euro Zone. Still, all major European stock exchanges had broken new records by year's end. The broad-based pan-European stock index, FTSE Eurotop 300, ended the year at a record 1,584, up 34 percent.

Most global exchanges peaked in March 2000 in tandem with the Nasdaq Composite. TSE 300, for instance, reached as high as 9,500 on March 10; Dax neared 8,000, and the French Cac, 6,500. As the Nasdaq sank thereafter, the world indexes followed suit, but not as swiftly. However, the global bull market was over, the Nasdaq contagion deadlier than the earlier Asian counterpart.

By October 9, 2002, most major indexes bottomed and crumbled nearly by half, in spite of Greenspan's frantic cuts in the funds rate.[17] FTSE Eurotop 300 fell by exactly 50 percent, from a high of 1,703 in 2000 to 851 by the end of 2002. The Nasdaq market crash climaxed into a planetary crash, with earlier heights nowhere in sight. In 2003 and

2004, the markets recovered around the world, but they had lost their zing and lure. Greenspan had finally discovered that once the bubble bursts, it is simply impossible to stop the crash.

Even the lowly Nikkei of Japan could not escape the carnage. Some smaller indexes in Mexico, Brazil, and Argentina suffered Nasdaq-like losses. At the worst point of this collapse, $7 trillion of wealth was wiped out in the United States; the world's loss was nearly as high. Many a youth, along with workers, CEOs, savers, homeowners, pensioners, and grannies were impoverished. Greenspan giveth, and Greenspan taketh away.

6

WHAT CAUSES A STOCK MARKET BUBBLE AND ITS CRASH?

A week before the October 1929 crash, Irving Fisher, the celebrated Yale economist and stock analyst of the Roaring Twenties, remarked: "Stock prices have reached what looks like a permanently high plateau." In May 1998, Greenspan boasted to President Clinton: "This is the best economy I have ever seen in 50 years." It is now clear that both celebrities were woefully wrong. Their hyperbole was a mirage that lured millions into a glittering quick-buck trap, hurtling some into destitution in the end.

What did Fisher and Greenspan have that made them hazardous to society? Partial knowledge. There is an old saw: a little knowledge is a dangerous thing. Why? Because its maxims sound so plausible. Ridiculous ideas are not perilous, because they lack credibility. But partial knowledge can be worse than ignorance, as it tends to fool the public. As Publilius Syrus, a Latin poet during the Roman Empire, once said, "Better to be ignorant of matter than half know it."

Economic theories abound but none can explain what triggers a stock market bubble and crash. Robert Shiller, a macroeconomist and best-selling author, remarks: "A great embarrassment for modern macroeconomic theory is that it has never achieved any consensus on the basic questions of what makes the stock market rise or fall."[1] Robert Hall, a Stanford University professor, is even more candid: "Economists are as perplexed as anyone by the behavior of the stock market."[2] Greenspan certainly was—perplexed yet boastful, without realizing what he was doing to the finances of millions of Americans and others around the world.

The maestro did stumble onto something—productivity as the main-spring for profit. We will now show that productivity captures only half the picture; what Greenspan left out was the other half—debt. This is because productivity is the main source of supply, whereas, in modern economies, wages and debt are the main source of demand.

If demand and supply are to be balanced over time, then either wages rise in sync with productivity, or productivity growth must be matched by the growth of wages plus debt. Of course, new debt becomes unnecessary, if wages keep up with rising labor efficiency, because then both demand and supply grow apace to equal each other. Such, however, has not been the case since the advent of Greenspan on the national scene; so debt growth was the only way to maintain demand–supply equilibrium from the 1970s till today.

In a low-wage economy of the type championed and engineered by the maestro, wages trail but profits outpace productivity; then new debt must grow exponentially to maintain economic balance. Profits and hence share prices then zoom, culminating in a bubble, but soaring debt growth one day halts this process, and brings it tumbling down. Both Fisher and Greenspan failed to fathom the debt requirement underlying a stock market bubble, which must crash one day, because the debt binge cannot be sustained forever.

It matters not who borrows money in a bubble economy—consumers, the government, or corporations. What matters is that, when wages trail productivity, someone has to spend money on goods and services to prop demand up to the level of rising supply. You may call it fiscal policy or monetary policy. Such euphemisms cannot mask the fact that, in reality, new debt is created, which in turn ensures a mega rise in profits. Neither Keynesian nor classical economics explains this process, which is expounded in detail below.

THE DEMAND–SUPPLY BALANCE

Two questions need to be answered. First, why doesn't every output boom generate a stock market bubble? Second, why do all bubbles burst in the end?

In twentieth-century America, output grew strongly during the 1900s, 1940s, 1950s, 1960s, and then in the second half of the 1990s, with annual GDP growth exceeding 4 percent—but market bubbles arose only in the 1920s and from 1982 to early 2000, when growth was mediocre, even below average. The behavior of wages and debt answers this puzzle. When wages grew smartly with productivity, output grew sharply without much rise in debt. Thus high wage growth alone produced high output growth, but no bubbles, because rising worker salaries precluded the sharp rise in profits. High profit growth is a prerequisite for the share-price mania, which cannot occur even in a booming economy if wages rise in sync with economic efficiency.

When wages trailed productivity, demand grew slowly, so debt soared to preserve the demand–supply balance. Output also grew slowly but profits increased sharply, so the bubble arose, lingered for a while, and crashed in the end. Thus some decades saw the rise of bubbles only because wages failed to keep up with productivity and the resulting demand deficiency had to be filled by gobs of new debt.

Let's begin with a very simple economy, approximating a libertarian utopia in which there is no government at all and no borrowing of any kind. This may be wishful thinking, but is a convenient starting point. The main components of aggregate spending or demand in such an econ-omy are spending by consumers for consumption and by businesses for investment, on newly produced goods and services. We thus begin with a simple formula:

Demand = Consumption + Investment

Let the formulas not deter you, because the analysis offered here is intelligible to anyone with an iota of common sense. All you will need is a calculator, or a working knowledge of addition, subtraction, division, and multiplication.

If there is government presence, then we need to add government spending to this formula, because the president and the lawmakers also spend money, on behalf of the State, on new goods and services; but we also have to subtract all the taxes that the private sector pays, because consumer and business spending goes down proportionately to the level of taxation. So if official spending matches tax revenue, or if the government balances its budget, then the above formula does not change significantly. As our starting point, let there be no debt or deficit of any type.

Let's assume that workers save nothing and spend their entire salary for consumption and that all investment comes from profits. This is a realistic assumption in today's American economy, where the saving rate is just 2 percent of people's income; this assumption in any case is just a simplification, and can be relaxed without any jeopardy to the analysis. Then consumption equals wage income, or employment multiplied by the average wage. Another level of simplification may be achieved by assuming for the time being that foreign trade is always balanced, so that exports never fall short of imports. Relaxing all these restrictions, as will be explained later, makes no difference to the central argument.

Suppose our economy consists of ten workers, who are all employed, and each on average earns $4 a year; then wage income and hence consumption equal $40. What about the wage rate of the CEOs and other executives? They are workers as well, and their salaries are part of the average wage; they also earn profits, which arise in the production process. On the other side, national output or supply is produced by capital (machines and land), labor, and available technology. The formula here is:

$$\text{Supply} = \text{Productivity} \times \text{Employment}$$

As an example, suppose a worker, using capital and technology, on average produces $5 worth of goods in a year. Then productivity, defined as output per worker, is $5. If 10 workers are employed, their total output is worth $50. This explains the supply formula. For economic balance,

$$\text{Supply} = \text{Demand}$$

Thus in this simple economy, wages are the main source of demand, productivity the main source of supply, and there are no debts, and trade deficit or surplus. Since supply is $50, consumption equaling wages is $40, investment must be $10 so that demand equals supply. What about profits? In a macroeconomy,

$$\text{Profits} = \text{Business Revenue} - \text{Wage Costs} - \text{Unsold Goods}$$

Don't we need to deduct other costs, like raw materials, etc., to obtain profits? Not at the national level. Raw materials are produced by labor and capital as well, and their revenue is also divided into wages and profits. The point is that when all output is aggregated in the macroeconomy, national output or income is shared by workers and the owners of capital. When the economy is in balance, unsold goods equal zero, and then

$$\text{Profits} = \text{Business Revenue} - \text{Wage Costs}$$

Business revenue is the value of total production or national supply, so that with business revenue also equaling $50, and wages costing $40, profits equal $10, which is the same amount as investment. In other words, investment is financed by profits in our economy.[3]

With all these formulas, I can see you wiping the sweat from your brow, but believe me the effort will be well worth it. If you understand even a bit of economics, then you can see through the shenanigans of people like Greenspan and politicians. And all I will ever use are simple numerical examples to explain complex questions.

Let our starting point be the simple economy presented above. Here, productivity is $5, average wage is $4, ten people are employed from the same level of labor force, and profit and investment are $10 each. In other words, we have a fully employed society—nirvana for a politician and policymaker. Let's see what the politician needs to do to maintain this state of nirvana in a growing economy.

Because of investment spending on new machines embodying the latest technology, productivity rises over time. Suppose the latter doubles to $10 per worker. If the wage rate matches the productivity gain, it will rise to $8. With employment equaling ten workers, supply increases to $100 (i.e., 10 × 10), and wages and consumption each to $80. Suppose further that investment also doubles from $10 to $20. This is quite likely because there is a powerful link between consumer spending and business expansion that requires increased investment. When employers find that sales are brisk, they are confident enough to plough their profits back into capital spending in proportion to rising output. So, after the doubling of productivity, wages, and investment, we have the following values:

Demand = Consumption + Investment = 80 + 20 = $100
          = Supply

Profit = Supply − Wages = 100 − 80 = 20 = Investment

Clearly when productivity and wages double, everything else also doubles; the demand–supply balance is automatically maintained over time, and there is no overproduction. Now suppose the wage rate lags behind productivity growth and rises, say, only to $6. With employment at ten workers, wages and hence consumption are now $60. Since supply is still $100, investment must rise further to $40 to fill the consumption gap and maintain the economic balance.

Thus even if wages trail productivity, economic equilibrium can still be maintained if investment picks up the slack. But this is a very big if. When consumer spending was $80, investment was $20. Now that consumption falls to $60 and firms are stuck with unsold goods, how can they possibly expand their business any further? New investment implies business expansion. Who would expand their business if goods were piling up on their shelves?

Would you sink more into your company if you could not sell all you currently produced? Of course not! With consumer spending falling, investment will be no larger than $20. Let's say that investment is normal when it rises roughly in proportion to output. In the long run, this clearly holds in the U.S. economy.[4] Since the investment/output relationship in our example is 10/50 or 20 percent, then the new output of $100 supports an investment of only $20. So now

$$\text{Demand} = \text{Consumption} + \text{Investment} = 60 + 20$$
$$= \$80 < \text{Supply} = \$100$$

This means an excess supply or unsold goods worth $20. With goods piling up on shelves, firms have to lay off some workers, leading to unemployment. Thus, *when wages trail productivity, other things remaining unchanged, there must be a rise in unemployment.* This is an important result, something that is lost on the acolytes of classical economics, supply-side economics, and Greenomics.

GROWTH IN DEBT

Let us now introduce the concept of wage gap, simply defined as productivity divided by the wage rate. In our example,

Wage Gap = 5/4 = 10/8

In other words, when both productivity and the wage rate double, the wage gap stays constant; but when the wage rate rises only to $6, while productivity climbs to $10, the wage gap equaling 10/6 or 5/3 goes up. What you have seen is that a rise in the wage gap generates unsold goods and hence joblessness. So the matching of wage growth with rising productivity is crucial to a smooth functioning of any economy. This is not to suggest that the wage rate equals productivity, only that salaries rise proportionately to economic efficiency.

If the wage gap rises then joblessness arises because investment is insufficient to fill in the resulting consumption or demand gap. Since investment is not forthcoming, can a full-employment equilibrium be maintained in the face of a rising wage gap? Yes, but only with the help of an ever-increasing amount of debt. Suppose confident and fully employed workers get into debt because of their rising salary. Earnings may lag behind productivity, but so long as they rise, employees may just borrow lots of money to buy expensive goods such as cars, homes, and furniture. This occurred in the 1920s and then again since the late 1970s.

Politicians also have to act, because joblessness disturbs their economic nirvana. They respond with expansionary fiscal and monetary policies. They raise the budget deficit and trim the interest rate to lure society into increased borrowing. For aggregate demand, it doesn't matter who does the borrowing—the consumer, the firm, or the government. Demand will increase, whenever debt rises, because people and governments borrow money primarily to spend it. But since firms are flush with profit because of the growing wage gap, the corporate sector as a whole is a net lender, although some inefficient or merger-prone firms may do the borrowing. Once new debt is introduced, then

Demand = Consumption + Investment + New Debt

The new debt equals borrowing by consumers, government, and firms, and comes out of savings or profits of rich corporations. It may also be financed by the Federal Reserve. Here the notion of consumer spending changes somewhat. It now includes wages plus a part of the new debt; the new debt may also include the government deficit, which is the difference between government revenue and receipts.[5]

Obviously, new debt must equal the value of unsold goods, equaling $20, to eliminate overproduction and preserve full employment in our model economy. Thus, if the government won't introduce reforms to ensure the rise of the wage rate in sync with productivity, then full employment can be maintained only through expansionary fiscal and monetary policies. Expansionary policies are therefore not independent, reflecting official compassion or wisdom. They become necessary in an environment with a growing wage gap to preserve full employment. Whenever Greenspan trimmed the federal funds rate to expand the supply of money or lure more people into debt, he did it, as we shall soon see, against the backdrop of wages trailing productivity.

Rocketing Profits and Share Prices

When debt rises to maintain the demand–supply equilibrium, profits must rise sharply. Suppose consumers and the government borrow money to raise aggregate demand to $100, and eliminate overproduction; then

Profit = Supply − Wages = 100 − 60 = $40

Here profit quadruples, not just doubles. When the wage gap was constant, the profit had doubled; but now, supported by debt growth, it jumps four times its original level. Herein lies the seed for the stock market bubble. Note that without the new debt of $20, profit would not rise to $40, because goods have to be sold before companies realize their incomes.[6] Note also that the entire increase in the debt goes into company profits and hence executives' incomes. No wonder CEOs love the system in which the government and the public borrow their savings that are deposited with financial institutions. CEO bigwigs are at once the lenders and the profiteers, that is, whatever money they lend goes back into their own coffers in the form of enhanced profits.

What about the workers—don't they benefit from debt creation in terms of preserved jobs? No, because they won't be losing work if they are being paid according to their productivity. You have already seen that unemployment results when a CEO fails to match worker pay with productivity gains; demand falls short of supply and triggers layoffs.

Share prices depend primarily on profits. Let's suppose, for the sake of argument, that initially the stock market index (the Dow or the Nasdaq Composite) equals the level of profit, and that, other things remaining the same, share prices increase in proportion to the rise in profits. In our illustration, when the wage gap is constant, the share market will double with the doubling of profit, and it will quadruple when profit grows to four times its original level. Thus *when the wage gap and debt grow, company profits rise sharply, and so does the share market*. The stock index now grows from 100 to 400.

When some other things change, the stock market escalation can be even sharper. Another factor that stimulates the share price is the fall in the interest rate resulting from the rising wage gap. Whenever Greenspan lowers the federal funds rate to push the public into increased debt, assets that compete with stocks lose some of their attraction.

Bonds and shares are very competitive with each other. When the rate of interest falls, bonds become less attractive, so more funds flow into share markets. This is then another avenue through which the rising wage gap fuels the stock market bubble, because the gap forces the Fed to bring the interest rate down in order to eliminate the shortfall in consumer demand. Thus, share prices outpace even profits in the wake of a rising wage gap. So after the fall in the interest rate, the stock index will exceed 400. Say it rises to 600.

Of course, the falling interest rate plays only a supportive role in stock market gains. The primary role goes to the rocketing level of profit. When profit falls, then the declining rate of interest may do little to shore up share prices, as occurred during the 1930s and recently from 2000 to 2002.

Overinvestment and Mergers

Let us take another look at our economy following the productivity increase and business expansion. In the new situation

Supply = \$100 = Demand, Consumption = \$60,
   Investment = \$20, Profit = \$40, and

New Debt = 20

With profits flying high it is possible that some firms disregard the long-term investment rule, whereby investment is roughly a fixed proportion of output, and spend excessively to purchase capital goods.

When profits quadruple, it is natural for firms to become overly optimistic. They may not realize that it is the growth in national debt that is keeping their business afloat. Even if they do, perhaps they won't care. What they see is their balance sheet with a surging bottom line, and the rest is immaterial to them. High profit itself may induce them to borrow funds from banks and sharply expand their investment.

Had wages kept up with productivity, there would be no growth in debt, and investment would be \$20. In the debt-prone atmosphere, however, where profit rises to \$40, firms may spend a part of the extra income either for further expansion of their own business or just to buy other companies, which also become attractive due to rising profits. The end result is a hike in business mergers along with overinvestment, which may be conceived as a jump in capital spending that outruns output.

With growing mergers among firms, even highly profitable companies start to borrow money from financial institutions. Corporate debt soars, and mergers in turn fuel another round of the share-price boom. Housing investment also zooms because of low interest rates resulting from the Fed policy to encourage debt. This in turn further inflates the investment bubble. The point is that with a soaring wage gap and profits, overinvestment, merger mania, and mushrooming indebtedness may all occur simultaneously.

Bubble Economy

What is a bubble? During the 1990s the Dow broke all bounds and jumped from about 2,500 in 1990 to its peak near 11,700 in January 2000. Was this a bubble? Look at it this way. The Dow Jones Index was first compiled in 1885, and following 1982 it permanently passed 1,000. The Dow took nearly 100 years to cross the one-thousand mark, and then in a matter of two decades it surpassed 11,000. This was not an ordinary bubble, but a bubble of the millennium.

The Nasdaq Composite index flew even higher, from about 300 in 1990 all the way up to 5,049 on March 10, 2000. Even as late as 1996, the index stood near 1,000, but then in the next four years it crossed 5,000.

What is a speculative bubble? *When the laws of demand and supply for assets break down completely, a speculative bubble or mania is born.* Normally, people avoid buying pricey goods, but in the hoopla surrounding bubbles they purchase assets simply because their prices have already surged and are expected to surge more. On the other side, the public shuns these assets even as their prices fall. Similarly, sellers' behavior contradicts the law of supply, as more selling occurs with a sinking price.

When Nortel went for $75 per share in 1999, it had few sellers, but Wall Street analysts coaxed the public into buying even more; when it crashed all the way down to $2 per share, the analysts counseled against its purchase, while sellers wanted to dump it on the market. Amazon.com once sold for $390 per share and still had a lot of suitors; then it sank to $5 and had few seekers. Such is the stuff of which bubbles are made. Buyers and sellers become irrational, and the laws of demand and supply fall apart.

The phrase "bubble economy" became popular during the 1980s, when Japan experienced a stock market euphoria, which at the time appeared to be much more potent than the corresponding euphoria in the United States. A bubble economy is born when collectively debt, business investment, business mergers, and share prices appear to flout the bounds of rationality. They all exceed the rise in productivity and the GDP. Speculation thrives, as the public and financial institutions rush to acquire various assets at exorbitant prices.

In Japan, the price of land leaped even faster than share prices. At one point Tokyo's real estate was valued above the real estate in all of California. The only thing that sinks in the bubble economy is sanity, and the fraction of GDP going into wages and possibly consumption. *If the wage gap continues to rise unchecked, a bubble economy is the inevitable result.*

Reverting to our numerical illustration, with soaring investment comes another jump in productivity. In fact, productivity now rises even faster than would be the case if investment had just doubled from $10 to $20. Suppose the average product of labor climbs to $30 from $10, but the real wage rises only to $15, and the wage gap rises again—this time from 5/3 to 30/15, or 2. With ten employees, supply rises to $300, and wages and consumption to $150. Since normal investment is one fifth of output by our assumption, the normal level of capital spending now equals 20 percent of $300 or $60. Therefore

Demand = Consumption + Investment = 150 + 60 = $210

Unsold goods now equal

Supply − Demand = 300 − 210 = $90

In order to plug the shortfall in demand, debt must rise by the amount of unsold goods, or by $90, compared to the previous rise of just $20. So *debt grows exponentially.* With the rise in this much debt, there are no unsold goods, and

Profits = Supply − Wages = 300 − 150 = $150

as compared to the level of $40 in the previous period; so *capital income also grows exponentially.*

With a constant interest rate, share prices rise in proportion to profit growth. So the stock index rises from 400 to 1,500, or exponentially. This is the minimum rise in the share market. But with a falling interest rate, the market swells even more. Again, a part of the rocketing profit may feed overinvestment and business mergers, and another part the rising indebtedness. In this case, *investment, mergers, profit, share prices, consumer and government debt all grow exponentially, and a bubble economy is born.* Asset valuations then lose sanity. The share market comes to fascinate the people. Having seen it vault higher and higher, even the general public becomes infected with greed, and starts diverting the bulk of its savings into the stock market. *Optimism breeds optimism, and for a while money seems to grow on trees.*

However, all this only succeeds in creating a fool's paradise. New dogmas, à la Greenspan's rationalization of the new economy, are born to explain the sky-high profits and share prices. People, even experts, come to believe, as they did in the Roaring Twenties and the la-la 1990s, that everyone can become a millionaire. They equate soaring share prices with a growing living standard for the nation. How is this ever possible? The living standard is not paper profit. It is realized capital gains or profits, which occur when shares are actually sold. Soaring share prices are like distributing a bucket of printed money to every citizen. Does this improve the nation's lifestyle? Those few who sell their shares in time indeed become millionaires and billionaires overnight, but if every one tries to cash out, the stock market will indeed crash. The entire nation cannot possibly see a jump in its living standard.

The living standard rises with an increase in the production of tangible goods and services. Suppose our ten workers live in only two houses. If the number of homes doubles, and people no longer live in cramped quarters, that is certainly an improvement in lifestyle. But if stock prices skyrocket with little rise in the availability of tangible goods, how can the living standard improve? In the hoopla of the bubble economy, however, rationality gives way to euphoria, euphoria gives way to mania, and the nation gets drunk, until it wakes up one morning and suffers a mega hangover.

The Inevitable Crash

A bubble economy is born when wages trail productivity for some time and result in ever-rising debt. Then profits grow faster than productivity gains, and share prices outpace GDP growth. However, a time comes when debt growth slows down, and demand falls short of output, resulting in the profit decline and a stock market crash. Thus, the very force that generates the stock market bubble seeds its crash.

The speculative bubble is supported by ever-rising debt growth, and common sense tells us that debt growth cannot endure forever. Around such times, experts may come out with various ratios such as the debt to investment ratio, the debt to GDP ratio, the debt to consumption ratio and so on, and offer pearls of wisdom assuring the public that these ratios are reasonable. But rationality dictates that the debt binge must come to a halt some day.

When the public is up to its neck in loans, the financial institutions simply slow their lending for fear of defaults by borrowers. A point comes when some households and corporations become risky customers. The government itself may loathe its mushrooming liabilities and raise taxes to eliminate its deficit, as happened in the 1990s. Few mergers live up to expectations. Companies begin to fail; some file for bankruptcy, banks become cautious in their lending, and for all these reasons credit growth slows down, starting a chain reaction that unravels the bubble economy.

The seed of the speculative bubble is also the seed of its destruction. The rising wage gap feeds profits on one side and debt on the other. A time comes when the debt binge slows. That is when the potential demand–supply imbalance, thus far masked by swelling debt and overinvestment, comes to the surface. That is when profit begins to fall, and the nation receives a sudden jolt. First, the stock market moves sideways. But as excess supply of goods continues, share prices begin to crash.

Most of the investors then head for the exit, in a stampede that cripples mega fortunes built on the foundation of paper profit or sandy capital gains. Those who were late in joining the bubble party suffer real losses; some even lose their retirement money and lifetime savings.

That is why governments should do all they can to suppress a specu-lative bubble. Capital gains may come and go, but debt is forever, until it is paid off or until the debtor declares bankruptcy, none of which is a pleasant prospect. Greenspan and other government officials—Clinton, Bob Rubin among others—had regarded the exploding stock market as a badge of honor. But it turned out to be a badge of shame, when millions around the world lost their savings in the subsequent crash.

Greenspan's little knowledge indeed turned out to be a dangerous thing, not for Greenspan but for society. The maestro failed to fathom the role of the debt in supporting soaring profits. As you have seen above, high productivity alone is inadequate to raise profits sharply. It is the combination of rising productivity, the wage gap, and debt that does the job. Thus the profit surge that Greenspan had effusively rationalized in the late 1990s, using the glitter of new technology in the new economy, actually required the help of something old-fashioned—oodles of debt.

The illustration above derives from several simplifying assumptions, none of which is crucial. In reality, not all wages are consumed, investment may not be in strict proportion to output, debt may not be zero initially, trade may not be in balance, and so on. None of this is material to the analysis. What really matters is the size of the wage gap; if the wage gap rises, the rest follows as a matter of cause and effect. Some of these simplifications will be relaxed in the pages to come, and they will only reinforce our analysis.[7]

In fact, the speculative process described above happened during the 1920s and later from 1982 to 2000. This is explained in Table 6.1 and Figures 6.1 and 6.2. Each time the wage gap leaped high. Take a close look at this table, which describes the wage–productivity relationship in the United States for two time periods—first the 1920s and then from 1962 to 2003. These periods are of interest because in both cases the American economy evolved into a bubble economy.

In column 2, the data, displayed usually at five-year intervals, start from 1962, which is a year of recovery for the economy. Actually the data series goes all the way back to 1959, but we have omitted the first three years because of a lingering recession that began in 1957, and kept the jobless rate high until the end of 1961. The first normal year of the 1960s was 1962, with business neither booming nor languishing.

If we divide the index of output per hour in the business sector by the index of real employee compensation, both available from the 2004 *Economic Report of the President*, we obtain a measure of the wage gap in the United States. If real incomes rise in sync with labor productivity, which is the same thing as hourly output, then the figures in column 2 should be more or less constant. In 1962, the wage-gap index stood at 85, and rose steadily thereafter, at first slowly, and then in a torrent, to reach an all-time post–World War II high of 111 in 2003. Clearly, real wages trailed productivity over time; in four decades the wage-gap index soared about a third.

When the wage gap remained more or less constant, as in the 1960s, economic growth was stronger than in any other post–World War II decade, yet there was no speculative bubble, and hence no crash. What about the 1970s, when the wage gap started to rise? There the rising price of oil hurt the growth in productivity and profit. So asset markets were subdued. The wage gap rise is only one prerequisite for soaring share prices; another is a steady rise in hourly output, so that an increasing

Table 6.1. The Wage-Gap Index in the United States in Selected Years: 1920s and 1962–2003

(1) Year	(2) Wage Gap 1	(3) Wage Gap 2	(4) Year	(5) Wage Gap
1962	85	21	1919	111
1965	88	21	1921	128
1970	87	23	1923	130
1975	91	26	1925	148
1980	91	30	1927	154
1985	96	33	1929	156
1990	99	37		
1995	104	40		
2000	106	43		
2003	111	45		

Source: Columns 2 and 3 from *The Economic Report of the President*, 2004, Council of Economic Advisers, Washington, D.C.; Column 5 from *The Historical Statistics of the United States: Colonial Times to 1970* (Washington, D.C., U. S. Department of Commerce, 1975), series D 685, D 727, and D 802.

share of productivity growth goes to profits and nourishes the stock markets. Sagging economic growth, along with high uncertainty, tends to hurt the share prices.

What is interesting, however, is that from 1962 to 1970, the wage gap was fairly constant, ranging from 85 to 88. It even fell a bit from 1965 to 1970. After 1970 it began a steady rise, never to fall back again. The wage-gap index in column 2 relies on an overall wage, which is highly aggregated and does not truly represent the general public in the United States, because it also includes the compensation of the CEOs of the Fortune 500 corporations.

The CEOs and management executives have seen a vast jump in their salaries since 1980, and their presence tends to distort the size of the real-wage data pertaining to the public, because a part of their wages represents soaring profits. A better measure of the wage gap is in column 3, which uses the average real wage of the non-supervisory or the production worker. This wage is usually called the production wage, which began to fall after 1973. The message of the second measure is the same from 1962 to 1970, as the index changes slightly. But after 1970 the wage gap soars, and in fact nearly doubles in three decades.

The other time period in Table 6.1 refers to the 1920s when the wage gap climbed from 111 in 1919 to 156 in 1929, or about 40 percent in one decade. This jump is comparable to the jump in column 3. It is

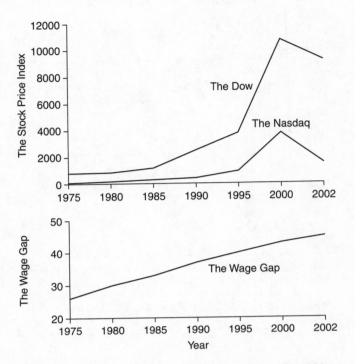

Figure 6.1. The Dow, The Nasdaq Index, and the Wage Gap, 1970–2002
Source: The Economic Report of the President 2003.

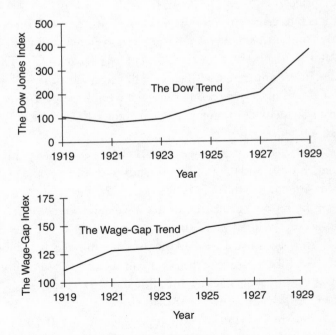

Figure 6.2. The Dow and the Wage Gap in the 1920s
Source: Table 6.1, and *P. S. Pierce, The Dow Jones Averages: 1885–1990*, Homewood, Ill., Dow Jones-Irwin, 1982.

clear that *the two decades of the 1980s and the 1990s have something in common with the 1920s, namely that wages badly trailed productivity in both cases.*

There are more similarities between the two time periods than meets the eye. Profits, stock prices, consumer debt, and business mergers soared in both cases. Then as now governments adopted a noninterfering approach to company behavior. The general belief was: what is good for big business is good for America. In both periods macroeconomic policy emphasized industrial and financial deregulation. Taxes were cut repeatedly to benefit the affluent in the 1920s, just as in the 1980s. In both periods, leading economists argued that such tax cuts foster efficiency and promote social welfare. Figures 6.1 and 6.2 display how the rising wage gap coexisted with stock market bubbles in the 1920s and from 1982–2000.

Then as now income and wealth inequality jumped while the State stood idly by. Finally, of course, in both cases the share markets crashed. To be sure, there are also striking differences in the two time periods. But differences are only natural over time. The element of surprise lies in all the similarities you have observed. Are they simply coincidences, or inevitable emissions of the soaring wage gap?

THE AMERICAN ECONOMY: 1962–2003

Let us closely examine the behavior of the U.S. economy from 1962 to 2001, especially its debt growth over these four decades. Table 6.2 displays various credit, deficit, and debt measures that, our theory says, are related to the wage gap. Column 2 displays consumer borrowing, column 3 the borrowing by the federal government, and column 4 is obtained by adding up columns 2 and 3; all of these values are expressed as percentages of GDP. Finally, column 5 displays the behavior of productivity growth.

Table 6.1 showed that from 1962 to 1970 the wage gap was virtually constant, and then began to rise in the 1970s. Table 6.2 reveals that there was not much of a trend from 1962 to 1980 in consumer credit, but following 1980, it generally began to rise. Apparently, the credit card became people's best friend thereafter. Consumer credit was at its all-time high in 2003, reflecting the growing impact of the rising wage gap on consumer demand.

Table 6.2. Productivity Growth and GDP Shares of Consumer Credit and Federal Debt in the United States (in Percent): 1962–2003

(1) Year	(2) Cons. Credit	(3) Fed. Debt*	(4) Con + Fed. Debt	(5) Productivity Growth
1962	11.6	42.3	53.9	4.5
1965	13.4	36.3	49.7	3.5
1970	12.7	27.2	39.9	2.0
1975	12.5	24.1	36.6	3.5
1980	12.6	25.5	38.1	−0.3
1985	14.2	35.7	49.9	2.0
1990	13.9	41.6	55.5	1.5
1995	15.4	48.7	64.1	0.6
1999	16.3	39.2	55.5	2.5
2000	17.2	34.7	51.9	3.1
2003	18.0	35.2	53.2	6.0

* Federal debt held by the public.

Source: The Economic Report of the President, 2004, Council of Economic Advisers, Washington, D.C.

The federal government's debt relative to GDP decreased until 1975 and then began to rise; so did the aggregate level of consumer and federal debt. After 1975 all types of debt measures generally display a rise. The debt measure that is most significant is displayed in column 4. It shows a steady increase until 1995. The reason lies in the fall of the production wage, which we utilized to obtain the second wage gap index in Table 6.1.

The production wage began a slow but steady decline after 1973, and since productivity continued to climb, debt had to rise to plug the demand shortfall. Productivity growth was very strong from 1962 to 1975, but then slowed considerably. After 1980, it picked up somewhat, while the production wage continued to fall. So the debt had to rise significantly to raise national demand to the ever-growing level of national supply.

These were the early and formative years of the bubble economy, which arrived after the recession of 1990. Share prices began to surge after 1982, but the public obsession with the stock market began only after the Gulf War in 1991. America's easy victory over Iraq in the war, along with the concurrent fall of Soviet communism, created a general aura of optimism, and share markets not only took off but also found enthusiastic public support.

However, this prosperity was clearly built on the sandy foundation of debt, which, as column 4 shows, peaked in 1995. Following that year the aggregate debt measure displays a drastic fall. The wage-gap theory says that when debt growth slows down, the demand–supply gap comes to the surface. This is precisely what happened by 1999, as aggregate debt as a percentage of GDP tumbled and then a few months later the share markets peaked—the Dow in January 2000 and the Nasdaq Composite index in March 2000. Global stock indexes also peaked around that time, and then crashed over the next two years. Ironically, as Professor James Galbraith argues, Greenspan himself contributed to the fall in debt growth by resisting "new government spending initiatives or tax reductions" in 1999 and 2000.[8]

By the end of 2000, the slowdown in debt growth showed up in terms of the gap between demand and supply, especially in the high-tech sector that included computers, communications, and cell phones. As unsold goods piled up it became abundantly clear that the share-market crash would be no longer contained, no matter how hard Greenspan and other officials tried.

According to our wage-gap theory, the rising wage gap creates exponential growth in debt, which in turn generates an exponential rise in profits, leading to the share price bubble. Eventually, debt growth slows, so the demand–supply gap, thus far hidden by the debt mountain, comes to the surface; profits plummet, and stock markets collapse. As you can see from Table 6.2, the wage-gap theory finds complete vindication from the U.S. experience in the 1920s as well as in the 1980s and the 1990s.

You may be wondering why the speculative mania lasted much longer this time around—in the 1980s and the 1990s—compared to the 1920s, even though the wage gap rose both times. The reason is Greenspan, who gave massive injections of new debt to the system whenever a potential disaster arose at home or abroad. Keynesian policies, which put band-aids on economic wounds, were unknown during the 1920s, so that the government didn't know how to respond to the stock market collapse of 1929. But Greenspan learned the trick after his successful handling of the 1987 crash. As the world hopped from crisis to crisis, the maestro applied the same medicine again and again. He would cut the federal funds rate around the start of a crisis, create new debt to close the demand gap, and then raise the rate back after the crisis had passed. He delayed the crash again and again but in the process generated a taller mountain of speculation that suckered far more people than in the 1920s.

The biggest irony is that global crises were created by Greenspan's own policies that encouraged regressive taxation and low wages and thus enhanced the wage gap not only in the United States but also in many other countries (see chapter 9). Debt injections became indispensable to prevent the system's collapse. So the world adored Greenspan for healing diseases that he himself had germinated. But in 2001 and 2002, his debt-generating artifacts proved ineffective, because by then the wage gap and the attendant demand gap had soared so high that the band-aids of the interest rate cuts could not stop the share-market bleeding. In other words, if the wage gap keeps rising, a crash becomes inevitable.

THE AFTERMATH OF THE CRASH

In the aftermath of the crash come recession and stagnation—even depression. A depression brings mega misery to the nation, similar to what a person feels when she loses her job. President Reagan once declared: "Depression is when you are out of work; recession is when your neighbor is out of work." A recession occurs when aggregate demand falls, leading to a decline in output. But a depression occurs when the initial fall in output is compounded by further falls in demand and output, and the process continues for months, sometimes even several years.

In the past a stock market bubble and the subsequent crash created depressions. In recent years they have primarily generated recessions, along with prolonged stagnation in employment. This is because Keynesian policies aimed at creating government and private debt have helped the countries avoid recurrent declines in aggregate demand.

The bubble economy of Japan is a case in point. Its stock market crashed in 1990. The government immediately lowered interest rates through the policy of monetary ease, bringing them down close to zero. It also expanded its budget deficit sharply. Did these policies help? Yes, indeed. They prevented an economic collapse, but failed to bring the nation back to lasting recovery. Japan has had four recessions in the past decade.

Once the fastest growing economy in the world, the country has been stagnant since its share-market crash. Its rate of unemployment is at 5 percent, compared to its NAIRU of just 2 percent. Its jobless rate is the highest since 1950. In terms of growing joblessness, Japan has been in recession for over ten years. Such is the aftermath of the bursting bubble.

Other bubble economies belonged to the Asian Tigers—South Korea, Hong Kong, Taiwan, Thailand, Malaysia, Indonesia, the Philippines, and Singapore. Their bubbles burst in 1997, and not surprisingly most of them also adopted expansionary monetary and fiscal policies. They managed to avoid the 1930s style collapse, but are still not out of the woods in terms of employment.

The U.S bubble burst in late 2000, with a recession arriving in the first quarter of 2001. Although the output decline ended nine months later, joblessness continued to rise. The downturn began with a fall in investment, especially in the high-tech sector. These are the areas that had attracted enormous investment during the 1990s; they were overbuilt in the prior decade and were the first to shows signs of overproduction. Business investment peaked in the second quarter of 2000, and then began to decline; however, consumer spending, aided by record consumer debt, continued to expand smartly, and prevented a decrease in aggregate demand until the first quarter of the next year.

THE 9/11 MASSACRE

The Fed rushed to cut the rate of interest in January 2001, and did it 12 times over the next 18 months. But the shock of the stock market crash was too great to be contained, and even though consumer debt continued to climb, investment fell so much that the slump could not be avoided. Then came the massacre of 9/11, when the Al Qaeda terrorist group attacked the Twin Towers in New York and the Pentagon in Washington, D.C., stunning not just America but the entire world. For the first time in history an outsider had been able to strike at America's heartland. The tourist industry came to a halt. Airlines alone laid off 100,000 people. So the recession continued.

The output decline finally ended at the end of 2001, but layoffs kept going and real wages shrank. By mid-2003 more than 2 million workers had been fired, and the rate of unemployment, which had receded to less than 4 percent in 2000, grew to 6 percent. Thanks to the American consumer and the government doing their patriotic duty of wallowing in debt, aggregate spending kept up its rise, but the excesses of the bubble economy were too strong to be overcome by monetary and fiscal policies.

In terms of fiscal action, President George W. Bush adopted the supply-side policy and in 2001 sharply cut the income tax rate for top earners. He also provided some tax relief to the poor, but the bulk of the benefit accrued to the affluent. This was expansionary fiscal policy, but its stimulating effect on demand was muted, because the relief to the opulent adds practically nothing to aggregate spending. It is the poor who spend all of their tax cut, not those with high incomes, whose needs have been already fulfilled. The tax refunds of the affluent go mainly into their savings accounts, because they have already met their daily living needs of shoes, clothing, furniture, appliances, and so on.

If the experience of Japan and the Asian Tigers is any guide, then the United States is likely to enter a long phase of stagnation, where jobless-ness remains stubborn and real wages go down. Such is the legacy of bubble economies. The chief reason for the post-crash stagnation is all the debt buildup among consumers, and the overinvestment among producers and homeowners that occurred during the prior euphoric years.

Heavily indebted consumers are not in a position to expand their spending substantially. Even if the interest rate falls practically to zero, as it did in Japan and more recently in the United States, consumer spending remains sluggish. Automobile sales in the United States did go up when General Motors and Ford offered zero-percent financing from 2002 to 2004, but overall consumption could not match the consumption growth of the late 1990s. Even then consumer credit soared, which essentially borrows sales from the future, because the loans have to be paid back one day or else the consumer has to declare bankruptcy. Either way, future spending cannot be anything more than lukewarm.

Business spending on capital goods cannot even respond to the lure of low interest rates because of all the overinvestment in the recent past. Even though the interest rate plummeted after the first quarter of 2001, business investment continued to sink until the end of 2002. Housing investment did pick up substantially, but not enough to make much of a dent in overall capital spending.

Economic growth must then suffer. Output may still rise, but not fast enough to absorb the new job seekers, who arrive every year from an increasing population. Even if the employment level stabilizes, the jobless rate continues to go up. At a minimum, the aftermath of the bubble burst is stagnation with a rising rate of unemployment and sinking wage rates; at a maximum, it is a depression.

THE WAGE GAP IN JAPAN

Does the wage-gap thesis apply to other countries? It is based purely on common sense, and seems to have universal validity. Let's see whether it applies to Japan, which developed a bubble economy in the 1980s. Japan's economic progress is truly a Cinderella story. The nation rose like a phoenix out of the ashes resulting from the devastation caused by World War II. Japan's economic growth is often described as miraculous. We will now see that the Japanese miracle occurred when the nation's wage gap was more or less constant, and troubles began when the gap started to rise.

Take a look at Table 6.3, which presents indexes for real wages, productivity, the wage gap, and per-capita GDP from 1960 to 2002. GDP per person, after adjustment for inflation, rose from a mere 0.77 million yen in 1960 ($2,139) to as much as 2.07 million yen in 1975 ($5,750). This is a jump of 168 percent in just 15 years. The real-wage index increased from 23 in 1960 to 73 in 1975, a rise of 217 percent over the same period. Similarly, manufacturing productivity made a leap from 14 to 51, or a climb of 264 percent. These are stratospheric numbers.

The numerical illustration presented above shows that an economy's expansion path is smooth when its real wage moves in sync with labor productivity. Japan is a sterling example of such a smooth functioning and prospering economy. Its affluence derives primarily from the relative stability of its wage-gap index, which was 61 in 1960 and 70 in 1975. This index is obtained by dividing column 3 with column 2 and then multiplying by 100 to express it as a percentage.

The wage gap actually climbed somewhat, but the rise was meager, given that hourly output in manufacturing more than tripled between 1960 and 1975 (see column 3). Over the 15 years the gap rose at the tiny rate of one percent a year. With wages nearly keeping up with productivity, national demand kept pace with output. As a result the country needed little artificial demand or debt to cope with soaring production.

Here's a clear-cut example of how wages are the main source of demand, the productivity the main source of supply, and if the two grow hand in hand with each other, the macroeconomy expands smoothly over time, without a prop from public or consumer borrowing. From 1960 to 1975, consumer debt was practically unheard of, the government budget deficit was more or less zero, and foreign trade was in balance. Corporate debt varied from industry to industry, but overall the corporations had a light debt load.

After 1975, however, some institutional changes, such as the decline in competition and feeble unions, began to raise the wage gap. The Japanese lifestyle would no longer be the same. First came the culture of budget deficits. As Japan's wage gap rose, national demand fell relative to national supply. The rising government deficit was one way to plug this shortfall; another was to adopt the mercantilist policy of surplus trade, so that the country began to depend on foreign demand. When demand trailed supply, the excess production was simply sent abroad.

A persistent rise in the wage gap inevitably creates a speculative bubble in stock markets, which in turn may generate bubbles in other assets such as real estate, silver, and gold. This is what happened in Japan. Between 1960 and 1975, when wage rates grew strongly along with soaring productivity, the index of share prices tripled (see column 6). This index is compiled by the IMF, and is different from the Nikkei. Share prices surged but no faster than manufacturing productivity, which also tripled. This was no speculative mania, as the share-price boom simply manifested a booming economy. This was genuine, not paper, prosperity.

Between 1975 and 1990, however, the wage-gap index climbed at a rate of 3 percent per year; and the inevitable happened. Stock prices sizzled, with the market index rising by 700 percent over the next 15 years. Between 1975 and 1990, productivity nearly doubled, but share

Table 6.3. The Indexes of Wage-Gap, Per-Capita GDP, and Share Prices in Japan: 1960–2002

(1) Year	(2) Real Wage Index	(3) Productivity Index	(4) Wage-Gap Index (in %)	(5) Per-Capita GDP (1900 = 100)	(6) Share Price Index*
1960	23	14	61	0.77	10
1965	32	21	66	1.12	9
1970	50	38	76	1.77	16
1975	73	51	70	2.07	31
1980	75	64	86	2.46	48
1985	81	77	95	2.85	100
1990	95	95	100	3.40	219
1995	107	109	102	3.80	100
2000	110	136	124	3.85	89
2002	121	140	126	3.85	56

* Starts from 1962.

Source: *International Comparisons of Manufacturing Productivity and Unit Labor Cost Trends*, Bureau of Labor Statistics (BLS), United States Department of Labor, 2004, and *International Financial Statistics*, various issues, The International Monetary Fund (IMF), Washington, D.C.

prices surged eightfold. The giant imbalance in the stock markets sparked frenzied speculation in land and housing.

Of course, everyone in Japan gloated: politicians celebrated, financial gurus danced in ecstasy, historians glorified Japanese institutions, and caution vanished. But then came 1990, the year of reckoning, when the IMF share-price index peaked at 219. First stock markets crashed, followed in turn by real estate markets, consumer confidence, and business investment. With them came soaring bankruptcies, shattered families, and, above all, the highest rate of unemployment ever recorded in Japan. By 2003, the Tokyo stock market had plunged an inconceivable, and inconsolable, 80 percent from its peak.

More than a decade has passed since the rupture of the bubble, yet Japan is still hobbled by stagnation and gloom. Such are the ultimate consequences of the growing wage gap.

THE WAGE GAP IN GERMANY

If Japan is the lion of Asia, Germany is the tiger of Europe. World War II destroyed both countries, but both astounded the world with their subsequent accomplishments. Germany is regarded as the locomotive that pulls the Euro Zone. Its economy is the largest in the continent and the third largest in the world.

Germany's economic growth has been unique in terms of its wage gains. As revealed by Table 6.4, the wage-gap index fell steadily for German workers over the 20 years from 1960 to 1980. The fruit of productivity growth accrued mostly to workers because of the presence of powerful unions.

The wage-gap tumble meant that there was little, if any, indebtedness in the economy. There was hardly any consumer debt; budget deficits at the state and federal levels were absent. Corporations also were mostly free from debt. The falling wage gap made all this possible.

Greenomics argues that rising wages hurt business investment as well as employment. It opposes the minimum wage, which it says ends up harming the unskilled worker by forcing him into joblessness. This is a self-serving argument, because it tends to back the affluent interests that finance such research through lucrative gifts and grants. The German development experience clearly belies this dogma, which is a standard item in almost every economics text used in American universities.

Table 6.4. The Indexes of Wage-Gap, Per-Capita GDP, and Share Prices in Germany: 1960–2002*

(1) Year	(2) Real Wage Index	(3) Productivity Index	(4) Wage-Gap Index (%)	(5) Per-capita GDP	(6) Share Price Index
1960	23	29	126	17,440	34
1965	33	39	118	20,650	28
1970	47	52	111	24,660	29
1975	61	66	108	26,870	29
1980	75	77	103	31,620	31
1985	81	89	110	33,800	68
1990	96	99	103	30,590	100
1995	109	112	103	35,710	103
2000	118	127	107	39,700	201
2002	131	121	108	39,700	117

* After 1990, the figures are for unified Germany and per-capita GDP is in terms of German marks.

Source: International Comparisons of Manufacturing Productivity and Unit Labor Cost Trends, Bureau of Labor Statistics, United States Department of Labor, 2004, and *International Financial Statistics,* The International Monetary Fund, various issues.

From 1960 to 1970, as the wage-gap index plummeted from 126 to 111, the rate of unemployment was below 1 percent in Germany, but three to ten times higher in its neighbors, in Canada, and in the United States. Nor did the wage-gap tumble trim the German rate of investment, which held steady at about 25 percent of GDP. The moral of the story is that rising salaries create no problems so long as productivity rises as well; in fact, trouble arises when wages fail to rise in sync with growing efficiency.

The German economy also supports the finding that a growing, or at least constant, wage gap is a necessary condition for a share-price boom. Since the gap declined in the nation from 1960 to 1980, we should expect the stock market to stagnate. Table 6.4 demonstrates that this is precisely what happened. In spite of soaring productivity, the German stock market index compiled by the IMF actually declined from 34 in 1960 to 31 in 1980. It soared thereafter, as the wage gap began to rise, but another reason for its rise was the booming New York Stock Exchange, which began to pull global share markets with it.

Following the global stock market crash of 2000–2002, the German economy, as expected, became sluggish. Germany's NAIRU is very high, around 8 percent. This is because the country now offers generous welfare and unemployment benefits that discourage people from holding unpleasant jobs. So, many jobless workers remain content with unemployment compensation and do not strive to find work. With a high NAIRU, Germany's real problem of unemployment arises only when the official jobless rate exceeds 8 percent. In the heady days of the share-price bubble, German unemployment fell and moved closer to full employment; but following the crash, its jobless rate began to rise and approached 10 percent by 2004.

As with Japan, the United States, and indeed much of the Western world, the latest market crash has caused employment and growth stagnation in Germany as well. Such is the aftermath of the bursting bubble, and Greenspan's legacy to the world. An example of the maestro's meager knowledge of economics is what Greenspan told President Clinton in May 1998: "This is the best economy I've seen in 50 years"— he reiterated the view in Congressional testimony two months later.[9] But in September, barely four months later, Clinton faced a business melt-down, which he called the "biggest financial challenge facing the world in a half-century."[10] How can an economy be the best and then face its biggest crisis in the same year?

7

THE INCOME TAX RATE
AND OUR LIVING
STANDARD

1981 was a watershed year in the annals of the United States, as Congress enacted the path-breaking, Reagan–Greenspan cut in income tax levies. Over the next three years, the top-bracket tax rate paid by the wealthiest people declined from 70 percent to 50 percent, and the first-bracket rate, paid by those with low incomes, fell from 14 percent to 11 percent. Most Americans were pleased to see their tax bills fall, but the top earners were euphoric. The fall from 70 to 50 overwhelmed the one from 14 to 11.

Of course, the tax cut had an unpleasant side effect—giant and unexpected budget deficits, which, as you have seen, lifted interest rates to the stratosphere. Greenspan and Reagan then scrambled to raise excise, gasoline, and payroll taxes, and gradually trimmed the federal deficit. Then came 1986, when the top-bracket income tax rate fell to 28 percent, and the first-bracket rate to 10 percent. Again the affluent had a reason to smile. But the smile turned into a frown in 1993, when the top rate jumped to 39.6 percent under Clinton; the bottom rate also went up to 15 percent.

When George Bush was elected in 2000, the affluent had a cause to celebrate again, as their tax rate fell to 35 percent by 2004, while the low-income groups also saw a slight decline in their tax bills, with the bottom rate sinking back to 10 percent. The Congressional Budget Office (CBO), a nonpartisan body, estimated that fully one-third of the Bush tax relief went to the top 1 percent of earners, with an average annual income of $1.2 million. Similarly, about two-thirds of the relief, according to the CBO report, accrued to the top 20 percent of families. "The report calculated that households with incomes in that top 1 percent were receiving an average tax cut of $78,460 this year, while households in the middle 20 percent of earnings—about $57,000 a year—were getting an average cut of only $1,090 . . . those in that bottom fifth of earnings received an average tax cut of only $250."[1] Only Reagan was able to outdo Bush's largesse to the wealthy.

Underlying all this tax churning since 1981 is the basic belief held by Greenomics that low income tax rates nourish economic growth and social prosperity, and that no harm comes to the economy from Robber Baron taxation, wherein the income tax, which is progressive, falls, and other taxes that are regressive go up.

Now I will prove that this theory itself can be seen as a fraud trumpeted by Greenspan. In a Senate hearing on February 12, 2004, recall that the maestro counseled lawmakers to perpetuate all of Bush tax cuts and raise other taxes under pay-go rules:

We do not know the extent to which increased taxes will inhibit the growth of the GDP and hence the revenue base . . . because it's very obvious that if you put very substantial tax rate increases in, you could slow the rate of growth enough so that the revenue base does not increase anywhere near the amount of expectations when you raise taxes.[2]

Thus Greenspan essentially argued that if Bush tax cuts were allowed to expire, top-bracket tax rates would rise "to inhibit the growth of GDP," but if those tax cuts were retained and other taxes went up under pay-go rules, then the economy would grow smartly. This theory derives from the belief, encouraged by economists and politicians on the payroll of the wealthy, that high tax bills leave the affluent with less money for job-creating investments. So the economy suffers. Let me give you a very simple example of why such policies, implemented between 1981 to 1983, always, yes *always*, hurt the economy.

As you may know, I make a living as a university professor. Recently, in spring 2004, I staged a mock drama in my class to explain why cutting the tax burden of the wealthy is always bad for the U.S. economy. It was a rather difficult task, because Texas is Bush country and my students were fond of their president, who has repeatedly lowered the top-bracket tax rates. I selected ten of those sitting in the front row, and formed two groups among them. I appointed one student as a company CEO (chief executive officer), and asked the other nine to play the role of his employees. I myself played the role of the government.

I then took out a ten-dollar bill from my pocket, handed it over to the CEO as his tax cut, and extracted a promise from him to use the tax relief for investment expansion and to provide jobs to new graduates. In other words, my student CEO offered to do what CEOs usually pledge, while demanding tax benefits from the government.

"But now my revenue has fallen by $10; so what should I, the government, do to pay my bills?" I asked my class. Someone answered: "You borrow money or raise other taxes." "Very good," I replied. Then I asked the drama participants to pay me one dollar each as their new Social Security tax in exchange for future benefits payable upon retirement. I told them this was essentially what Reagan and Congress, following Greenspan's advice, had done from 1981 to 1983. This way I collected ten dollars, just enough to meet the government's deficit. The student CEO now had only $9 left as his tax relief.

"Are you now ready to increase your investment by the amount of your tax cut?" I asked the CEO. "Yes, sir," came back a confident reply. "Wait a minute," I said, "your sales have now fallen by $9, because your employees, who buy your goods, are that much short of money, while the government has no additional revenue to spend. Your shelves are piling up with unsold goods. Would you, in your right mind, expand your business in these circumstances?" The student CEO paused, pondered the question a bit, and then said no.

"In fact, you will fire some employees because of declining sales," I added. The student agreed reluctantly.

That year there were more than 100 students in my class. I said to them: "Assume that you all own your own company; now tell me if you would expand your business and risk more funds in investment in the face of dwindling sales, even if the government substantially cuts your taxes." Not a single hand went up. I asked them to think it through and tell me if anything would prompt them to expand their investment in an environment of unsold goods piling up on their shelves.

There were some smart-alecks in my class. One girl said, "I might buy a new machine to cut my costs if I could borrow money from a bank but did not have to pay it back." A student added that he could see himself investing more if the sales decline was temporary. Another said she would expand her business if the tax cut financed it 100 percent. I was pleased that they were thinking for themselves, but told them they had come up with some of the excuses that a supply-sider offers to justify mega tax relief for the wealthy. In the end they all, every man and woman, agreed that investment expansion in an environment of declining sales was extremely unlikely, if not impossible.

At this point, a staunch Bush supporter raised his hand. "But President Bush," he said, "hasn't acted like Reagan or Greenspan, because he has not raised anyone's taxes. He has only cut them. So there can be no sales decline in this case."

"Very good," I replied. "I was about to come to Bush's case. Do we agree then that Greenomics has hurt our economy?" Most hands went up in the affirmative.

"Let's now discuss the other option." I added. "Suppose we don't raise other taxes at all; then how does the government pay its bills? Obviously by borrowing money." After a slight pause, I said to my students, "Remember I am playing the role of the government in our mock drama, and I have already handed $10 dollars to the CEO as the tax cut. Now, who has the money to lend me? Which one of the ten drama participants is loaded enough to be the government's lender?" Everyone in the class looked at the student CEO, who then handed the ten-dollar bill back to me.

"Would you expand your business now?" I asked him again. "No, I just gave the tax relief back to you." "Case closed," I said. "The CEOs demand tax relief so they would have more money for investment, but if the government borrows it all back from them to pay its bills, then they are back to where they were before the tax cut. So how can investment rise even in Bush's case?"

"But while investment does not respond," I continued, "precious time has been wasted in tackling the economy's problems that had prompted the tax cut to begin with. In addition, the government debt goes up, its interest expense will rise, and future generations will have to pay the debt bill. You employees, all nine of you, will have to foot the bill when you retire. So in any case, the CEO benefits at the expense of you all."

By then the 50-minute class was over; normally the students would be itching to close their notebooks to get to their next class; but that day some sat there, wanting to learn more, their faces reflecting the glow of enlightenment. My message, though unpopular with the majority of Bush acolytes, seemed to change some opinions.

HIGH HISTORICAL GROWTH WITH A 92 PERCENT INCOME TAX

Now you can clearly see why and how cutting the income taxes of the CEOs, or the rich, always hurts the economy when you raise the levies paid by their employees to finance the tax cut, because sales fall, and the CEOs actually have to trim output and employment. In the other case, when the government borrows the tax-cut back, precious time is lost even as the problems fester, while future generations are stuck with new debt and its interest expense. Either way, trimming the top-bracket tax rates harms the vast majority of people, and hence the economy.

Since this argument is so simple and derives from common sense, it should find ready backing from history. It does. In fact, the supporting evidence is so strong and stunning that you may wonder about the motives of those backing low income taxes to stimulate economic growth. All you have to do is to look at average GDP growth in the 1950s and the 1960s, when the income and corporate taxes were sky-high, and compare them with the growth rates in the 1980s, 1990s, and thus far in 2000s (till 2004), when such taxes were low.

Look at the link among the top-bracket income tax rate, corporate tax, and the average annual growth of GDP in Table 7.1. Economic growth fluctuates from year to year, and is influenced by a number of factors including taxes. For example, war normally stimulates growth, because government spending jumps to fuel demand, which invites increased production from businesses. It's well known that World War II ended the depression of the 1930s. Wars, therefore, generate above-average growth.

When peace returns, government spending on arms and related materials plummets and a recession follows, with zero or negative growth for the year. Fast growth during wartime is then balanced by the low growth years. Similarly, the volatile price of oil has had a significant impact on GDP growth. The point is that growth fluctuations generally average out over a decade, so most decades ought to have approximately the same level of real GDP gains, unless something unforeseen, or a faulty policy, interferes with the economy.

Table 7.1 lists average annual GDP growth rates per decade. These are obtained by adding annual growth rates, positive or negative, over a decade, and then dividing the sum by 10. Thus the average growth of the 1990s equals the sum of the annual growth rates from 1990 to 1999 divided by ten.

Table 7.1. GDP Growth, Corporate Income Tax and Top-Bracket Income Tax Rate in the United States: 1950s–1990s and 2000s (in Percent)

Decade	Corporate Income Tax (%)	Average Annual Growth Rate	Top-Bracket Income Tax Rate (%)
1950s	52	4.1	84–92 (89)
1960s	52–48	4.4	91–70 (80)
1970s	48–46	3.3	70–70 (70)
1980s	45–34	3.1	50–28 (39)*
1990s	35–38	3.1	31–39.6 (36)*
2000s (2000–04)	33	2.8	less than 36 %*

* Author's estimate.

Source: *Economic Report of the President, 1988 and 2004*, Council of Economic Advisers, Washington, D.C.; *Historical Statistics of the United States: Colonial Times to 1970*, U.S. Department of Commerce, Washington, D.C., 1975, p. 1095; *Statistical Abstract of the United States*, 1981 and 2004, U.S. Department of Commerce, Washington, D.C. (Tax data provided to these sources by the Internal Revenue Service.)

The top-bracket income tax rate has also varied every decade. Column (4) in the table displays the tax range and the average rate in parentheses. The highest income taxes after the war prevailed in the 1950s—92 percent in 1953 and 91 percent between 1954 and 1963. The average of the tax rates on top incomes in the 1950s, as revealed by the Internal Revenue Service data, was 89 percent. Out of every dollar earned above $200,000 (about a million dollars in today's prices), the taxpayer had to pay 89 cents to the government. Most people would call this confiscatory taxation, and with good reason. Not only the individuals but wealthy corporations were also subject to heavy taxation (see column 2). But did it kill economic growth? Hardly. Growth averaged 4.1 percent per year during the 1950s.

Such is the message of Figure 7.1 as well, where the upper part tracks the behavior of the top-bracket income tax rate, and the lower part the behavior of the average growth rate each decade. The direction of the trend lines make it clear that as the income tax rate plunged, so did the growth rate.

During the 1960s, the average income tax charge fell slightly to 80 percent, and the growth rate also moved up a little to 4.4 percent per year. The top-bracket income tax rate was still confiscatory, but growth was exceptionally high. Thus, *the experience of the 1950s and 1960s reveals that extraordinary growth coexisted with exorbitant income tax rates.*

In addition to affluent individuals, big business also faced extremely high taxes, because the corporate tax rate exceeded 50 percent; over a

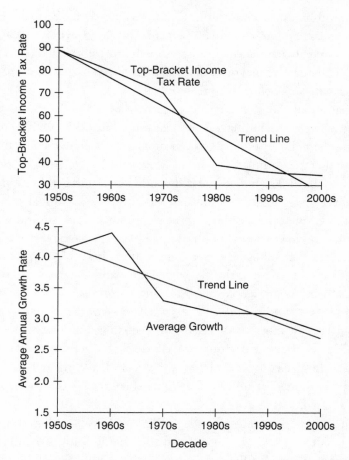

Figure 7.1. GDP Growth and the Top-Bracket Income Tax Rate (in Percent): 1950s–1990s

Source: Table 7.1.

quarter of federal receipts came from corporations, compared to less than 10 percent today. According to Greenspan and supply-siders, the American economy should have then imploded. Did it? No; it flourished instead.

In the 1970s, the corporate tax rate fell slightly and the top-bracket rate averaged 70 percent, below the levels of the 1960s. The rates were not as high as before, but average growth tumbled with lower taxes on the affluent. Some may legitimately argue that the vast jump in energy prices crushed growth during the 1970s in spite of lower taxes. They may be right, but let us examine the record of the next decade before we jump to this conclusion.

The top-bracket tax rate during the 1980s ranged from 28 to 50 percent and the average plummeted to 39 percent. Did the growth rate soar? No, just the opposite happened. Average growth rate sank to 3 percent in the 1980s. The international price of oil also declined sharply after 1985, yet GDP growth sank below the rate in the 1970s.

What about the 1990s? Average growth over the decade remained mediocre, not withstanding the boom lasting from 1995 to 2000. We will examine the real cause of that boom in chapter 9. The income tax rate jumped after 1993; but the share of taxes paid by the corporations fell sharply. In the 2000s, both the wealthy individuals and corporations paid even lower taxes, as the tax rates fell for the incomes, capital gains and dividends of the opulent. Thus top earners, corporate and individuals, generally paid lower tax rates after the 1970s, even as the tax burden on the poor and the middle class went up sharply. This is because for almost 75 percent of taxpayers, the Social Security and the sales tax burden exceeds their income tax payment. *So much for the notion that low income taxes on affluent individuals and corporations nourish economic growth.*

High energy prices do afflict a nation's economic performance. During the 1970s, oil prices rose frequently. As a result, the country went through the wrenching experience of low growth and leaping inflation. One reason why the 1970s suffered a mediocre economy was the sharp jump in the international price of oil.

But what is the excuse for the 1980s and beyond, where oil prices began to fall after 1982 and nosedived after 1985? It turns out that there were three culprits for the growth stagnation during the 1980s, 1990s, and 2000s. One, of course, was the sharp decline in the top-bracket income tax rate. Another was a sharp reduction in corporate income tax rates, which fell from a high of 52 percent in the 1950s to as low as 34 percent in the 1980s, and stayed close to that level during the 1990s. The third culprit is explained below.

HIGH TAXES ON THE POOR AND LOW GDP GROWTH

The economic performance of the 1980s and beyond is so poor relative to that of prior decades that there must be another culprit to share the blame. Indeed there is. It is the combination of the giant Social Security tax, the excise tax, and the sales tax that rendered the tax system ultra-regressive.

A progressive levy such as the income tax rises with a person's rise in income, whereas a regressive tax rate declines with the jump in income. All taxes in the United States have been regressive except the income and the corporate tax. So when income taxes decline and other taxes go up, then the tax system is bound to become ultra-regressive.

In 1983, Greenspan had proposed a value-added tax, which works like a national sales tax, the kind generally imposed by the states. His proposal was never enacted but, if adopted, it would have worked as the state sales tax, which jumped from an average 2 percent in the 1960s to over 7 percent today. Let us revert to the economic record within each decade and see how rising taxes on the poor and the middle class hinder prosperity. Conversely, we can see how low taxes on the destitute and middle-income groups promote development.

We already know that growth slowed sharply in the 1970s and further in the 1980s and beyond, even though tax rates paid by the wealthy fell. One reason for the slowdown in the 1970s was, of course, the big jump in the price of oil. Clearly, another was the giant leap in the Social Security burden, which rose from 9.6 percent in 1970 to 12.3 percent by 1980. (These are tax rates for both employers and employees.) Thus, high oil prices and Social Security hikes combined to lower economic growth in the 1970s.

Even though energy prices tumbled during the 1980s, the growth blight continued with increasing virulence. So what happened? The income and corporate taxes plummeted, whereas the Social Security, excise, and the state sales tax jumped. The tax system became ultra-regressive and coexisted with growth decline. Thus, the total transformation of the tax system in the 1980s and beyond is the true culprit behind the growth blight. In other words, the conclusion is unavoidable that the poor performance of the economy in recent decades stems from confiscatory taxation of the poor.

When the tax burden declines on those who can better afford it, it has to be transferred to those who can bear it the least, because governments cannot run free on air. This is what happened in the 1980s and beyond, when the income and corporate tax rates plunged but the Social Security and other tax rates soared. This, however, was blatantly unethical and could not be done without a solid justification. Thus was born the dogma that low income and corporate taxes stimulate investment, work effort and economic growth. Experts came up with this dogma simply to rationalize the transfer of the tax burden from the affluent to the poor and the middle class.

However, unethical policies rarely work. They might work in the short run, but never in the long run. In the case of Greenomics, they failed from the start. Economic growth was mediocre in the 1980s in spite of the tumbling price of oil. If energy prices had been unchanged, the growth record would have been even worse. In spite of fortuitous assistance from OPEC, the oil cartel, the 1980s could only produce what until then was the worst economic performance of the post–World War II period—an anemic annual growth of 3.1 percent per year.

In sum, the record of economic growth since the war shows that low taxes on top earnings and big corporations hurt economic development. When the affluent and corporations paid high taxes, as in the 1950s and the 1960s, the economy grew much faster than in the 1980s and beyond, when they paid low taxes. In other words, a sharply progressive income tax system has been the lifeblood of the postwar U.S. economy. Once progressiveness vanished, growth turned mediocre.

In fact, the tax system and other economic policies matter more for economic growth than even dazzling new technology. The computer and the Internet revolution, which has vastly magnified labor productivity, came into full swing in the 1980s and beyond; yet growth during this period sank below average. GDP growth during the 1950s and the 1960s would have vaulted even higher if those decades also had the benefit of information technology. Thus, ethical policies—or the lack thereof—are the keys to a lofty living standard.

LOGIC OF HIGH INCOME TAXES AND HIGH GROWTH

A puzzle remains: why do high taxes on those who can afford to pay them spur growth and prosperity, whereas high taxes on the poor and the middle class generate poorer growth? The answer comes from the simple macro demand-and-supply framework that is familiar to you from the previous chapter. If you recall,

Demand = Consumption + Investment = Supply

in a simple economy with no debt or deficit of any kind. Assuming that all wage income is consumed, consumption equals wages. If taxes are imposed on the wealthy as well as others, then consumer spending must fall. But the spending declines mainly for the poor and the middle-income groups, not for the opulent. Even Greenomics does not claim that taxes adversely affect the consumption spending of the wealthy, who earn incomes from their labor as well as capital.

A family with an income of $200,000 a year can still afford to buy most goods and services for adequate consumption even if they have to pay $50,000 in taxes. Their taxes come mostly out of their savings, or their share of profits. But those families earning $60,000 or less have little in savings and taxes will reduce their spending by an almost equal amount. Therefore, in the presence of taxation, as a close approximation, consumption falls by the amount of taxes paid by the poor and the middle class. That is,

Consumption = Wages − Taxes Paid by Low-Income Families

It should be clear by now why the Robber Baron type of taxation that raises taxes on the low income families (LIF) and showers tax breaks on the upper income families (UIF) must lower real GDP and employment. Consumer spending then sinks, and so does output, because no businessperson produces goods for her own consumption. Thus, tax cuts should only be reserved for the LIF group.

In an advanced economy like that of the United States consumer spending is at the center of production. In recent years consumption expenditures have been as much as 70 percent of GDP, of which about 20 percent comes from the UIF group and the remaining 50 percent from the LIF group. The LIF group consists of families that earn up to $80,000 a year, whereas the UIF group comprises the rest of the households, earning a 40 percent share of GDP. The UIF constitutes about 20 percent of American families, and the LIF, the remaining 80 percent. The lower income groups spend their entire after-tax income that derives chiefly from labor, and save practically nothing. It is the UIF group that does all the saving in our society because the average UIF income, at over $250,000, is very high. Therefore,

LIF Consumption = LIF Net Wages = Half of GDP

Here net wages are labor income after taxes. From this relationship, it is very simple to demonstrate that[3]

GDP = Twice the level of LIF Net Wages

The formula thus highlights the importance of the role played by the poor and the middle class in sustaining our economy and the living standard. The middle class is truly the backbone of the American capitalist system. Without its spending, investment would be next to nothing.

Now you can clearly see why raising the tax burden of low-income groups inevitably reduces GDP growth, because such taxes enter negatively in the GDP formula. Businesses cannot afford to produce more than what is purchased by society. When population rises, demand increases, and so does output. But if taxes rise on low incomes, then demand growth slows, and so does GDP growth.

It is interesting to note that such a simple formula describes our highly complex economy with all its debts and deficits. This is because the LIF net wages being 50 percent of GDP is an empirical relationship that prevails after all complications have been taken into account. Despite its simplicity, its message is profound and is confirmed by the entire post–World War II history of the United States.[4]

Now, a low tax burden for the poor and the middle class automatically means a high burden for the rich. That is why a progressive tax system produced much higher growth in U.S. history, and a regressive system did the opposite. Every society needs government. You can argue whether the government should be large or small, but you cannot do away with the State and taxes. So if you want a system that grows sharply and steadily, and even maintains adequate profit, then the tax burden has to fall mostly on those who can afford it. Taxes have to be high on the affluent and practically zero for the poor. Otherwise, demand is mediocre, growth is low, and even profits are anemic, because the CEOs need well-paid employees to buy all their goods.

GREENOMICS: ANOTHER FRAUD

You have seen before that Greenspan committed a variety of intellectual frauds by repeatedly changing his economic theories. But even if he had not altered his views, the supply-side part of Greenomics itself is fraudulent. How can you miss the fact that the top-bracket income tax rates were as high as 92 percent in the 1950s, even as the economy roared? In his Senate hearing about Bush's tax cuts held on February 12, 2004, Greenspan said, "it's very obvious that if you put very substantial tax rate increases in, you could slow the rate of growth."

Even critics admire the maestro for his mastery over facts, data, and American economic history. He, of all people, should know that high taxes on the affluent coexisted with exceptional growth in the 1950s and the 1960s, and when regressive taxes went up then the growth rate declined—not just in the oil-parched 1970s, but also during the 1980s, 1990s, and the 2000s. How is it then "obvious" to him that high taxes paid by the affluent "slow the rate of growth"? If the top-bracket tax rates were lower from 1950 to 1980 than those prevailing thereafter, then the maestro could justify the claim he made in the Senate hearing. However, his statement should have been that "it's very obvious that if you put very substantial tax rate increases in [on the affluent] and lower other taxes, you could increase the rate of growth."

The top-earner tax rates during the 1950s and the 1960s were not just a bit high, they were extraordinarily high—as high as 92 percent. How could you possibly ignore their effects and evidence? They left no scope for ambiguity that giant taxes on the wealthy stimulate growth and prosperity by avoiding taxation of the destitute and by taxing the middle class gingerly. The implication is clear: Greenspan misled the senators when he testified that high taxes on the affluent obviously inhibit economic growth.

While high taxes need not restrain growth, fairness demands that they should not be confiscatory. However, that is a separate issue altogether. The point is that even confiscatory taxation promotes economic growth, so long as the poor and the middle class pay puny taxes.

8

DOES THE MINIMUM WAGE CREATE UNEMPLOYMENT?

An important tenet of Greenomics is that the minimum-wage legislation is detrimental to the labor force and the economy, because it creates unemployment, especially for unskilled workers, such as teenagers, and hurts small businesses such as restaurants, hotels, grocery stores and the like. The argument is that such companies rely strongly on unskilled work, and if the minimum wage goes up their profits and hence hiring would decline, leading to increased unemployment. I will now show that all these claims are not just illogical, they are absurd, and constitute another fraud on the people.

In fact, I will demonstrate that employment and economic growth generally improved whenever the minimum wage went up to match the rate of inflation. When prices increase, the purchasing power of the minimum salary, which remains fixed until raised by legislation, falls. I will show that not only does this create hardship for those earning that salary, but also for the public at large.

There are ten million workers in America who earn the minimum wage; another 20 million, such as those in retailing and temp jobs, have their salaries tied to this wage. These people are all victims of inflation, for their incomes are fixed year after year, while prices advance relentlessly, until Congressmen and the president, out of the goodness of their hearts, swing into action and, instead of giving themselves a raise, legislate an increase in the minimum wage.

The U.S. minimum wage in 2004 was $5.15, and had remained constant since 1997 when it last rose following the recommendation of Labor Secretary Robert Reich. By contrast, the corresponding wage in the late 1960s was close to $8 in terms of today's prices. Clearly, the purchasing power of the minimum wage has eroded sharply since 1970. Typically, a minimum-wage employee is an unskilled worker, with very little bargaining power, and his/her plight gets no attention from the lawmakers.

Let's first see how the rise in the minimum wage has no deleterious effect on anyone's profit, so long as it is no faster than the general rise in prices. Take the case of the restaurant industry, which generally howls whenever someone tries to match the minimum wage with the rate of inflation. For any single firm, in contrast to the economy as whole,

Profit = Business Revenue − Wage Costs − Other Costs

This is a simple formula that is valid by definition. Now, business revenue equals a worker's production times the product price. Suppose you own a McDonald's franchise; a teenage cook makes ten hamburgers per hour for you, and each hamburger is sold for $2. Your hourly business revenue from hiring that cook is $20, i.e., price times the cook's output. Suppose all other costs add up to $12 per hour of production, and the minimum wage you pay the cook is $5 per hour. Then your hourly profit from hiring that cook is

Profit = Price × Cook's Output − $5 − $12
     = 20 − 5 − 12 = $3

Now suppose all costs and prices double, that is, a hamburger fetches $4, the minimum wage becomes $10, and other costs rise to $24. Your hourly profit becomes

Profit = 4 × 10 − 10 − 24 = 40 − 34 = $6

Your hourly profit from hiring that cook has doubled, but so have prices (or the rate of inflation), which means that the purchasing power of your profit remains unchanged. Thus it should be clear that as long as the rise in the minimum wage does not exceed the rate of inflation, there can be no decline in your real profit. Economists usually add the term "real" to any value that is expressed in terms of its purchasing power. Thus the claim that a rise in the minimum wage lowers the real or inflation-adjusted profit of small businesses is downright false, provided that rise remains within the bounds of inflation. On the other hand, a constant minimum wage in the face of generally rising prices will raise your real profit but surely decimate the cook's living standard.

If your profit fails to decline when all prices including the minimum wage double, there is no reason for you to fire your cook, even if such wage rates go up. You will fire your employee only if such a wage increase surpasses the general rate of inflation. So the assertion that a rise in the minimum wage lowers teenage hiring is simply bunkum, because it cannot possibly do this in an environment where prices rise year after year.

Of course, if the minimum wage rises while other prices are constant, then your profit will indeed decline. But when was the last time that prices fell or remained unchanged? They increase every year.

GREENSPAN AND THE MINIMUM WAGE

What does Greenspan have to say about the minimum wage, even though as Fed chairman he has no business interfering with such legislation? Plenty. For instance, he told the House Banking and Financial Institutions Committee in February 1999: "My main concern is . . . the issue of individuals who become unemployed because of the minimum wage." Greenspan's retort came in response to queries from some committee members. Then Vermont Representative Bernard Sanders interjected, "What we're seeing is CEOs now make 200 times what workers make." And, Mr. Sanders added, "You're expressing your concern about raising the minimum wage over $5.15 an hour, but I would hope we would see that same concern about CEOs . . . getting golden handshakes worth tens and tens of millions of dollars."

Greenspan responded: "Well, in both cases, I'm arguing that the government should not be involved. . . . I'm being consistent in that respect."[1]

You have to have a really bad memory lapse to forget that just six months before Greenspan had arranged a $3.6 billion bailout of that hedge fund, Long Term Capital Management, but now he was back to laissez-faire economics. You see again that once his pet project of enriching the rich has been accomplished, he rushes back to the principle of government nonintervention when the interests of the poor are involved. His statement that he is "being consistent" in that he dislikes government involvement in setting either the minimum wage or the maximum salary for CEOs reminds you again of his "unrelenting justice," which treats the indigent and tycoons alike.

Greenspan doesn't see any difference between what has happened to the purchasing power of the minimum wage and that of the CEO wage. The first has plummeted since 1980 whereas the second has rocketed. So what if some of the minimum-wage earners are homeless and unable to afford three meals a day. The government, argues Greenspan, should be evenhanded in its treatment of CEOs and unskilled workers, except, of course, when the CEO profits are threatened by their own speculative horrors; at that point, the maestro seems to hold, the government should intervene in order to preserve laissez-faire.

Two years after his exchange with Rep. Bernie Sanders, Greenspan had another spat with the Congressman on July 18, 2001. When asked by Sanders if he would abolish the minimum wage, Greenspan replied, "I would say that if I had my choice, the answer is, of course." The Congressman, now stunned by the maestro, remarked, "I believe this is the first time Chairman Greenspan has ever acknowledged that he not only opposed increasing the minimum wage, but would outright abolish it." Greenspan had said earlier: "The reason I object to the minimum wage is I think it destroys jobs. And I think the evidence on that, in my judgment, is overwhelming."[2]

"Overwhelming?" You have already seen above that a rise in the minimum wage to catch up with persistent inflation cannot possibly lower anyone's profit. So it cannot possibly destroy jobs. In fact, it can easily be shown that a rise in such a wage actually raises employment. Let us recall the GDP formula from the previous chapter:

GDP = 200 % of LIF Net Wages

where net wages are the total after-tax earnings of the low-income families (LIF). In order to eliminate the effects of inflation from our analysis, let us speak in terms of the real wage. Suppose we divide both sides of the above formula by a price index, such as the GDP deflator or the Consumer Price Index (CPI).[3] Then the formula will remain exactly the same, but its interpretation will be in terms of the purchasing power of the variables. The formula will then tell us that real GDP or output is 200 percent of the LIF net real wages, which equal real wages minus real taxes paid by people with low incomes.

Real GDP = 200 % of LIF Net Real Wages

Suppose product prices keep rising but the minimum wage rate does not. It has indeed remained constant since 1997 at $5.15. Then the real minimum wage of low-income groups falls, so that the LIF net real wages decline. This means that output or real GDP must also fall, and businesses have to resort to layoffs, causing a rise in unemployment. Thus, if the real minimum wage is allowed to fall, the end result is a rise in the ranks of the unemployed. *In other words, a constant minimum wage in an inflationary environment generates increased joblessness in the economy— an outcome that blatantly contradicts Greenspan.*

U.S. history confirms this idea resoundingly. The effects of a falling minimum wage are more or less the same as those of regressive taxation examined in the previous chapter. The purchasing power of this wage has been sinking fast, especially since 1980 when the Greenspan era essentially began. As already stated, today the minimum wage stands at $5.15, whereas in 1968 it was $8 in terms of 2004 prices. The sinking real minimum wage also shrinks aggregate demand as well as demand growth for the same reason as a regressive tax system.

Minimum wage workers, for sure, consume everything they earn, and when their real earnings decrease, there is some loss in aggregate demand. The decline in demand tends to lower output and employment, whereas the fall in demand growth lowers output growth and raises the rate of unemployment. So a falling real minimum wage tends to increase joblessness and lower GDP growth.

The classical model underlying Greenomics blames joblessness on the minimum wage legislation. Let history settle the question again. At the end of the 1960s the jobless rate was a puny 3.5 percent, just when America had the highest minimum wage. The real minimum wage began a slow but steady fall from 1970 on, and America could never regain that low a rate of unemployment. Even in 2000, the last year of the bubble economy boom, when joblessness had been sinking for several years, the unemployment rate was 3.9 percent.

In fact, 1997 was the last time the minimum wage was allowed to catch up with recent increases in prices. That year the rate of unemployment was 5 percent, but fell to 3.9 percent by 2000, because the rise in the minimum wage was partly responsible for raising aggregate demand. It is clear that over the long run, the rising minimum wage in pursuit of rising prices actually raises, not lowers, employment, theoretically as well as historically.

However, even in the short run, employment generally goes up. Take a look at Table 8.1, which presents data for the year the minimum wage

Table 8.1. The Change in the Minimum Wage, and in Employment a Year Later: 1950–1997

Year	Minimum Wage	Employment Change*
1950	$0.75	1,043
1956	1.00	272
1961	1.15	956
1962	1.25	1,062
1967	1.40	1,542
1968	1.60	1,982
1974	2.00	–948
1975	2.10	2,906
1976	2.30	3,265
1978	2.65	2,776
1980	3.10	1,094
1981	3.35	–871
1990	3.80	–1,075
1991	4.25	774
1996	4.75	2,850
1997	5.15	1,905
1968	**7.92 in 2000 prices**	**Highest Minimum Wage**

* In thousands.

Source: Statistical Abstract of the United States: 2002; The economic report of the President: 2004. (The minimum wage was the highest in 1968, when it bought what $7.92 would buy in 2000.)

went up in column 2, and for the change in employment a year later in column 3. For instance, this wage remained constant from 1950 to 1955, and then increased by 25 cents in 1956, or by a whopping 33 percent. In one year, i.e., between 1956 and 1957, employment rose by 272,000 because of a giant rise in the minimum wage. Thus, the table above traces the immediate effects of a minimum-wage rise on changes in employment from 1950 to 1997, the last time such a rise went into effect.

According to the table, the minimum wage rose 17 times in 47 years, and, a year after this change, employment increased 14 times. There are only three years in which the minimum-wage rise was followed by a fall in employment within 12 months. They are 1974, 1981, and 1990. Each time there had been a major jump in the price of oil in the same or preceding year. So the moral of the story should be clear.

Raising the minimum wage to catch up with rising product prices generally increases employment, except when the price of oil goes up substantially. Even then, the negative employment effect vanishes quickly.

For instance, when the minimum wage went up in 1974, employment fell by 948,000 within 12 months. But when the minimum wage rose again the next year in 1975, employment rose by 2,906,000, easily overtaking the job loss of the previous year. Thus, even the short-term effects of a minimum-wage rise are overwhelmingly positive for job creation. This holds true logically as well as historically.

The policy implication of our analysis is that the real minimum wage should be kept constant at the 1968 level, when the United States faced the lowest postwar rate of unemployment. In other words, such a wage should be indexed with the cost-of-living formula; otherwise, it may have to be raised abruptly, as in 1974, when it went up 25 percent in one year.

Incidentally, the table also reveals that from 1982 to 1989, there was no change in the minimum wage for eight long years, even as the CPI jumped 28 percent in the period. The 1980s were generally a period of low growth. History shows that while Reagan and Greenspan played Scrooge with the destitute, the lawmakers were busy raising their own salaries. This way they took care of themselves, reduced GDP growth, and decimated the poor.

So why blame the minimum wage for unemployment? Output, employment, and investment are lubricated by wages that are consistent with labor productivity, and so long as the minimum wage does not push the average economy-wide wage above the level of labor's average product, there is no harm to the economy. Problems, as you saw in chapter 6, arise only when income inequality rises as the real wage trails productivity gains, because then debt has to rise incessantly to maintain a balance in the economy.

You have already observed that the main reason for the growth blight from the 1980s and beyond was the sad transformation of the revenue system that shifted the U.S. tax burden from the rich to the poor. Now you can add another reason, namely the sharp decline of the purchasing power of the minimum wage, which was the highest in the 1960s, the decade with the highest rate of growth and the lowest rate of unemployment since World War II.

GREENSPAN AND LABOR

You may recall that classical economists generally opposed minimum wage laws; some of them, swayed by classical liberalism, also believed that laborers work hard only under the compulsion of starvation, so wage rates should be kept as low as possible. During the 1990s, a variant of this anti-labor attitude showed up in Greenspan's concern for inflation and economic growth. In his congressional testimony in October 1997, Greenspan worried about low unemployment and a tight labor market.

> The imbalance between the growth in labor demand and the expansion of potential labor supply of recent years must eventually erode the current state of inflation quiescence and, with it, the solid growth of real activity. . . . If the recent 2 million plus annual pace of job creation were to continue, the pressures on wages and other costs of hiring large numbers of such individuals could escalate more rapidly.[4]

Greenspan has often been accused of what is called "Fedspeak," which is a synonym for obfuscation, or an intentional use of words with multiple interpretations. So, it is sometimes hard to understand what he is trying to convey. Greenspan's remarks above essentially meant that labor demand was so strong that wages had to rise soon and that would force companies to raise prices rapidly, which in turn could derail the long economic expansion. Thus, to Greenspan, low real wages and hence "inflation quiescence" were the keys to "solid growth." But you can see from the growth formula presented above that if real wages decline and fail to keep up with productivity, you get lower, not higher growth.

In January 2000, Greenspan spelled out his concern about rising wages in detail:

> There has to be a limit to how far the pool of available labor can be drawn down without pressing wage levels beyond productivity. The existence or nonexistence of an empirically identifiable NAIRU has no bearing on the existence of the venerable law of supply and demand. To be sure, increases in wages in excess of productivity growth may not be inflationary, and destructive of economic growth, if offset by decreases in other costs or declining profit margins. A protracted decline in margins, however, is a recipe for recession. Thus, if our objective of maximum sustainable economic growth is to be achieved, the pool of available workers cannot shrink indefinitely.[5]

A day after these remarks, financial writer Richard Stevenson summarized the maestro's thinking about labor earnings: "In assessing current economic conditions, his focus, as it has been for months, was on the possibility that the country could run short of workers, which would push up wages and then prices in an inflationary spiral that could derail the long expansion."[6] In the same month, Greenspan even suggested relaxing the immigration laws to cool down wage gains and thus control inflation.

> It's clear that under existing circumstances, not only in high tech and in the farm area, but indeed, throughout the country, aggregative demand is putting very significant pressures on an ever-decreasing available supply of unemployed labor. The one obvious means that one can use to offset that is expanding the number of people we allow in, either generally or in specifically focused areas. And I do think that an appraisal of our immigration policies in this regard are really clearly on the table.[7]

Greenspan's bias against American labor now becomes crystal clear. This poster boy of free markets, who protected the profits of wealthy corporate barons time and again from their own speculative errors, who hardly ever spoke out against the skyrocketing compensation of CEOs, now sought to interfere with the free operation of U.S. labor markets by tinkering with immigration laws. He could not stand a decline in profit margins, which had soared above the historical norm during the 1980s and the 1990s, whereas rising wages might have just restored the historical average.

Greenspan's tirade against American labor amounted to this: free markets are great, except when they raise wages sharply, because then inflation may result. The government should then intervene by relaxing immigration quotas, or, as he himself had done in 1994–1995, by raising interest rates. It is interesting that the maestro favors government intervention to protect the interests of Wall Street brokers on one side, as in the case of LTCM and the Mexican crisis, and to maintain low wage growth on the other side, so that again the profit margins stay high. Either way, from left to right, Greenspan acts to prey on the interests of working families.

How can rising wages possibly cause recession or output decline? According to the classical economics that underlies Greenspan's theology, a profit-maximizing business never hires a worker if his/her productivity is below the real wage. So the real wage cannot exceed a laborer's output— not for long anyway. Even if wage rates were to exceed productivity temporarily, profits would fall and some workers would be fired, thus easing the tightness of the labor market. The real wage would then come down to the level of labor productivity, easing inflationary pressures.

Greenspan conveniently forgot the dictum made famous by his friend Milton Friedman that inflation anywhere and everywhere is a monetary phenomenon. In other words, inflation results from persistently high money growth, and little else. The very fact that the real wage is not independent of the laws of demand and supply suggests that free labor markets seldom cause inflation.

Greenspan also overlooked the fact that real earnings had not kept pace with productivity since the early 1970s; that the real production wage, according to the *Economic Report of the President*, had been sinking since 1973, and never regained that year's peak. He never talked of restraining immigration when the vast majority of Americans saw the average production wage fall.

Clearly, to Greenspan, markets become free when profits are unfettered, but not when wages are unfettered. Thus, to him, free profits define free markets. So pervasive and vocal was the maestro's bias against American labor that, just before the election of 1996, Aaron Zitner, staff writer for *The Boston Globe*, remarked: "The next president will have little chance of raising American wages and job prospects without the support of a lone, dour-looking numbers-cruncher: Alan Greenspan. . . . History shows it will not be an easy sell."[8]

It is not that the maestro was unaware of the real cause of inflation. In a speech on September 5, 1997, he said: "We recognize that inflation is fundamentally a monetary phenomenon, and ultimately determined by the growth of the stock of money."[9] Then why did he harp on wage escalation as the culprit behind spiraling prices? Obviously, to keep profits and hence CEO wages humming. He conveniently forgot that the CEO compensation is also part of the cost of production and could act in the same way as soaring wages to foment inflation. What is appalling is that wage pressures were quiescent in the 1990s, whereas escalating CEO salaries were a fact of life, and yet the maestro chose to ignore the "infectious greed" of his favorites, and occasionally raised interest rates to contain wages.[10]

What CEO compensation can do to escalating prices becomes clear from the upward trend in the cost of health care. Princeton's Professor Krugman argues that CEO and management salaries are a big reason for ever-increasing health costs, because "private insurers and H.M.O.s [health maintenance organizations] spend much more on administrative expenses, as opposed to actual medical treatment, than public agencies at home or abroad."[11] When Reagan–Greenspan took over the levers of the economy in the United States in 1981, the CPI for medical care stood at 83; it climbed all the way to 297 in 2003—a jump of over 250 percent in about two decades. But the maestro, to my knowledge, never blamed the CEO salaries as a potential threat for inflation in consumer prices or health costs.

A puzzle remains to be explored: Why was general inflation quiescent in the late 1990s in spite of constantly falling unemployment and a relentless rise in CEO compensation? The answer lies in the emergence of an unprecedented phenomenon that permitted the United States to import vast quantities of high-quality but cheap foreign goods without fully paying for them in exports—in other words, the unprecedented trade deficits. This is what we examine next.

9

GREENSPAN AND THE GALLOPING TRADE DEFICIT

By now it is clear that Alan Greenspan is an unconventional and wavering economist. Few know what he really stands for. His early life reveals that he used to have a bevy of core convictions, but that was before he became the CEA chairman in 1974 and acquired a taste for the forbidden fruit of government authority. Since then his priorities and loyalties have shifted repeatedly; he has abandoned those convictions time and again, mostly to benefit his rich constituency of Wall Streeters. So it should not come as a surprise that once upon a time Greenspan used to rail against the rising tide of trade deficit facing the United States. But not any more. Here's a sampling of the views that various articles in *The Washington Post* ascribed to him from 1984 to 1986.

1. "If the trade deficit continues to narrow, U.S. manufacturers will pick up an increasing share of consumer demand, which they had been losing to foreign sales during the past few years, according to economist Alan Greenspan."[1]
2. "Alan Greenspan, former chairman of the Council of Economic Advisers and now a private economist, also blamed imports for many of the economy's ills."[2] Furthermore: " 'The tremendous pressure from imports has created, up until very recently, very significant downward pressure on manufacturing operating profit margins,' said economist Alan Greenspan."[3]

3. "Greenspan and Bergsten appeared with Pzifer Inc. Chairman Edmond T. Pratt Jr. before a joint hearing of two House foreign affairs subcommittees. . . .

"All three witnesses agreed that the huge U.S. budget deficit is a primary cause of most of the present international economic problems."[4]

It is clear from these excerpts that Greenspan attributes a variety of negative effects to the growing American trade deficit. First he says if the deficit narrows, then manufacturers will gain a bigger share of consumer spending, which essentially means that they will raise output and employment. Thus, eliminating the trade shortfall is good for the economy.

Second, he blames many of the economic problems on rising imports, especially their squeeze on companies' profit margins. Third, he contends that the U.S. trade imbalance is the primary source of global economic dilemmas. In addition, you can see that Greenspan gives great importance to the manufacturing sector of the economy. He is worried that rising imports are hurting the profit margins of U.S. manufacturers.

Now let's see how he has changed his tune in these matters as well. Let's look at some excerpts from the press and Greenspan's testimony in 2003:

1. "Chairman Alan Greenspan said ballooning trade deficits have not hurt the U.S. economy so far. . . . To date, the widening to record levels of the U.S. ratio of current account deficit to GDP has been 'seemingly uneventful.' "[5]
2. Greenspan wonders and answers in his House testimony on July 15, 2003: "Is it important for an economy to have manufacturing? There is a big dispute on this issue. What is important is that economies create value, and whether value is created by taking raw materials and fabricating them into something consumers want, or value is created by various different services which consumers want, presumably should not make any significant difference so far as standards of living are concerned."[6]

In 2003 the chairman no longer cared about the harmful effects of the U.S. trade or current account deficit. The deficit records being broken were "seemingly uneventful" to him. Nor did he fret over the loss of manufacturing in the United States. It did not matter to the living standard if the public was employed, or value was created, mostly in services. This view of manufacturing reminds you of what

Michael Boskin, the CEA chairman of President Bush Sr., is supposed to have said in the early 1990s: "Computer chips, potato chips, what's the difference?"

THE TRADE-MANUFACTURING FLIP-FLOP

What accounts for this flip-flop? Greenspan's other intellectual somersaults were perhaps dictated by his self-interest to remain Fed chairman and stay on the good side of the powers that be, but why shift his position in the matter of manufacturing and trade in the U.S. economy? This does not seem to be crucial to the retention of his post.

This flip-flop appears to be mostly a matter of sour grapes. After his appointment as Fed chairman, Greenspan had occasionally assured the U.S. public that the depreciation of the dollar in foreign markets would take care of the trade deficit in due time. The dollar did fall, once in a while, but not the deficit, which in the long run kept increasing regardless of the greenback's value.

Greenspan also used to blame the trade shortfall on unprecedented U.S. budget deficits, but then the budget turned into a surplus from 1999 to 2001, while the trade deficit set ever-new records. The following press reports in 2004 describe Greenspan's positions in the past:

1. "In remarks before the Economic Club of New York, Greenspan said the declining U.S. dollar should help reduce the nation's huge trade deficit."[7]
2. "Federal Reserve Chairman Alan Greenspan said yesterday that cutting the federal budget deficit would make it easier to shrink the huge U.S. trade deficit without hurting the economy."[8]

The Washington Post, for instance, wrote this on August 2, 1987: "In his confirmation testimony, Greenspan explained that only limited progress has been made so far in bringing down the trade deficit, despite a cheaper dollar."[9] Clearly the maestro believed that the cheaper dollar should improve U.S. trade arrears. Similarly, in his Congressional testimony in February 1990, he recommended the creation of a federal budget surplus to eliminate the trade deficit. Obviously, none of Greenspan's theories panned out. Finally he gave up and claimed that neither the manufacturing loss nor the current account deficit mattered to the

U.S. economy. Let's see where the maestro, the world's best economist, went wrong.

There is a well-known theory in the area of international economics that currency devaluation eliminates a nation's trade deficit, usually in two to three years. Indeed this is what happened during the 1970s, when the dollar's fall took care of the American shortfall in trade. *Since 1983, however, the dollar has waxed and waned, but the U.S. trade deficit is as stubborn as ever.* In fact, it is now climbing at an unprecedented rate. At nearly 6 percent of the GDP, it threatens to vault even higher.

During the 1980s and the early 1990s, the most popular hypothesis was one of twin deficits, wherein the unprecedented federal budget deficits coexisted with an escalating trade deficit. The idea was that the big jump in government spending and deficits caused national demand to exceed national supply year after year, so that this excess American demand for goods had to be satisfied by foreign companies, which then had a corresponding trade surplus.

A variant of the twin-deficit thesis blamed the high value of the dollar on high American interest rates resulting from the budget deficits. The expensive dollar in turn spawned the trade deficit. But then the government budget deficit began to decline after 1992, while the trade shortfall kept on rising. At the same time, the budget deficit soared in Japan along with its soaring trade surplus. That was the end of the twin deficit hypothesis, at least among scholars.

So the crucial question is this: Why did the much higher budget deficit of Japan not create a trade deficit there, while a smaller deficit did create one in the United States? During the 1990s Japan's budget was in arrears by as much as 10 percent of its GDP, whereas the corresponding U.S. deficit never came close to that figure, and even moved into surplus at the turn of the millennium.

It turns out that Greenspan, like most economists, relied on a tautology in macroeconomics, something that always holds and has no cause-effect relationship. The simplest version of this tautology says that if a nation's investment matches its savings, then

Budget Deficit $=$ Trade Deficit

So the higher the budget deficit, the larger the trade deficit. But this is not a theory; it is true simply by the way macroeconomic variables are defined. It always holds, but does not say that the budget deficit causes the trade deficit. For all you know, from the twin-deficit viewpoint, the trade deficit itself could cause the budget deficit. But Greenspan relied on this naïve idea and confidently proclaimed that the trade shortfall resulted from the budget shortfall. From 1999 to 2001, America indeed had a budget surplus, yet its trade deficit broke records, thus refuting Greenspan's prognostication.

In fact, it is more plausible that the trade deficiency is the cause of the budget deficiency, rather than the other way around. Let's see how. Recall Greenspan's own statement mentioned above: "If the trade deficit continues to narrow, U.S. manufacturers will pick up an increasing share of consumer demand." These words suggest that U.S. output rises if the trade deficit falls. Conversely, U.S. output falls if the trade deficit increases.

Falling American output means rising unemployment, declining tax receipts, and rising government spending for unemployment compensation. And that is mostly what the budget deficit is made of. So by generating joblessness, the trade shortfall creates falling tax receipts and rising government spending. Thus the thesis that the trade deficit may cause the budget deficit is just as plausible as the one that blames the budget deficit for the trade shortfall.

THE PERSISTENT TRADE DEFICIT

The dollar has been depreciating relative to foreign currencies ever since the early 1970s. A dollar bought 360 yen in 1969, 226 yen in 1980, about 110 yen in 2004. The story with respect to other currencies is basically the same. With all these devaluations, American trade remained in balance during the 1970s and ended the decade with a slight surplus.

Following 1983, however, U.S. trade moved into red ink that peaked in 1987, but then began to return to balance. The dollar depreciation engineered by the Plaza Accord of 1985 did help some and by 1990 the deficit had fallen sharply. After 1991, however, the deficit started rising again and has been increasing ever since regardless of the value of the dollar.

In fact, according to the 1996 *Economic Report of the President*, "The trade balance is a deceptive indicator of economic performance and of the benefit that the United States derives from trade. Trade policy is neither responsible for, nor capable of significantly changing, the overall trade balance."[10] American policymakers simply gave up and declared that trade policy could not balance trade any more. Such benign neglect of the trade balance is similar to Greenspan's description of the record trade deficit in 2003 as "seemingly uneventful."

Why does the dollar depreciation not improve the U.S. trade balance any more? Furthermore, how come devaluations by other countries, such as Japan and the Asian Tigers, successfully eliminate their trade deficits or raise their trade surpluses? Remember the Mexican crisis resulting from Mexico's trade arrears and the subsequent peso devaluation in December 1994. Within six months, the country's commerce turned into a surplus. There must be some reason why an impoverished country like Mexico can use devaluation to transform its foreign account within six months, something the United States could not do for 21 years, from 1983 to 2004. That reason, as it turns out, is manufacturing—or the lack of it.

Table 9.1 reveals that the foreign currency value of the dollar fell under almost every presidency, starting with Nixon's. A dollar bought 303 yen in 1972, 296 in 1976 under Ford, 226 in 1980 under Carter, and 237 yen in 1984 under Reagan. By that time, U.S. trade, specifically the current account, had turned from a $2.3 billion surplus under Carter into a $94 billion deficit under Reagan. Alarmed at the unprecedented short-fall (called current account deficit in the data), officials of G-7 countries met in New York in 1985 and decided to bring the value of the dollar down in the Plaza Accord.

The currency had already depreciated a lot, with mediocre success; yet, the government once again tried the largely unproven policy. The dollar fell to 128 yen in 1988, but the deficit only went up. Under Bush Sr.

Table 9.1. U.S. Current Account Deficit and the Yen–Dollar Exchange Rate in the Last Year of Each Presidency: 1972–2004

Year	President	Yen per Dollar	Trade Deficit (billions of dollars)
1972	Nixon	303	5.8
1976	Ford	296	−4.3 (surplus)
1980	Carter	226	−2.3 (surplus)
1984	Reagan	237	94.0
1988	Reagan	128	121.0
1992	Bush Sr.	127	48.0
1996	Clinton	109	127.7
2000	Clinton	108	441.5
2004	Bush	110	640.0

Source: *Economic Report of the President*, Council of Economic Advisers, Washington, D.C., 1996, pp. 392 and 400; 2005, pp. 328 and 336.

the dollar remained stable, and the deficit declined somewhat, presumably reflecting the delayed effect of the dollar's cheapness. Clinton resumed the failed policy, and, of course, it led to a soaring deficit—once again. The dollar remained more or less stable under George W. Bush, yet the deficit broke new records.

Why is it that Mexico's devaluation in late 1994 ended its trade deficit almost overnight, whereas the United States has been unable to do this since 1983? The reason lies in the lack of U.S. manufacturing. Not that Mexico is an industrial powerhouse. But the relocation of many American companies in Mexico has given it a large manufacturing base that is geared primarily for exports to the United States.

In general, we find that countries that export manufactures have surplus trade, while those exporting services and/or farm products have deficits. This pattern is unmistakable in the case of free markets undisturbed by trade barriers; but it is also usually valid in the case of tariff-driven economies. In the nineteenth century, the United States imported manufactured goods in exchange for farm goods and raw materials. The country's trade was generally in deficit, which was usually financed by foreign investment.

At the turn of the century, America began to export more manufactured goods than it imported, so that it became a net exporter of manufactures, and not surprisingly its foreign account, specifically its trade balance, turned into a surplus. The surplus lasted until the early 1970s when the country again became a net importer of manufactures. The foreign shortfall at the time was meager and did not adversely affect growth. But in the 1980s, the red ink turned into a gusher with no end in sight so far.

Table 9.2. Trade Deficit in Manufactures-Importing Countries, USA, United Kingdom, and Australia (billions of dollars): 1985–2002

Year	USA	UK	Australia
1985	122	4	1
1990	108	32	0
1995	172	19	4
2000	450	50	4
2002	479	70	15
Mfg. Employment in 2002 (%)	14	17	12

Source: International Financial Statistics: Yearbook, 1992 and 2004; Statistical Abstract of the United States, 2004.

Other countries also confirm what the United States experienced with respect to its trade balance. Table 9.2 lists three countries with persistent deficits in commerce between 1985 and 2002—the United States, the United Kingdom, and Australia. They are all net importers of manufactures, with the United States as the ringleader at an unprecedented deficit of $479 billion in 2002.

Table 9.3 displays the other side of the coin, detailing the trade performance of countries that are net exporters of manufactures. This group includes Japan, Germany, and the new manufacturing power-house, China. All three were virtually destroyed by World War II. Once they regained independence from war victors in the late 1940s, they launched a vigorous program of industrialization. Initially, Germany and Japan imported investment goods in large quantities from the United States and endured big deficits in foreign commerce. But after 1970, the two began to enjoy the fruit of thriving manufacturing. They became net exporters of manufactures with a positive balance of trade.

China's emergence on the world economic scene was delayed by socialist policies at home and confrontation with the West until about 1972, the year President Nixon visited the country. Following that year, China began to modernize its economy and gradually opened up its industry to foreign investment. With its disciplined and cheap labor, the country induced many multinational corporations to open plants on its soil. Today there is hardly any Fortune 500 corporation that does not have a subsidiary in China.

With all that international investment, local expertise, and hard work, China grew into an industrial behemoth and became an exporter of

Table 9.3. Trade Surplus in Manufactures-Exporting Countries, Japan, Germany, and China (billions of dollars): 1985–2002

Year	Japan	Germany	China
1985	56	29	−13
1990	64	72	9
1995	132	64	18
2000	117	58	35
2002	94	128	44
Mfg. Employment in 2002 (%)	21	24	21

Source: *International Financial Statistics: Yearbook*, 1992 and 2004; *Statistical Abstract of the United States*, 2004; The Conference Board, 2004.

manufactured goods. After 1985, it began to enjoy a surplus in its current account, which has continued to this day.

What's the difference between the two groups of trade surplus and trade deficit countries? The deficit nations are those where manufacturing has been on the decline; the manufacturing employment share in this group was below 20 percent in 2002, with the United States and Australia falling even below 15 percent. By contrast, the manufacturing employment share in the surplus nations exceeded the 20 percent benchmark.

This is not to say that all nations suffering from the manufacturing debacle will have trade deficits. There may be cases where the country is well-endowed with oil, such as Saudi Arabia and Kuwait, or it has ancient landmarks and a thriving tourist industry, such as France. A positive foreign balance may then persist for a long time. In general, however, manufacturing importers have trade deficits and exporters have surpluses.

Currency depreciation succeeds in turning the trade balance around if the country has a growing base of manufacturing. Otherwise it works for a while, but then the nation goes back into the same old hole. The United States and the United Kingdom have frequently suffered currency depreciations, but with little lasting success.

Devaluation of the dollar means that a greenback buys less in foreign exchange. This tends to raise prices of foreign goods in the United States, so Americans buy fewer imports. But they may still spend more on foreign goods because their dollar-denominated prices have risen. On the other side, other countries get more dollars for their currency, so that U.S. goods become cheaper abroad. Foreigners then buy more American goods, but that does not mean American exporters receive more foreign exchange. This is because prices of U.S. goods abroad have fallen. Currency depreciation, in other words, may or may not succeed in eliminating the trade deficit.

Manufactured goods, such as cars, air conditioners, televisions, computers, furniture, and carpets, are far more expensive than farm goods and raw materials. They are also in general priced higher than service products such as airline tickets, restaurant meals, education, healthcare, banking and insurance activities, among others. The United States mostly exports farm goods and services, and imports practically everything else.

When a country constantly exports low-ticket items and imports expensive products, it is bound to have large deficits no matter how often it devalues its currency. That is why U.S. devaluations have failed since the early 1980s, whereas the 1994 Mexican devaluation had a resounding success.

Thanks to U.S. corporations, Mexico is now a big exporter of manufactures to the United States.

The official position used to be that trade deficits result from low savings and high budget deficits. This is only partly true. In the 1990s, Japan had one of the largest budget deficits in the world. Yet it had the largest, and most persistent, trade surplus. Low savings may indeed create a high foreign shortfall, but the responsibility for dwindling savings lies with regressive American taxation. In the 1950s and the 1960s, the U.S. saving rate was higher, but it still paled before the saving rates in other nations. Yet America had a trade surplus at the time. In the end, the state of manufacturing primarily determines the state of the trade balance. In order to eliminate our persistent deficit, we have to put America back on the trajectory of reindustrialization.

Today there is hardly any manufacturing activity left in the United States. The country imports almost everything—VCRs, autos, bicycles, motorcycles, baseball bats, tennis rackets, shoes, textiles, toys, and even American flags; the list goes on and on. Even if the dollar falls sharply, what can we possibly export? Perhaps a few airplanes, computers, wheat, lumber, some machine tools—things you can count on your fingertips. Not much is built in America. So the lack of manufacturing means that it will take an enormous amount of dollar devaluation before the trade deficit vanishes or even falls.

THE U.S. MANUFACTURING DEBACLE

What caused the manufacturing debacle in the United States, a nation that emerged as the global industrial behemoth following World War II? Manufacturing employment peaked in 1979 at a little over 21 million. Ever since then the new entrants in the job market have gone primarily to service-producing industries. In 2004 manufacturing employment stood at a pathetic 14.8 million, about 11 percent of non-farm employment.

The share of manufacturing jobs as a fraction of employed labor began its rapid decline after 1965, when this number stood at 30 percent, roughly the same as in 1930. In the long interregnum of 35 years, the globe went through the wrenching of the Great Depression, a world war, and the onset of the Vietnam War, among others, but the U.S. employment share in manufacturing was essentially unchanged. The United States remained the industrial leader and continued to enjoy the highest living standard.

The growth experience of most countries reveals that prosperity lies primarily in the development of manufacturing rather than services. Agriculture is also important, but only to an extent. In the absence of a thriving farm sector, prosperity is, of course, difficult to achieve. But there is only so much of farm goods that you can consume. If your income doubles, your food consumption will not normally double. You may switch to a better and more expensive diet, but your calorie intake is unlikely to jump, and if it does, you could be in real trouble.

Once a country has developed its farming, its further prosperity can come only from an expansion of manufacturing, which is really the foundation of advanced economies today. This is because in manufacturing, a country builds something tangible, whereas in other sectors such as services, the manufactured product mostly undergoes an improvement in the form of transportation to the market, packaging, repair, and salesmanship. The service product is often intangible.

Manufacturing includes the production of iron, steel, aluminum, copper, television sets, VCRs, cameras, watches, cars, railroads, airplanes, computers, thousands of spare parts, and so on. In the service sector, these products are relocated to retail shops and malls, packaged properly and then sold by sales people. Clearly then the service sector cannot thrive without a developed manufacturing sector.

Other service products such as banking, insurance, and real estate also depend crucially on healthy manufacturing, where productivity and hence wages tend to be high. From high wages people can afford to save money, which then creates the need for banks and savings associations. Savings, in turn, enable people to make a down payment for a house and borrow money from the financial institutions. Banks lend money not only to homebuyers, but also to various industries, which all thrive on the foundation of manufacturing.

The United States and other G-7 countries also have a prosperous service sector that includes healthcare, education, transportation, tourism, banking, real estate, insurance, restaurants, hotels, and, lately, information technology, among others. All these countries have some manufacturing, which is closely connected to their service industries.

Manufacturing is the locomotive that pulls most enterprises. It is a dynamo that powers the rest of the economy. In its absence, even new technology fails to flourish. New ideas and innovations materialize only if there is a healthy manufacturing sector at home. Otherwise, a country will invent new products, but their production will occur in other countries. New technology industries normally enjoy the fastest growth, because the demand for new products generally outpaces that for old products. That is why high-tech companies pay higher wages. But if the manufacturing sector is not robust, then the actual production of new inventions usually occurs abroad. The inventor benefits, of course, but people in his country do not. Listen to the words of two economists, Stephen Cohen and John Zysman:

> Manufacturing matters mightily to the wealth and power of the United States and to our ability to sustain the kind of open society we have come to take for granted. If we want to stay on top—or even high up—we can't just shift out of manufacturing and into services.[11]

The history of G-7 countries shows that their economies were built on the sturdy foundation of manufacturing. How did they build that foundation? With the help of tariffs. They protected their industries from foreign competition through high import taxes. Table 9.4 gives us an idea of how pervasive protectionism was in some of today's advanced economies, of which the United States was the ringleader. The fact that the developed countries had exorbitant tariffs on manufactured goods and not on all products shows that they understood the importance of manufacturing in the process of development.

Being a vast area, the United States tended to be self-sufficient in most products and could afford to impose one of the largest tariffs in the world. But the country also became the world economic leader by the end of the nineteenth century. Such was the crucial role that the manufacturing tariff played in the affluence of the United States.

Table 9.4. Manufacturing Tariffs in Industrial Countries (%)

Country	1875	1902	1913
Canada	NA	17	26
France	12–15	34	20
Germany	4–6	25	13
Italy	8–10	27	18
Japan*	6	10	20–35
United States	40–50	73	44

* Average tariff on dutiable imports.

Source: *World Development Report*, The World Bank, Washington, D.C., 1991, p. 97; Ryoshin Minami, *The Economic Development of Japan: A Quantitative Study*, 2nd edition, Macmillan, London, 1994, p. 194; Ravi Batra, *The Myth of Free Trade*, p. 178.

Following World War II the United States felt the need to create a bulwark of nations to resist communism. It needed to link the free-world economies through international trade and direct foreign investment. Now if all democracies had opened up their markets and lowered their tariffs, the effects would be roughly the same for most nations.

As it is, among the G-7 all nations except Japan liberalized their trade. The Asian nation did not join the G-7 assembly initially and preferred the historical American model of competitive protectionism. It retained stiff tariffs on most imports, but broke up its domestic monopolies into small competing units. Thus, competitive protectionism means high industrial competition at home but little from abroad.

At first, Japan focused on low-tech, labor-intensive industries such as textiles, leather goods, fountain pens, bicycles, and the like. Its industrial base had been devastated in the war, and, above all, it lacked raw materials and sufficient arable land. In short, it faced the worst economic prospects among all economies.

But the people of Japan face adversity well; they are well educated and hardworking. The country imported technology and capital equipment from the United States in exchange for small industrial products produced at home. Slowly but surely, Japan's disciplined and diligent labor force began to excel in manufacturing. The country had ready access to the U.S. market, and by 1965 it began to outcompete American industries. That was the beginning of de-industrialization in America.

On its part, the United States continued to pursue trade liberalization and slowly persuaded Japan to open up its markets. U.S. policy picked up steam under Reagan and his advisers such as Greenspan. They wanted the world not only to liberalize trade but also to pursue financial deregulation, whereby controls were lifted from the transfer of funds across borders. Thus globalization came to mean free foreign investment as well as free foreign trade.

Historically the two ideas had developed along divergent tracks. Economists were interested more in the removal of tariffs than the unrestricted international movement of funds. However, Greenspan favored both ideas, and it is his version of globalization that came to pervade the world. Gradually, the trading partners lifted most tariffs as well as controls over capital transfers. By 1995, even Japan relaxed its capital controls, and the dollar became the currency of choice among the richest people in the world. Another competing currency, the euro, came into being in 1999, and is fast emerging to have the same status as the mighty dollar.

Freer trade had started to hurt the American manufacturing base in 1965; freer international capital movements simply decimated it, because they enabled the United States to run a seemingly limitless trade deficit in return for paper dollars. Global financial deregulation enabled exporters around the world to park their dollars in the New York Stock Exchange, the Nasdaq market, U.S. Treasury bonds, real estate, and so on. Tons of foreign money came from abroad to chase American assets. This capital inflow financed the U.S. addiction to foreign goods, but in the process crippled American manufacturing.

Essentially, the United States has been exporting its goods and assets to pay for its imports since 1983. It is the policy of global financial deregulation that facilitated the export of American assets to other countries. Thus Greenspan and his acolytes from big business who usually benefit from his actions are mainly responsible for the American manufacturing debacle. Now the nation produces so few goods at home that its trade imbalance has a faint connection with the value of its currency. No wonder the maestro was unconcerned about the carnage of U.S. manufacturing as well as the mushrooming trade deficit. He was, and is, their chief perpetrator. Finally, he woke up to reality and in late 2004 acknowledged that the U.S. trade shortfall could not grow forever.

GAINS AND LOSSES FROM TRADE

Nations normally benefit from international trade under most circumstances. Such benefits are diverse and many. Consumers gain from cheaper imports of goods and services; producers benefit from inexpensive importation of raw materials, spare parts, and capital equipment, and from access to larger markets; economic growth thrives when a nation acquires the latest information and technology from abroad. Product quality improves from enhanced foreign competition. All these gains are clear-cut and definitive if a country exports as much as it imports.

But once imports regularly exceed exports, gains from trade may turn into losses. The persistent trade deficit kills domestic industries and real wages. In general, freer trade benefits exporting industries and hurts those firms that compete with imports, and if exports match imports, the losses generally offset the gains, but society as a whole prospers, because producers in trading countries are forced to become more efficient under the threat of increased competition. Overall, there is productivity or efficiency gain from trade, which shows up in increased profits.

However, if exports consistently fall short of imports, then the losses of import-competing industries surpass the gains of exporting sectors. This may be called the trade deficit loss to the economy. It leads to a fall in the real wage. With freer trade, export industries gain jobs, whereas the import-competing sectors fire workers. If trade is in deficit then job losses exceed job gains, and the demand for labor declines. When the demand for something falls, its price also falls. The real wage is the price of labor; therefore under deficit-ridden trade, the country's real wage sinks, because of shrinking labor demand.

Thus deficit-ridden free trade generates two effects for an economy— one positive and one negative. Productivity rises on one side, the real wage falls on the other. The overall effect then depends on which side is dominant. If the trade deficit continues to rise, it is clear that the wage loss will be dominant in the end, and the nation will end up losing from trade, although profits will still be higher because of efficiency gains. Thus the deficit-ridden trade, at least in the short run, does not cause a profit loss, only a wage loss.

Does it mean the nation should abandon free trade? No, not in today's world where the economies have become extremely intertwined with each other, so much so that the disruption of global commerce itself could cripple the trading partners. But it does mean that the country should abandon deficit-ridden free trade and act swiftly to restore balance in its foreign commerce. How this can be done will be pursued in the final chapter dealing with economic reform.

When Adam Smith championed free trade, he expressed his logic in terms of the productivity gain from trade, wherein foreign commerce was in balance. His rationale was accepted by most economists, and it did not change much from 1776, when Smith's *Wealth of Nations* appeared, all the way till 1987, when Greenspan became Fed chairman. For more than two centuries economists simply assumed balanced trade in their free-trade arguments. No one could envision anything else. A nation had to export to pay for its imports—it was as simple as that. Or else the deficit country had to make payment in terms of gold, which could not last indefinitely.

But Greenspan changed such centuries-old practices by pushing financial deregulation. With the dollar dominating global commerce, countries became content to accept the greenback in exchange for their goods and services. Any surplus dollars of foreign exporters could now come back to the United States to buy its productive assets. For a while, this created a party atmosphere in America, which was happy to consume all those high quality yet cheap foreign goods coming from abroad, but it made a mish-mash of its own industries. American manufacturing all but disappeared, as did millions of lucrative jobs.

Greenspan, a Good Samaritan, pressed financial deregulation at the behest of Wall Street and big business, which, according to him, was America's persecuted minority. He didn't realize that the legislation born from his advice would result in an ever-growing trade deficit and decimate American manufacturing, which appeared important to him before he became Fed chairman. He thought that the dollar devaluation, as with currency effects in other countries, would contain the U.S. trade arrears. But when the deficit kept soaring, he changed his tune in a reminder of sour grapes, and in 2003 declared the record deficits as "seemingly uneventful"; still he again assured the Americans that the dollar decline would improve the trade imbalance. Similarly, he slighted the loss of manufacturing, because there was nothing he could do about it.

THE TRADE DEFICIT AND THE RATE OF INTEREST

Normally the trade deficit, as shown above, hurts a nation, but for the United States it played an unexpected and positive role during the 1990s. While weakening the manufacturing base, it lowered the rate of interest. As foreign exporters accumulated dollars, they passed some of them on to their central banks in return for local currencies. The central banks in turn purchased U.S. government bonds, raising bond prices in the process. It is well known that a rise in such prices is the same thing as a fall in the rate of interest.

Suppose you spend $100 to purchase a government bond paying 6 percent per year. If you pay $200 to buy the same bond, then the bond price doubles, while the interest rate is cut in half. Thus rising bond prices automatically mean a fall in the interest rate.

The trade deficit generated two additional effects in the United States. It lowered the interest rate on the one hand, and ate into consumer demand for domestic industries on the other. But the interest-rate effect dominated for a while, because it stimulated housing, which is the largest sector in the United States. Most people purchase homes on credit, and cheap credit is the best tonic for the housing industry.

When someone buys a house, they also buy many high-ticket goods—furniture, appliances, rugs, paintings, curtains. Low interest rates stimulate the auto industry as well. Thus the interest-rate effect on aggregate spending in the United States is huge, and it overwhelmed the normally negative demand impact from the trade deficit. So demand growth jumped in America after 1995. The same year saw the Japanese lift capital controls from their economy. Individuals in Japan, not just exporters, began to purchase dollar-denominated assets, so bond yields fell even more.

Take a look at Table 9.5. Demand growth, and hence GDP growth, remained strong from 1996 to 2000, even as the trade deficit jumped. Nothing like this has ever happened in the history of the world. Normally, the deficit nations have to raise interest rates in order to attract foreign funds and finance the red ink. So a rising deficit leads to a rising interest rate. But the United States experienced what may be called the interest rate paradox, which actually produced a fall in bond yields.

As the trade deficit surged interest rates fell, demand growth jumped and so did GDP growth. From 1990 to 1994, growth averaged only 1.8 percent, but over the next five years the average climbed to 4.3 percent, approaching the peak growth decade of the 1960s. The country went through a boom, which added fuel to the share-price bubble. Thus the boom of the 1990s did not just result from the excellence of the new economy, as contended by Greenspan; it also had fortuitous assistance from an unexpected source—the mushrooming trade deficit. Stated another way, the new economy also had something brand new in U.S. history—record American borrowing from abroad.

During the 1990s, the United States borrowed almost a trillion dollars from trade-surplus nations to finance its foreign shortfall. Even a pauper can become a billionaire through debt. There is no doubt the growth spurt of the late 1990s derives from Clinton–Greenspan policies. But the spurt was a mirage, built on the sandy foundation of borrowed money. The boom of the second half of the 1990s may be called the *foreign money boom*. American interest rates would have been higher without those foreign funds. The foreign capital not only financed the housing splurge but also the slight gain in investment.

Greenspan and Clinton pursued financial deregulation under the umbrella of the WTO (World Trade Organization) and facilitated the inflow of capital from abroad. The boom was engineered by massive

Table 9.5. Trade Deficit, Interest Rate, and the Boom of the 1990s: 1995–2000

Year	Trade Deficit as % of GDP*	30-Year Govt. Bond Interest Rate	GDP Growth
1995	1.4	6.88	2.4
1996	1.5	6.71	3.8
1997	1.5	6.61	4.8
1998	2.3	5.58	5.3
1999	3.1	5.87	5.3
2000	4.2	5.94	4.4

Source: The Economic Report of the President, 2004.

U.S. indebtedness to foreign countries. Even then it fell short of the growth record of the 1960s, when the United States was a lender, not borrower, to the world. The economic policies in the two decades were drastically different; they produced a win-win situation in the 1960s but an illusory bonanza in the 1990s that quickly fell apart at the turn of the millennium.

Financial deregulation brought short-term gains to the United States, but devastated its manufacturing and generated a long-term mess in the process. Now the country produces so few goods that it could suffer mega trade deficits for years to come. Even moderate doses of dollar devaluation no longer work to ease the red ink.

IMBALANCES ABROAD

Ultimately, all economic imbalances can be traced back to the growing wage gap in the United States and other countries. Please recall that this idea was developed in chapter 6, and it is relevant here as well. We live in a global village today, and an imbalance in one market is bound to spawn imbalances elsewhere. The labor market is the one crucial segment of any economy, because workers are producers on one side and consumers on the other. When the labor market is distorted in the sense that the wage growth trails productivity growth, then all other markets get distorted as well.

Record indebtedness in the United States, chiefly the result of the rising wage gap, has been partially financed by record trade deficits. On the flip side, foreign countries have persistent trade surpluses, which reflect their own rising wage gap. Surplus trade means that a nation produces more than it consumes, and the surplus production is shipped abroad. Thus

Trade Surplus = Exports − Imports = Supply − Demand

Since wages are the main source of demand, and productivity the main source of supply, trade surplus grows only when the real wage fails to keep pace with growing productivity, because then supply outpaces demand. Thus, for different reasons, American deficits and foreign surpluses are mirror images of the same phenomenon—the growing gap between the real wage and productivity.

In the United States, the growing wage gap produces rising indebtedness, which spurs demand; it also reflects the country's de-industrialization, and the two together reflect the growing trade shortfall, which seems immune to the value of the dollar. Elsewhere, in China, Japan, and Europe, the rising wage gap causes supply to exceed demand, and the two together spawn surplus trade that mirrors the U.S. deficit. At the root of all these imbalances lies the increasing divorce of wages from productivity gains.

In 1992, the United States actually had a slight trade surplus with the 15 countries that formed the European Union (EU); but by mid 2004, the EU had a surplus of $100 billion with America. In the same period, China's surplus with the United States had jumped from $18 billion to $140 billion.[12] To all this, add Japan's surplus of $70 billion, and the three regions accounted for nearly 60 percent of U.S. trade arrears in 2004. The rest belonged mainly to the OPEC, the Asian Tigers, and India.

Does the United States have a meaningful trade surplus with any nation today? Yes, there is one indeed—Australia—whose manufacturing base, employing barely 11 percent of the labor force, is just as depleted as that of America. We have learned before that the global share-price bubble of the 1990s was rooted in the rising wage gap throughout the world. Now you can see that this wage gap is also the root cause of worldwide imbalances in international trade, and indeed of many other economic troubles.

GLOBAL WAGE GAP

What is raising the wage gap around the world? In one word, Greenomics, or its caricature, Greedomics. As stated before, for much of U.S. history wages kept up with productivity, but not during the 1920s or since the 1970s. So stock market bubbles and persistent trade deficits are rare occurrences, because real wages refuse to trail hourly output all the time. But sometimes a variety of institutional changes occur to bring about a growing wage gap.

Why does the wage gap rise? Like most puzzles in economics, this one also depends on the laws of supply and demand. In general, anything that generates a decline in labor demand or a rise in labor supply produces a rise in the wage gap. Since the labor force consists primarily of the poor and the middle class, anything that increases their tax burden can force them to work longer hours. Regressive taxation has generally increased the labor-force participation in the United States. People have to survive and feed their families. Their rising tax burden then induces them to increase their labor supply.

While the virus of regressive taxation has hit the United States hardest, it has not spared the world. Corporate taxes have been slashed in Europe, Australia, Canada, and Japan as well, while the Social Security taxes remain as high as ever. Most of these nations also have an exorbitant value-added tax, which is like a sales tax and is extremely regressive.

Regressive taxation tends to increase the supply of labor and trim demand and GDP growth. For that reason, it also restrains the demand for labor, because if growth falls, businesses don't need to hire as many new workers as before.

The merger mania around the globe is another factor behind the rising wage gap. When product markets lack intense competition, they become monopolistic. The firms then have the capability to control their prices by controlling their output. They realize that to sell more of their product they have to charge a lower price, which they despise. So they reduce their output and employment, and raise their price. The end result is a lower real wage and a higher wage gap.

Business mergers climbed in the 1920s and then again between 1982 and 2000, crimping rivalry among firms. Some markets became monopolistic, even oligopolistic, where just two or three firms dominate the industry. Microsoft in the software industry became a giant, as did some pharmaceutical firms in the field of medicine. The 1996 merger between Exxon and Mobil generated a petroleum-industry behemoth with enormous production, profits, and financial clout. Such developments could not but raise the wage gap.

Labor unions normally exert a powerful influence on the real wage of their own members. They tend to offset the negative impact of business mergers. But during the 1920s, as well as since 1970, the union influence, for a variety of reasons, declined in the United States, Britain, and Australia. The real wage of union members suffered as a consequence. However, the result percolated throughout the national labor markets, because the employers have to pay a wage that competes with the union wage. Otherwise, workers could join the unions, which the producers regard as adversaries. Therefore, when unions lose their influence, the real wage declines relative to productivity in the entire economy and generates a rise in the wage gap.

The average U.S. wage is far above the minimum. How does the minimum wage then affect the average salary? It serves as a benchmark for the salaries of production workers. Both the employer and the employee look at the minimum wage and add the skill premium to it in their wage negotiations. The greater the skill, the higher the premium.

Thus the benchmark wage sets the standard for the salaries of most nonsupervisory workers, who constitute up to 80 percent of the work force. When the benchmark declines, naturally production workers experience a drop in the purchasing power of their pay, and the wage gap rises.

In countries like China and India, the minimum wage is pathetically low. It translates into pennies per hour, and goods produced at such abysmal wages put a damper on wages in advanced economies that compete with the developing nations through freer trade. The low-wage competition from the NICs (newly industrialized countries) is perhaps the largest locomotive propelling the growing wage gap in affluent nations. Another factor is the giant increase in CEO compensation around the planet, because companies have less money left to pay workers.

Some economists contend that new technologies of the new economy tend to make labor redundant, as fewer workers are needed to perform the same chores. Computers are a case in point. A PC can double a person's productivity overnight, but we all know that salaries don't rise so fast, if at all. So computers may have also caused the rise in the wage gap, although I have my doubts about this idea, because new technology rarely, if ever, caused wage stagnation in eighteenth- and nineteenth-century America.[13] Whatever the reason, the growing wage gap around the world is the major cause of global economic imbalances. That is what we need to tackle to cure our thorny dilemmas.

DORMANT INFLATION

A puzzle that went largely unanswered during the 1990s related to the dormancy of U.S. inflation in spite of rocketing CEO compensation and a relentless fall in the rate of unemployment. The jobless rate at the end of the millennium was just 3.9 percent, the lowest in three decades. Yet the rate of inflation stood at a paltry 3.4 percent. A lower jobless rate of 3.5 percent had last occurred at the end of 1969, when the inflation rate was 6.2 percent.

The experience of the late 1960s and the early 1970s had spawned the concept of NAIRU (the non-accelerating inflation rate of unemployment), which considers inflation to be linked negatively to the rate of unemployment, at least in the short run. In other words, inflation rises when joblessness declines. But nothing like this showed up during the record economic expansion of the 1990s. The reason lies in the mounting American trade deficit.

As usual, product prices are ultimately determined by supply and demand. The reason why persistently high money growth engenders inflation is that monetary ease raises demand faster than supply, so inflation escalates. During the 1990s, U.S. imports grew much faster than U.S. exports. All those imported goods created a big jump in supply that stayed ahead of demand, even though the latter also soared because of the bubbly stock market and the mushrooming consumer debt, which was fed by gobs of foreign money. With supply outrunning demand, the inflation rate remained subdued from 1990 to 2000.

Even when oil prices began to rise after 2001, the rate of inflation remained below 3 percent. Again the mounting trade deficit, with cheap imports flooding American malls, was responsible for the price restraint. However, the price restraint, while laudable, is not a goal in itself. The goal is the rise in the real wage, or the purchasing power of your salary. While the trade deficit slowed down the rise in prices, wage growth also slowed, so that the real production wage barely budged. From 1990 all the way till 2004, the 14 years in which America borrowed almost $3.6 trillion from abroad to finance its trade shortfall, the real production wage climbed 6 percent.[14]

Such is Greenspan's proud bequest to the American working family. Finally, there came a period when the real production wage recovered somewhat, though even in 2004 it was way below its 1972 peak, and also below the 1980 level, when Reagan was elected.

10

THE LEGACY OF GREENOMICS

Greenomics has been an ever-evolving subject. With the maestro changing his colors like a chameleon, the world usually sees a new version or package when there is a changing of the guard at the White House. At times, he offers old wine in a new bottle, at others new wine in the old bottle. With Greenspan things are never boring, only destructive of the poor and the middle class.

What has Greenomics wrought for the United States since 1981, when it first got its full, and as it turned out, enduring expression? What do we have to live with until there is a new guard and a period of time to settle into a consistent and more favorable economic state? Let's begin with the American living standard that the maestro contends has been rising under his guidance. He claims that the real wage has been moving up in the United States. The real wage, if you recall, is the purchasing power of the average salary for all American workers, rich and poor, supervisors as well as nonsupervisors. His claim is correct as far as it goes, although even there the real wage gain has trailed the productivity gain, which has rarely happened in the long U.S. chronicle.

You have to go back to the 1920s, when the wage gap last rose steadily in the American economy. Otherwise real earnings have usually kept up with the rise in productivity. Even with respect to labor earnings, there is more to it than meets the eye. For most people, consumption, housing, and savings are directly related to their wages. However, a small minority earns the bulk of income from their assets, which include savings, bonds (or loans), real estate, and company shares. This way they earn interest, rent, dividends, and capital gains arising from the sale of assets at a profit. GDP includes all forms of incomes, but for the vast majority of people, wages are the principal source of living.

Wages may differ sharply among people, but they can be represented by an average. Adding up the salaries of all workers and dividing the sum by the number of employees yields the average wage. The purchasing power of this average may be called the average real wage.

However, the average wage is a highly aggregated concept and may not capture the reality about general living conditions. The few who are well endowed with property or assets generally control big companies and are in a position to command high salaries. Their sky-high wages may distort the economy-wide average enough to create a deceptive picture of society's standard of living. That is why we need to explore the average wage of the asset-poor people, i.e., those who have little or no financial assets that could assist them in getting good jobs.

THE SHRINKING PAYCHECK

The U.S. department of labor has devised a category for what it calls a production worker, who, in any occupation, operates under the supervision of someone else. That is why such an employee is also known as a non-supervisory worker. The production or nonsupervisory workers generally fit the portrait of the asset-poor. Their compensation depends purely on merit, hard work, and the state of the economy, rather than connections, luck, and inheritance.

The average real wage of production workers, called the production wage, offers by far the best measure of the general living standard in the United States not only because their salaries are independent of their mea-ger assets but also because they constitute at least 75 percent of the labor force. According to some they are as much as 80 percent of the workforce. They and their families are the vast majority, practically the entire society.

Almost everyone is a nonsupervisory worker. The supervisors are generally those in management or those who are self-employed. Thus, clerks, foremen, farm laborers, busboys, truckers, secretaries, teachers, pilots, nurses, engineers, and accountants are production workers.

By contrast, anyone who has some say in setting their schedule and the work environment is a supervisory worker. This category generally includes doctors, managers, educational administrators, team leaders, and the like. Towering atop the pyramid of all workers is a company's CEO, or chief executive officer, who, of late, has been able to set his own salary, which may be thousands of times the production wage or even the economy-wide wage. The CEO of Citigroup earned close to $290 million in 2000; that of Oracle earned over $700 million in 2002 alone.[1]

If wages and incomes related to assets rise, the GDP rises as well. However, if asset incomes soar, it is possible for GDP to climb even as the production wage sinks. Here, then, the living standard actually drops, because losers then vastly outnumber the gainers. For much of U.S. history real per-capita GDP, the average real wage, and the production worker's real wage conveyed the same message. They all went up every decade. Unfortunately, since 1973, the three have followed divergent paths. Per-capita GDP has continued its upward trend, but the average real wage has stagnated, while the production wage has sunk. *Thus, the vast majority of Americans, over three-fourths of the labor force, has seen a drop in their living standard ever since 1973.*[2]

This is a startling and unnerving statement. Yet it is true, as shown by Figure 10.1, whose data source is none other than the *Economic Report of the President*, prepared annually by the government. The figure displays the weekly real wage of production workers for selected years from 1950

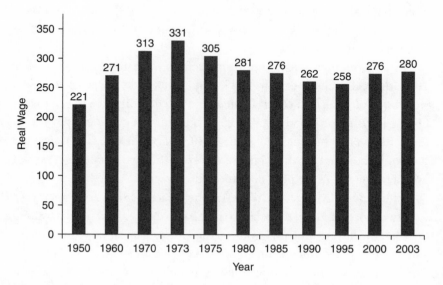

Figure 10.1. Real Production Wage in the United States, 1950–2003
Source: The Economic Report of the President, 2004 and 1990.

to 2003, including 1973, which turns out to be the peak year of the production wage.

The real wage is an inflation-adjusted quantity, which is an estimate of the purchasing power of your salary in terms of prices of some previous year, called the base year. In the figure, the base year is 1982. If prices rise, as they now do year after year, your money buys less than before, so a higher salary may not amount to much if your raise lags behind the pace of inflation. Your salary has to be adjusted for inflation in order to obtain a true gauge of your living standard.

This is done by estimating the equivalent of what your salary buys today compared to its purchasing power in the base year.

The figure shows that the real production wage went up after 1950, almost in a straight line, reached a peak of $331 per week in 1973, and then started a slow but steady decline. By 1995, it had plummeted all the way to $258, but then recovered somewhat to the level of $280 in 2003. The real-wage drop, for two reasons, is actually worse than that depicted by the figure, because first it does not include what are called fringe benefits, such as health insurance and pensions, and second it is a pre-tax figure.

The fringe benefits were steadily rising until 1973, but then started to decline, so much so that by 2004 pension and health benefits for production workers were the lowest in three decades. Ultra-regressive taxation, which has seen a steady rise in the tax bite since 1982 and 1983, makes the wage fall even more destructive of the poor and middle class than indicated by the graph.

Even though the take-home production wage began to sink after 1973, the real decline began in 1983. The events of the oil-parched 1970s were beyond American control, but after 1982, the oil price began to fall. Owing to rising productivity, the real production wage should have risen thereafter, as had been normal since 1940, but because of Greenomics, it did not; and, of course, the high payroll taxes, effective since 1984, caused even a bigger fall in the post-tax production wage.

The sinking living standard in America since 1980 is confirmed by a variety of social trends, especially rising bankruptcies and mushrooming debtors, the fastest-growing group in the United States. It is now acceptable to be in hock, to consume more than you make, simply because the expenses of two-earner families barely match the combined income of husband and wife. Even two earners cannot do today what a sole provider could do for the family in the 1950s and the 1960s.

Another indicator of the shrinking living standard is the drastic decline in the household savings rate. During the 1950s, 1960s, and 1970s Americans earned enough to save about 8 percent of their after-tax income. But since 1980, the picture has changed substantially. The U.S. savings rate is now a laughable 2 percent or less. Most households live from paycheck to paycheck. According to a survey done by the Census Bureau in 1995, almost half of all American families had less than $1,000 of financial net worth.[3] A similar survey has not been undertaken since then perhaps because of government fears about what it would reveal. The finances of a median family have not changed much since then.

What are $1,000 of net financial assets? Something like having that much money in your checking account. How secure do you feel with such a whopping amount in your bank deposit? For most families the money is shy of their expenses for one month. That is what half of America has been reduced to.

Since 1980, Americans have scrambled to maintain their lifestyle in three ways—by working longer hours, by sending more and more of their family members to work, and by borrowing. In 2003, 66 percent of able-bodied Americans worked compared to 64 percent in 1980; total debt in the economy, excluding the government debt incurred during World War II, was almost twice the level of GDP in 2003 compared to that in 1980; average working hours had jumped by 15 percent.[4] With real per-capita GDP soaring over the years, there should be no rise in debt at all. Instead, all major sections of society—the government, households, some corporations—are now indebted as never before.

American families today are caught in a "two-income trap," a phrase made popular by writers Elizabeth Warren and Amelia Tyagi in a much-discussed book published in 2003.[5] Two earners do indeed raise family income, but they also have bigger expenses. In many cities, they need two cars to commute and babysitters to care for their toddlers; they face higher auto insurance and larger payroll taxes from two incomes. Many such families fall into bankruptcy if one paycheck disappears, as has happened to some of them since the recession of 2001. In spite of two earners, millions of Americans have very little financial net worth.

Where did all the growth go? Much of it to CEOs. The chief executive officers have done exceptionally well, in times good or bad. If America goes into a recession, their incomes grow; when America booms, their wages grow even faster. The end result is what you see in the bar chart of

Figure 10.2, which displays CEO compensation as a multiple of the production wage.

American CEOs, with all their perks, have always been the envy of the world. As early as 1960 they were paid 41 times the average production wage, and their pay went up as the economy boomed during the 1960s. Then came the inflation and stagnation of the 1970s when the economy repeatedly suffered recessions; CEO compensation slowly declined and by 1980 was down to the multiples last seen in 1960. Thus, until 1980 CEO salaries behaved much like the rest of the economy. They fell and rose together.

Ever since 1980, during the Greenspan era, the CEO wage has generally moved up. The state of the economy seems to have little bearing on the CEO's reward, which jumped in 1990, a recession year, and then kept climbing at a dizzying pace during the 1990s. The Nasdaq stock index sank during 2000, but the CEO ended the year with a grin, his multiple over the production wage, 525, being the highest in history.

The CEOs, however, are not the only gainers since 1980. Supervisory workers in general have enjoyed large gains, mostly because of their higher education. Greenomics has so transformed the macroeconomy

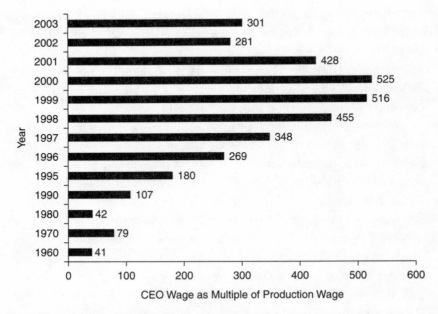

Figure 10.2. The CEO Wage as a Multiple of Production Wage: 1960–2003

Source: Business Week, Annual Pay Issues, Compiled by United for Fair Economy (Courtesy of UFE.com).

that people with high skills have benefited at the expense of those with lower levels of education and skills. The end result is a horrendous rise in income and wealth inequality.

As MIT economist Lester Thurow writes: "In the decade of the 1980s, all the gains in male earnings went to the top 20 percent of the workforce and an amazing 64 percent accrued to the top 1 percent. If incomes rather than earnings are examined, the top 1 percent gets even more—90 percent of total income gains."[6] However, by the end of the 1990s, female earnings were just as skewed as male incomes.

INEQUALITY AND WEALTH CONCENTRATION

Another gift of Greenomics to America is arguably the worst income and wealth disparity at least since 1929. Until Enron became a household name in early 2002, most Americans were unsure, or cared little, about the extent of income and wealth inequality in the United States. Yes, CEOs were raking in millions every year, but they were also making others richer through the biggest bull market in history. All that changed when the market crashed at the turn of the millennium, and millions of people lost trillions of dollars in paper profits that they thought were going to provide a cushy nest egg upon retirement. Some were wiped out. A search was on for the culprits, real and imaginary, who had deceived the public into parking its precious savings in a casino called the Nasdaq market.

Just when the share markets seemed to recover, Enron's chief executive, Ken Lay, mired in an accounting scandal, stunned the world by filing for his company's bankruptcy in January 2002. This was followed by a wave of scandals by the likes of WorldCom, Global Crossing, and Tyco International, among others. The giant salaries and shenanigans of the CEOs, at once bustling and now insolvent companies, then captured headlines.

Americans learned that Ken Lay had been paid over $300 million in the last four years; Bernard Ebbers, the WorldCom chief, made only $35 million in 2002, but he had borrowed $408 million from his own company in the past. Some others, not belonging to defunct companies, had done even better than the Enron chief. Oracle's Lawrence Ellison earned $706 million in 2002 in just one year, followed by Michael Dell, who ended up with only $201 million; Citigroup's Sanford Weill had made almost $1 billion over the past decade.[7]

Such eye-popping numbers finally made a believer out of Americans; yes, the nation's income and wealth concentration had indeed grown out of hand. As Professor Paul Krugman put it:

> The messy divorce proceedings of Jack Welch, the legendary former C.E.O. of General Electric, have had one unintended benefit: they have given us a peek at the perks of the corporate elite, which are normally hidden from public view. . . . In monetary terms, however, the perks must have meant little to Welch. In 2000, his last full year running G.E., Welch was paid $123 million, mainly in stock and stock options. . . . *For at least the past 15 years it has been hard to deny the evidence for growing inequality in the United States.*[8] (My italics)

Similarly, Debra Watson details the horrendous jump in income disparity in America in the Greenspan era that started in 1981:

> By the year 2000 the annual income of the top fifth of U.S. families had risen to 10 times the income of families in the bottom fifth, up 30 percent from 1980.
>
> Recent Census Bureau reports . . . show that last year . . . income inequality was at a post–World War II high. Last year nearly half the total income—49.7 percent—went to the top 20 percent of households and just 3.6 percent to the bottom 20 percent. *The gap in household income and in individual earnings is far greater today than at any time since the late 1960s.*[9] (My italics)

It is hard to imagine the bottom 20 percent of the populace, some 56 million people, subsisting on a mere 3.6 percent of national income. This is one of the worst levels of income inequality in the long U.S. chronicle, nearly as bad as it was in 1929, when the corresponding figure was 3.2 percent.

Does Inequality Matter?

The question that concerns a macroeconomist is: Does inequality matter? First let's see what Professor Krugman tells us about the current fad. "The concerted effort to deny that inequality is increasing is itself a symptom of the growing influence of our emerging plutocracy. So is the fierce defense of the backup position, that inequality doesn't matter—or maybe even that, to use Martha Stewart's signature phrase, it's a good thing."[10]

The study of the link between inequality and economic growth goes back at least to Keynes, who suggested that rising income inequality was one of the main causes behind the Great Depression. His argument was that income concentration in a few hands tends to lower consumer demand and raise the level of savings. High savings, when unmatched by investment, lower real GDP as well as employment. Keynes's remedy was a progressive income tax, which exempts the poor from such taxation, and imposes high levies on the affluent to reduce the level of savings.

Later, some economists turned the Keynesian logic around and offered a contrary opinion. They argued that rising inequality is beneficial to the country, simply because it generates high savings, which can be turned into higher business investment and capital stock to stimulate output growth. In the end, this raises everyone's living standard, including that of the poor. This came to be known as the growth argument for inequality, which was reinforced by the supply-side part of Greenomics that the income tax reduction promotes GDP gains. Some other economists called it the equity–efficiency tradeoff, meaning that there is a tradeoff between efficiency and equality, or that higher growth requires greater inequality.

However, the equity–efficiency tradeoff is false. There is no positive effect of inequality on economic growth. All the fastest-growing economies since World War II—Japan, the Asian Tigers, even China—have sharply lower levels of inequality than the United States, Canada, and Australia, the trio with the highest inequality in the world.

Let's re-examine our simple formula for GDP developed in chapter 8:

GDP = 200% of Net Wages of Low-Income Families

From this formula, it can be easily shown that

GDP Growth = Growth of Net Wages of Low-Income Families

where net wages equal wage income net of taxes.[11] The only restraint on this formula is that the real wage growth does not exceed productivity growth, because then employers have to lay off workers and output declines. But this is a condition that, to my knowledge, has been rarely, if ever, violated in the world. In fact, the world's problem, at least since the 1980s, is that the real wage trails productivity gains.

The simple growth formula suggests that economic growth is positively related to the growth of net wage income of the low-income groups in any economy. This means that (i) taxes should be low on the poor and the middle class, an idea that has been explained already, and (ii) the real wage should rise to the upper limit of productivity growth. If the real wage keeps up with productivity, then profits also grow proportionately to productivity, but no faster. Income and wealth disparities thus remain subdued.

A rise in inequality, by contrast, trims net wage growth and thus economic growth and prosperity. No wonder the growth record of the U.S. economy since 1970 pales before the record of the 1950s and the 1960s, and, in fact, falls short of the average for the entire U.S. history.

Reliable growth data go back to the 1870s and pin average growth for the entire recorded period at 3.8 percent, which clearly exceeds the average of 3.1 percent prevailing between 1970 and 2004. The difference of 0.7 percent appears to be trivial, but if it occurs year after year it adds up, so much so that by now the living standard of the production worker, or as much as 80 percent of Americans, has declined over the past three decades. And Greenspan has covertly or overtly shaped economic policy for at least two of the three decades of this decline. Congressmen and presidents have come and gone, but he remains entrenched in the seat of power, swaying not just monetary policy but also tax legislation. His imprint on the U.S. economy dwarfs any other influence.

In 1980 real GDP per person was $21,521, and had risen to over $33,000 by 2004. With so much output gain, there should be few, if any, economic problems today. Yet household debt is at an all-time high, and bankruptcies are breaking new records. Why? This is because almost all of the growth gain accrued to the top 20 percent of earners, mainly to the CEOs and business bigwigs. The other 80 percent saw practically no benefit of economic growth, while their tax burden climbed.

In 1980, 52 percent of American families constituted the middle class, as defined by households with incomes ranging from $25,000 to $75,000. After adjusting for inflation, the middle class had shrunk to just 45 percent of families in 2003.[12] The retirees were among the greatest victims of Greenspan's scramble to prevent the stock market crash, as the federal funds rate sank to just 1 percent in 2002, the lowest in 45 years. The interest income of the elderly then took a huge tumble, while CEOs continued to wallow in affluence.

THE RATE OF POVERTY

When inequality surges, poverty usually swells. The poverty rate for individuals, according to the Census Bureau, was 12.5 percent in 2003, not far from the rate of 13 percent in 1980. However, the absolute number of the poor has jumped.

The economy has been in such a mess that even the $3.6 trillion foreign capital inflow since 1990 could not do much for the nation's destitute. The rise in poverty derives mainly from the steep fall in the real minimum wage since 1980. How many individuals suffered from Greenspan-inspired policies in 2003 and lived below the poverty line?— 36 million, compared to 29 million in 1980! In 2003, the Census Bureau defined the poverty line for an individual by an income of $9,573 and for a family of four by an income of $18,660.[13]

Economic deterioration has accelerated since the start of the new millennium. Median family income sank by $1,500 in just three years from 2000 through 2003, or by 3.4 percent, while worker productivity soared 12 percent. Of course, profits and CEO salaries remained high.[14] The picture is also ugly on the debt side. The economy's propensity for debt has jumped further. It used to take less than $2 of new debt to produce $1 of GDP. Since 2001, it has taken over $3 to do the same.[15] On top of it all, workers are losing health insurance and pension benefits left and right.

REGRESSIVE TAXATION IN OTHER COUNTRIES

In view of its persistent trade deficit, the United States may not export much to the world, but it certainly exports unseemly ideas in abundance. The virus of Greenomics and the ultra-regressive tax structure that evolved in America after 1981 gradually infected other G-7 countries as well. Slowly but surely the tax burden switched from the rich to lower income groups, as Social Security fees soared, and income and corporate tax rates tumbled. Simultaneously, a value-added tax (VAT) on most purchases by consumers accentuated the public misery.

Currently the VAT ranges from a low of 5 percent in Japan, to 10 percent in Australia, 17 percent in the UK, 20 percent in France and Italy, and as high as 25 percent in Sweden. The United States has no VAT, but the states impose sales taxes averaging 7 percent. Here's what economist Andreas Haufler writes in his *Taxation in a Global Economy*, published by Cambridge University Press in 2001.

> Since the 1980s, *following the lead of the United States* and the United Kingdom, most EU member states have introduced significant changes to their schemes of personal and corporate income taxation. . . .
>
> Top personal rates of taxation were reduced in 1990s, but the changes remain modest for most countries. . . .
>
> Ten out of the fifteen EU member states now apply personal tax rates on interest income that are well below the top marginal tax rates applicable for wage income. . . .
>
> The average of statutory corporate tax rates in the EU fell by more than 13 points since the mid-1980s.[16] (My italics)

While income taxes sank for wealthy individuals and corporations in Europe, the payroll taxes, already high, rose further. Table 10.1 captures the direction of what has happened to payroll tax rates in G-7 nations and Sweden from 1980 to 1995. They have risen in all countries, and the picture has changed little since 1995. The tax structure also became ultra-regressive in other European countries as well as Australia. The economic consequences were predictable. See what a United Nations survey has written:

> Among many of the developed market economies, increased earnings inequality is one of the major factors responsible for the deterioration in the distribution of income among households. Since the early 1980s,

Table 10.1. Payroll Tax Rates for All Social Security Programs in Selected Countries: 1980–1995

Countries	1980	1985	1990	1995
United States	16.81	18.9	19.72	21.00
Canada	8.44	9.24	8.88	14.10
France	48.45	51.33	53.03	52.58
Germany*	34	34.3	36.18	34.54
Italy	55.02	55.91	53.11	56.96
Japan	20.57	25.50	23.40	26.62
Sweden	32.43	31.56	34.11	32.31
UK	20.45	19.45	19.45	22.20

* After 1990, the figures are for unified Germany.

Source: Statistical Abstract of the United States, 1981 and 2004, U.S. Department of Commerce, Washington, D.C. various issues.

profits have tended to grow faster than wages. The gap between the
average earnings of the educated and the non-educated has grown.
The phenomenon is discernible in Australia, Canada, France, the
Netherlands, Sweden, the United Kingdom of Great Britain and
Northern Ireland and the United States.[17] (My italics)

Regressive taxation could not but create the same results as in the
United States—slow growth and societal agony. However, the agony in the
G-7 nations of Canada, Europe, and Japan has been felt not in plunging
wage rates but in the form of mounting joblessness. For over a decade,
especially after 1990, voodoo economists and politicians in Europe
parroted the same line as their U.S. counterparts, namely, taxes should be
lowered for wealthy individuals to stimulate the economy. Much like the
United States, the rest of the G-7 group also shifted to borrow-and-spend
policies with the same inevitable consequence.

The countries, more properly their poor and middle class, are
saddled with huge debt to their rich denizens. In some cases the interest
burden is crippling the people; in others the tax toll is so high that nearly
half of the GDP goes into taxes. The rich collect the interest, while others
pay the levies. The same forces that have destroyed the American dream
are now demolishing the dreams in Canada, Britain, France, Italy,
Germany, and Japan. Greenomics has spread its vast tentacles to many
nations. The faster it is laid to rest, the better for us all.

Because of globalization the giant corporations of most rich countries
have been exporting factories and jobs to low-wage areas. As a result manufacturing employment has dropped in G-7 nations, although in the
United States the fall has been the steepest. Unlike America, the other
advanced economies do not have large and persistent trade deficits. That
is why globalization has not been as destructive for them. The damage has
been limited to the rate of unemployment rather than to the manufacturing base and real wages.

Manufacturing employment was 32 percent of employed workers in
Germany in 1990, only 24 percent in 2001. In the United Kingdom the
corresponding fall was from 22 percent to 17 percent over the same period.
The trend was the same in Canada, where the manufacturing employment
share tumbled from an already low 16 percent in 1990 to 15 percent in
2001. The story is the same in all G-7 countries, as well as the rest of Europe
and Australia.

Those who were laid off from manufactured goods industries in America
reluctantly accepted lower wages and went to work in services. This way

unemployment remained low in the United States. In other nations, however, this adjustment process broke down. They had earlier developed what is usually called a welfare state, which provides generous benefits to the unemployed, along with aid for healthcare and education. Official generosity seems to have hindered the migration of workers from industries to services. As a result their unemployment rate began to rise. Real wages did not fall—at most they stagnated—but the jobless rate began a slow but steady rise.

Wages and unemployment are two sides of the same coin. They are both linked to economic growth and the degree of manufacturing, and when the latter declines, something has got to give. In America, where regressive taxation along with low-wage competition from abroad did the worst damage, the result was the real wage blight over three decades, ever since 1973. In Europe and Canada, it was the scourge of unemployment. Japan did not suffer as much from any one of them, but then Japan does not follow free trade, either, and dutifully intervenes in foreign exchange markets to protect its industries from foreign competition. (This issue will be reexamined in the next chapter.)

However, the pervasive welfare state in Europe is not as responsible for the rise in unemployment as the current structure of regressive taxation. The welfare state, after all, is nothing new; it was established soon after World War II. But in the 1950s and the 1960s, the tax structure in Europe as well as the United States was progressive. The state sales tax in America was generally below 3 percent, whereas Germany had no VAT until 1968; Sweden introduced the VAT in 1969, the United Kingdom and Italy in 1973, Canada in 1991, and Australia in 2000. Payroll taxes were also lower in the 1950s and the 1960s, whereas the income tax rates on rich individuals and corporations tended to be high.

As Professor Junko Kato of the University of Tokyo writes: "Progressive income taxation and a large social security program were an indisputable part of the welfare state in the 1950s and 1960s."[18] But not any more. Now, and since the early 1980s, it is the regressive tax system that finances social welfare in Europe, Canada, and Australia, while in the United States a large portion of the welfare state was dismantled in 1996, when Congress passed a law "to end welfare as we know it," a slogan made popular by Clinton during the 1992 election campaign.

During the 1950s economic growth was extremely strong in Europe. This was not surprising because France, Italy, Germany, and the United Kingdom were devastated by the world war and started out with a low output base. Italy and Germany suffered from high joblessness, but by

1960, all four nations were at full employment. Thus, economic policy including progressive taxation and the welfare state did not matter much for these nations during the 1950s. But by the 1960s, the war-ravaged economies had come of age, and then their welfare states could have derailed their prosperity and caused unemployment, but did not. The reason was progressive taxation.

Once their tax system became regressive, their growth rates fell and unemployment rates went up. This much is clear from Table 10.2, in which the jobless rates are presented in parentheses. Other G-7 nations have had stronger welfare states than the United States. For instance, they offered free health insurance, which America did not. Yet their jobless rates generally paled before the U.S. rate in the 1960s and the 1970s.

Because of geographical proximity, Canadian growth and unemployment rates closely matched the U.S. experience. As the tax structure turned regressive, growth rates fell in all G-7 nations from the 1970s on. This tended to lower labor demand relative to labor supply. As a result, the labor markets had to adjust. In the United States this adjustment took the form of tumbling real wages, especially for production workers, whereas in other G-7 nations, it took the form of soaring unemployment.

Take Germany, for instance. Its growth averaged 4.5 percent per year in the 1960s, and, in spite of a strong welfare state, its jobless rate was a miniscule 0.6 percent. In the 1970s, German growth fell sharply, and although the unemployment rate jumped, it still remained low. But as the tax structure became increasingly regressive, Germany's growth plummeted and joblessness soared. And what happened in Germany was repeated verbatim in France and Italy as well.

The United Kingdom experience diverges markedly from that of the European continent. Britain has not enjoyed robust growth since World War II, but its unemployment rate was generally below that of the United States, at least from the 1950s to the 1970s. Exceptions occurred in the 1980s and the 1990s, when the country suffered from persistent and horrendous unemployment.

At one point, in 1982, one in eight people was out of work, which was even worse than British joblessness during the Great Depression.

Britain's anemic economic performance resulted from a very different factor—socialistic economic policies. The country did not have big welfare expenditures, nor stifling payroll taxes, but it nationalized its major industries soon after the war. Unlike its neighbors, France, Germany, and Italy, the other nations crippled by the war, Britain

Table 10.2. Annual Average GDP Growth and Unemployment Rates* in G-7
Countries: 1961–2003

Countries	1961–1970	1971–1980	1981–1990	1991–2000	2000–2003
United States	5 (4.7)	2.8 (6.2)	2.7 (7.3)	2.8 (4.6)	2.8 (5.1)
Canada	5 (4.6)	4.5 (6.7)	2.9 (9.0)	2.4 (8.1)	3.1 (6.6)
Japan	11.7 (1.3)	4.7 (1.7)	3.8 (2.5)	1.3 (2.9)	1.4 (5.1)
France	5.7 (1.6)	3.8 (3.9)	2.3 (9.3)	1.7 (9.0)	2 (9.0)
Germany	4.5 (0.6)	2.6 (2.1)	1.8 (5.2)	1.8 (6.8)	1 (9.6)
Italy	5.7 (3.1)	3.1 (3.7)	2.4 (5.6)	1.3 (7.7)	1.4 (9.6)
UK	2.9 (2.7)	1.9 (4.6)	2.4 (10.1)	2.0 (7.5)	2.2 (5.2)

* The unemployment rates are in parentheses.

Source: The Economic Report of the President, 1988, 2000, and 2004.

nationalized major industries—telephone, electricity, steel, gas, railways, coal, airplanes.

With so many industries under state control and management, labor unions flourished; they came to exercise virtual monopoly power over industries, and monopoly in any form is a recipe for inefficiency and stagnation. As a result, British manufacturing could not compete with the relatively free enterprise of its neighbors. Britain came to be known as "the sick man of Europe," with mediocre economic growth and productivity.

A major change occurred in the United Kingdom in 1979, when Margaret Thatcher was elected the prime minister. She began to undo the socialist flair of the industry, and privatized one enterprise after another. This restructuring, along with the steep recession in the United States induced by Greenomics in the early 1980s, caused massive unemployment in Britain. However, slowly, British industry moved out of the dark shadows of nationalization, and the country's economic performance gradually improved. Now British unemployment pales before that of the continental countries. So with Britain, the tax structure was not as stifling as its industrial policies.

In sum, the welfare state is not primarily responsible for the high rates of unemployment prevailing in Germany, France, and Italy today. It is their regressive taxation that is the chief culprit. Sweden and Denmark have even larger welfare states, with about a third of their GDP going into social transfers to support the indigent, yet their unemployment rates are no higher than 5 percent, compared to over 9 percent in their larger neighbors.

Let's now come to Japan, where the tax system became somewhat regressive in the 1990s. The end result was anemic growth and rising unemployment, although the stock market crash in the early 1990s accentuated the economic ills. Greenspan's main influence on Japan came in the form of financial deregulation that enables ordinary Japanese, not just the country, to pour funds into the United States in search of higher returns. Japan now invests heavily in American assets to prop up its own industrial machine.

In short, Greenspan's legacy to the United States as well as the world is regressive taxation and the stock market crash, both of which are responsible for slow growth and rising joblessness. Almost all governments are up to their neck in debt, which has become crucial to sustain their economies. Greenspan's forte is to create debt at the consumer, government, and corporate levels to solve economic problems. Rarely has he opted for genuine economic reform to raise the living standard of all.

It should not be surprising that Greenspan is no longer revered the way he was prior to the global stock market crash. See how the *Financial Times* greeted the maestro with an irreverent headline on September 14, 2002: "Mr. Greenspan's Tarnished Legacy." Later, Steven Pearlstein of *The Washington Post* gave the main reason for the media ire: "Most of the criticism of the Fed's bubble policies has come from Wall Street, where the vaporization of $7 trillion in market value has been keenly felt."[19] Alan Abelson of *Barron's* wrote in the same vein: "Pure and simple, save for the Fed, the stock market bubble could have never reached the monstrous dimensions it did, and its bursting would never have caused such a widespread and profound misery as it has."[20]

In a House hearing on July 15, 2003, Vermont's Representative Bernie Sanders best summed up Greenspan's legacy to America. Addressing the maestro, he said:

> You talk about an improving economy while we have lost 3 million private sector jobs in the last two years, long-term unemployment has more than tripled, unemployment is higher than it's been since 1994. We have a $4 trillion national debt, 1.4 million Americans have lost their health insurance, millions of seniors can't afford prescription drugs, middle-class families can't send their kids to college because they don't have the money to do that, bankruptcy cases have increased by a record-breaking 23 percent, business investment is at its lowest level in more than 50 years, CEOs make more than 500 times of what their workers make, the middle class is shrinking, we have the greatest gap between the rich and the poor of any industrialized nation, and this is an economy that is improving. I'd hate to see what would happen if our economy was sinking.[21]

Greenspan responded gamely: "we are doing an extraordinary job over the years, and people flock to the United States. Our immigration rates are very high, and why? Because they think this is a wonderful country to come [to]." Rep. Sanders replied: "That is an incredible answer." Indeed it is. Even if the real production wage declined another 25 percent, the United States would still attract hordes of immigrants from Mexico, Latin America, Asia, and Africa. But it is doubtful that America will lure people from Canada and Western Europe, the areas that have yet to see a major drop in real wages and benefits. Being a haven for immigration is no sure sign of a rising living standard.

The moral of this story is: You can fool all markets some of the time, or some markets all of the time, but you cannot fool all markets all the time.

11

ECONOMIC REFORM

A clichéd Chinese maxim, "may you live in interesting times," best describes the economy of the United States of America today. In 2004, per-capita U.S. output was the highest in history; so was the number of Americans without health insurance. Worker productivity breaks records every year; so does consumer debt. Homeownership is at all-time high; so are personal bankruptcies. What explains such monumental absurdities? In one word—Greenomics. Who is responsible for this ugly state of affairs? In one word—Greenspan. Presidents and lawmakers come and go, but the maestro seemingly remains in power forever, and sways not only monetary policy but also fiscal legislation. Does anyone else have this double-edged clout? No.

As we have explored in great depth, Alan Greenspan first came to prominence in 1974, when a Republican president and a Democratic Congress appointed him the CEA chairman. The appointment turned out to be ominous for working families, because the real production wage crested and the number of destitute Americans bottomed the year before. 1974 thus established a landmark for the U.S. economy and society, as it set the tone for things to come. It was a Nixon–Greenspan year, with Nixon leaving and Greenspan coming on board. Corruption departed, but expediency bordering on chicanery arrived.

Figure 11.1 reveals the two seemingly contradictory trends in the U.S. economy. Real per-capita GDP rises almost in a straight line between 1965 and 2003, but the number of poverty-stricken Americans first falls until 1973, to 23 million, and then peaks in 1993, at 39 million. Of course, poverty fell from 1996 to 2000 during the era of the foreign money boom. But even after borrowing close to $3.6 trillion from abroad since 1990, the poor Americans still numbered 36 million in 2003, not far from the 1993 peak.

The economic expansion since 2001 was often called the jobless recovery, but Bob Herbert of *The New York Times* described it better: "This alleged economic upturn is not just a jobless recovery, it's a job-loss recovery. The hemorrhaging of jobs in the aftermath of the recent 'mild' recession is like nothing the U.S. has seen in more than half a century. Millions continue to look desperately for work, and millions more have given up in despair," because the private sector laid off more than a million workers after output started to rise.[1] Let's take a bird's eye view of the U.S. economy today:

1. The share of wages in GDP is the lowest in 38 years.
2. The share of after-tax corporate profits is the highest since 1947.
3. Over 36 million Americans subsist below the poverty line; 45 million have no health insurance.
4. Job creation is extremely sluggish, so much so that for the first time since the 1930s a president, George Bush, saw virtually zero employment growth in his entire term—from 2001 to 2004.
5. Manufacturing employs just 11 percent of the workforce, something close to what the economy did prior to the Civil War.
6. The country borrows over $600 billion, or 6 percent of its GDP, from the rest of the world to finance its trade deficit.
7. The federal budget deficit lingers around $400 billion even after including the Social Security surplus.
8. The Social Security Trust Fund, having collected over $1.5 trillion in excess taxes from working families over two decades, is all but empty.
9. The richest 1 percent of Americans own close to 40 percent of wealth, more than the bottom 90 percent of people, who mostly live from paycheck to paycheck.
10. The stock indexes have crashed since 2000 and are still below their 2000 peaks.

This is the top-ten list of thorns needling America today. If nothing is done to banish Greenomics, the thorns will only grow sharper in the future. The country desperately needs an antidote to revive the comatose economy. It faces bleak and bleaker prospects without genuine economic reforms, which are offered in the ensuing pages.

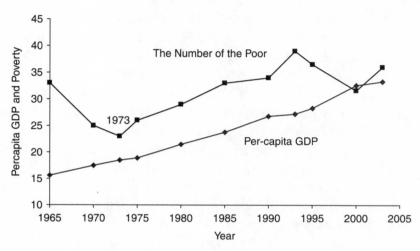

Figure 11.1. Real Per-capita GDP (in thousands in terms of 1996 prices) and Poor Americans: 1965–2003

Source: *The Economic Report of the President*, 2004 and 1990, Council of Economic Advisers, Washington, D.C.; *Statistical Abstract of the United States*, various issues, U.S. Department of Commerce, Washington, D.C.

MY QUALIFICATIONS

A tree is known by the sweetness of its fruit; likewise, an economist and his theories are known by the accuracy of their forecasts. I have been making predictions since 1978, on a wide variety of subjects. I have done this in my books and newspaper interviews. Between 1978 and 1998, I made about 33 predictions, of which, if I may say so at the risk of sounding less than humble, two or three have been wrong. They are all listed on my website—www.ravibatra.com—and in my 1999 book, *The Crash of the Millennium*, which made some new forecasts.

Two of my most memorable prophecies were made in the late 1970s. In 1978, I predicted that Soviet communism would collapse, at the earliest, around 1990.[2] The Berlin Wall fell on November 9, 1989, which is pretty close to 1990, and Soviet communism is no more. The same year I also declared that the Shah of Iran would be overthrown and replaced by a group of priests in 1979, which would be followed by an Iran–Iraq war lasting from 1980 to 1987. You can confirm that both these events came to pass.

Another forecast that you might find interesting in today's political milieu is what I wrote in 1979 in *Muslim Civilization and the Crisis in*

Iran: "It is now the turn of India and Islam to cause an upheaval in the Western world and Russia. It is the orient that is now poised to determine the future of the occident."[3] Stated another way, I predicted that the oil and internal turmoil of some Muslim nations, along with India's ideas, would cause an upheaval in the Soviet Union and capitalism. And my time frame for all these predictions made during the late 1970s was 1990 to 2010. The Islamic world, by way of the Soviet–Afghanistan conflict, has already caused the downfall of communism and continues to churn through Russia in the guise of Chechen rebels. On the other side, the 9/11 massacre in New York and Washington, D.C., in 2001 affirms how Islamic nationalism spearheaded by radical Islam is now convulsing the United States and the Western world.

Let me present some of the forecasts I made in *The Crash of the Millennium* that appeared in September 1999, because they deal with economic events still fresh in your memory and are germane to the global markets today.

> 1. The American market mania comes along once in a thousand years, and it will peak by the end of 1999. . . .
> The bubble is likely to explode all of a sudden, at the height of business and consumer optimism. . . . *Alan Greenspan* along with the rest of the world will react again by *lowering interest rates*, but the positive effects will be brief and ineffectual.[4] (My italics)

This is almost exactly what happened. The Dow peaked on January 14, 2000 at 11,723, 14 days after the predicted date. Later, Greenspan along with other central bankers worldwide feverishly lowered short-term interest rates to stem the market disaster, but to no avail.

> 2. Once the Dow Jones Index begins to crash, the so-called hedge funds will collapse quickly. . . . If we are lucky enough to escape financial disaster in the fall, we could get it sometime in the next six months.[5]

Isn't this what happened? Fall begins in the month of September. Adding six months to fall 1999 then takes us to March 2000, and that is exactly when the Nasdaq Composite index, along with the Dow, started to crash.

> 3. When the Dow plunges, the dollar will fall almost immediately. . . .
> Where would the foreign money go? Some of it would go back home; some into the euro. . . .[6]

This scenario has also materialized since 2000 and the dollar has fallen sharply relative to the euro, which hovered around $1.35 at the end of 2004 compared to less than a dollar in 2000.

> 4. Trigger-happy American companies will immediately resort to layoffs. . . . It will not take long before the stock market crash induces massive unemployment. . . .
> The employment depression is likely to endure. . . . the nation will have to endure years of growing poverty. . . . The US bubble . . . rupture could spark something that has never plagued the nation before—*falling real wages as well as employment.*[7] (My italics)

Much of this forecast has come true, although, thank goodness, we don't have massive unemployment. Still, employment and real wages have fallen together and poverty has been growing since 2000. There is no employment depression, only employment recession, but if Greenomics remains in force, depression could be next.

> 5. Just as in the 1970s . . . we are likely to see huge budget deficits, not surpluses over the coming years. . . . the budget deficit will rise to *dizzying heights.*[8] (My italics)

I made this forecast in response to all those future budget surpluses that economists from left and right were predicting in 1999. Soon after President Bush took over, America's fiscal health deteriorated and the budget deficit made a resounding comeback. In fact, the $413 billion deficit in 2004 turned out to be the highest in U.S. history, even after including the Social Security surplus. Furthermore, federal deficits are now expected as far as the eye can see.

Did I make any incorrect forecast in 1999? In terms of direction, not a single one has turned out to be wrong, although in terms of intensity, some have. I have already noted one of the errors, namely, we have had an employment recession, not depression. Similarly, I suggested that the dollar would collapse and lead to inflation. The dollar has indeed fallen sharply but not collapsed, while inflation, though picking up, remains subdued.

In my defense, let me note that these forecasts were meant for the entire decade of the 2000s, and I am afraid that if nothing is done in time to purge Greenomics, they could still come true. I have indeed made some errors, but who has not, and I would be happy to compare my record with Greenspan's or with that of any other economist.

REFORMING SOCIAL SECURITY

Social Security, you may recall, started out as a pay-as-you-go system and shifted to a tax-in-advance program in 1984 to create a surplus in its Trust Fund. The shift was wrong-headed for two reasons. First, it was subject to fraud, as the Social Security surplus was, and is, diverted to meet the operating expenses of the federal government. Second, it was, and is, bad economics, because the tax-in-advance system tends to lower GDP growth. Stated another way, even if the lawmakers had fulfilled their promise of separating the Trust Fund's finances from the federal budget and created a genuine surplus, their action would have hurt the country further. This is because an overall surplus in government tends to reduce aggregate demand.

In order to isolate the effect of the Social Security surplus on demand, recall the demand formula from chapter 7 that, in a simple economy with no deficits,

$$\text{Demand} = \text{Wages} + \text{Investment}$$

Now suppose payroll taxes are imposed in excess of Social Security benefits to create an overall government surplus. Then the formula becomes

$$\text{Demand} = \text{Wages} + \text{Benefits} - \text{Payroll Taxes} + \text{Investment}$$

because benefits tend to raise demand, whereas the tax tends to lower it. Since payroll taxes minus benefits equal the Trust Fund surplus,

$$\text{Demand} = \text{Wages} - \text{Social Security Surplus} + \text{Investment}$$

Clearly, the Social Security surplus affects demand negatively. As demand and demand growth decline, GDP and GDP growth will decline as well. So even the idea underlying the Social Security surplus is questionable. The nation would be better off with the old pay-as-you-go system, which thus offers two advantages over the current system. First, it will raise GDP growth; second, with the annual surplus gone, it won't be vulnerable to Congressional fraud.

The Trust Fund currently accumulates about $170 billion in surplus per year. Suppose the first $10,000 of a worker's wages are exempted from the combined payroll tax, which is currently 12.4 percent. The revenue loss per worker would then be $1,240. About 138 million people were employed in 2004, so the total revenue loss would be about $171 billion, i.e. 1,240 times 138 million. This figure is very close to the annual surplus. So exempting the first $10,000 of wages would take us back to the old pay-as-you-go system.

As more people retire and the system's revenue needs to increase in the future, we could simply raise the taxable wage base, which was capped at $87,900 in 2004. Suppose the wage base is increased by 20 percent over and above that provided by the law now in force. Then the wage ceiling in 2004, for example, would be close to $105,000, raising another $30 billion in payroll tax receipts, given that about 10 percent of workers earn in excess of $100,000 a year. This way the ceiling cap could be raised every year and, if necessary, abolished altogether.

The baby boomers are expected to retire in large numbers after 2010, but there is no need to worry about that now. No matter how bad *The Coming Generational Storm,* the title of a highly informative book by Laurence Kotlikoff and Scott Burns, there is no point in maintaining the current level of payroll taxes.[9] Why pay higher taxes for this purpose when they are being squandered anyway? Let's focus on raising the GDP growth to 4 percent or higher, the way it was in the 1950s and the 1960s, and the rest of the problems will become more tractable. Payroll taxes should be raised when the solvency of the Social Security system is really in jeopardy, not in advance.

PRIVATIZING SOCIAL SECURITY

In early 2005, some proposals appeared to privatize Social Security. The idea was that workers should be allowed to set aside about 4.2 percent or one-third of their combined payroll tax rate of 12.4 percent into individual accounts, which could then be invested in the stock market and possibly earn a higher return, enabling the government to cut future benefits and thus ensure the solvency of the Social Security program. George Bush offered this proposal during the election campaign of 2000, but failed to pursue it after he was sworn into office. In the 2004 campaign he raised the issue again and seemed to be serious about it this time. Another version of privatization would have the government invest a part of payroll receipts in the stock market, something that Greenspan has opposed, and rightly so, because it won't increase the nation's savings, which is ultimately what a household, and a country, have to do to meet their retirement needs adequately.

The biggest drawback of the privatization plan is that it is the pet project of Wall Street, which means that it will hurt working families. "Wall Street," wrote financial writer James Grant in 2001, "though not always corrupt, is almost always bullish."[10] Can you think of any program offered by big business in the last three decades that helped the American worker? I can't think of any, whereas I can name many of Wall Street's pets that ended up tormenting the poor and the middle class, while adding trillions to the federal debt. The privatization proposal could add trillions more, because the government would have to borrow billions of dollars every year to finance the transfer of payroll receipts to private accounts. The Social Security law of 1983, the income tax cuts of 1981 and 1986, and NAFTA are some of the boondoggles that raised CEO incomes while slashing the after-tax real wage of production workers. Once a law is passed, it is practically impossible to repeal it even when it is clear that it devastates working families.

Privatizing Social Security will undo the humanitarian basis of the program. The poor and women will especially suffer from it. Currently, those with lower wages get disproportionately higher benefits upon retirement. The idea is that retirement income should at least provide subsistence or the necessities of life. Privatization in exchange for sharp cuts in guaranteed benefits would do away with the redistributive aspect of the system and thus contradict the spirit underlying the very meaning of Social Security, which is to provide a minimum income shelter to the elderly regardless of their contributions.

At times, share markets turn negative, as they have since 2000, and it is not sensible to gamble with one's pension plan. If someone happened to pick lousy stocks, their holdings could be completely wiped out. Then what will they do in their old age? In the end, stocks offer higher returns than government or corporate bonds because they are risky, and it's not prudent to take undue risk with one's retirement. Social Security has been one of the most popular government programs, and it is better not to tinker with it. If you want to reform it, then the best thing that can be done is to restore its cash holdings that have been frittered away since the mid-1980s. In fact, as long as the government keeps devouring the Trust Fund's surplus, the shrill chorus of reforming the system will sound hollow and hypocritical.

If stock returns are so sure-shot, then the government can end all its budget dilemmas by selling more bonds and investing the proceeds into the stock market. Why does it not follow the advice it offers the payroll taxpayer? Suppose the government borrows $200 billion at 3 percent, invests it in index funds that on average have earned 10 percent over the long past, and reaps a net gain of 7 percent. Since the government economists argue that share markets will repeat past performance, within two decades that $200 billion would bring a net gain of $774 billion. If such investing is done regularly over ten years, then over three decades, the government would earn more than $10 trillion, enough to wipe out its entire current and projected debt.

However, no administration economist has suggested doing anything like this. Why? Because the entire scheme seems phony and sounds too good to be true. But if such a scheme won't work for the government's own debts, it also won't work for privatization, wherein the government would end up borrowing money on behalf of payroll taxpayers, who would be expected to put the money into company shares. In return for this dubious privilege, the future retirees would be required to forego a part of guaranteed benefits. People will bear the risk of stock investing, but the government will enjoy the savings, which, as usual, will be passed on to the wealthy in the form of further cuts in the income tax. Some such agenda is what the supporters of privatization seem to have in mind.

If it was so easy to steer clear of debts, some government would have surely tried this borrow-and-invest plan, but to my knowledge none has. Economist Jeff Madrick examines the pros and cons of potential privatization plans and concludes: "Americans who think privatization will necessarily preserve their retirement incomes should think again. Most privatization plans involve a decided cut in average benefits." And "a significant number of American retirees will do poorly."[11]

ETHICAL ECONOMIC POLICY

The verdict of history is that ethics works, and deception designed to foster the interests of the few does not. Ethical policies start out with direct benefits to the poor and the middle class, whereas deceptive policies directly favor the affluent in the name of benefiting the poor and the middle class. Ethical actions generate a trickle-up of prosperity, whereas deceptive actions offer a trickle-down. Trickle-up means that the poor benefit the most, followed by the middle class and the affluent. Trickle-down, by contrast, signifies that the wealthy reap maximum reward, possibly followed by the middle class and the destitute.

Ethical prescriptions keep the tax burden low on the poor and those in the middle, while unethical policies transfer the tax burden from the wealthy to the poor and the middle class. Ethical ideas keep aggregate demand high through high wages stemming from free enterprise, whereas deceptive practices try to revive demand in the name of free enterprise by generating debt. *Ethical measures work for the benefit of all, while unethical measures benefit the few and torment the most.*

Let's take another look at the 1950s and the 1960s, when high economic growth coexisted with confiscatory income tax rates, as high as 90 percent on top incomes, but never below 70 percent. Those were the halcyon days of ethical economic policy. The sales tax rate hovered around 2 percent, whereas the Social Security tax for an individual worker barely averaged 3 percent on the first $5,000 of wages.

The tax system was ultra-progressive in the 1950s and the 1960s. In addition, the minimum wage in the period averaged $1.25, which is about $8 in 2004 prices. The economic policy was highly ethical; it was designed to provide a living wage to the unskilled and minimize the burden on those who can least afford to pay taxes. It produced vast benefits for society. Growth averaged 4 percent in the 1950s and 4.4 percent in the 1960s even without the bonanza of the computer revolution; real wages soared for all, at the average rate of 2.5 percent per year; consumer, corporate, and government debt was extremely low. Unemployment fell to as low as 3.5 percent in 1969.

The Legacy of Unethical Policy

Now let's see what unethical policies, such as Greenomics, have accomplished. Between 1981 and 1983, the tax system became ultra-regressive, and has remained so to this day. Today the payroll tax is 6.2 percent on a wage base of $87,900, along with a Medicare tax of 1.45 percent. Overall, the Social Security tax burden is now much higher than in the 1950s and the 1960s. You can see what an enormous weight these levies place on the poor and middle-income groups. The top-bracket income tax rate is now just 35 percent, with capital gains and dividends barely facing taxation. The ultra-regressive system is going to be even more regressive in the future, because just as tax rates fall at the federal level, those enacted by states are expected to rise to make up for lost federal aid.

What did Greenomics have to show for itself in 2004? A trade deficit exceeding $600 billion a year? A federal budget deficit in excess of

$400 billion? A federal debt over $6 trillion, compared to just $366 billion in 1969? An overall debt level that is twice the level of GDP? Net foreign debt in excess of $3 trillion, compared to a surplus in 1969? An unemployment rate of 5.5 percent. An after-tax production wage, earned by 80 percent of working Americans, that is just three-fourths of its level in the 1960s? And, of course, a CEO wage that is several hundred times the production wage, compared to just 40 times during the 1960s. It is abundantly clear that the CEO club now owns the government and economic policy.

The fall in the after-tax minimum wage is really unbelievable. In 1968, the hourly minimum was $1.60 per hour. Since the cost of living has risen by a factor of five, the equivalent minimum wage in today's prices is $8, compared to the actual level of $5.15. This amounts to a wage decline of 36 percent. Furthermore, the Social Security tax rate in 1968 was just 4.4 percent, compared to 6.2 percent today. So after the payroll tax deduction, the minimum-wage drop approximates 40 percent.

Such is the legacy of Greenomics—an effective minimum wage less than two-thirds of the level in the 1960s. There are 30 million Americans whose wages are directly tied to the minimum pay; the remaining 80 million production workers have their earnings indirectly tied to the lowest wage. The effective wages of all these employees have plummeted beyond imagination. No wonder the average consumer is up to her neck in debt, saves a miniscule 2 percent of her income, and despite record indebtedness, does not generate enough demand to provide employment to all the job seekers.

Greenspan's Forte: Debt, Debt Everywhere

Greenspan is often said to be a poster boy for free enterprise. But he is actually a poster boy for free debt. His policy mantra since 1987 has been: "Whenever economic problems arise, create new debt." He did this in the wake of the 1987 crash, the Mexican crisis, the Asian crisis, the Russian default, the threatened bankruptcy of the hedge fund called Long Term Capital Management, and most recently in the stock market crash of 2000–2002. The debt mantra moved him to open up the money pump and lower the federal funds rate 12 times in 2001 and 2002.

The story in terms of tax legislation is much the same. What a bizarre irony! The disciple of Arthur Burns and Ayn Rand, the duo that despised government budget deficits, helped create the biggest federal debt buildup in

U.S. history, all in the name of public prosperity. From 1789 to 1979, the gross federal debt added up to less than $1 trillion. Then Greenomics went into effect in 1981, and by the end of Reagan's two terms, the federal debt exceeded $2.5 trillion. Greenomics generated more red ink in just eight years than was created in almost two centuries. And the 2004 *Economic Report of the President* expects the federal debt to exceed $8 trillion in 2005. A trillion here, a trillion there, and soon you are likely to face calamity.

Fiscal and monetary policies are just euphemisms for debt creation. Fiscal expansion does this for the government, monetary expansion for consumers and corporations. Economists have believed for a long time that monetary ease, within limits, can heal the economy whenever there is a downturn. But see what it really does: it creates a nation of debtors. In the 1990s, experts frequently lamented the rising consumer debt. Then when the recession was about to hit in 2001, some of them applauded, even demanded, a quick fall in the interest rate, so consumers could go more into debt.

The Fed indeed obliged them, hoping to lure people into increased borrowing. Is this a sign of sound economic policy, which will work only if people succumb to the debt temptation? Isn't this just a way of postponing the problem to the future? Oscar Wilde once said, "The only way to get rid of a temptation is to yield to it." That's what fiscal and monetary policies do: they create the debt temptation, and the public, oppressed by lower wages and higher taxes, cannot but yield to it.

Both fiscal and monetary expansion put the nation into hock—creating either government debt or private debt. When such prescriptions are used repeatedly over time, their cumulative effect is a debt mountain, which can become a big burden on the economy and posterity. That is why such policies are only short-run panaceas, not lasting cures. A time comes when they no longer work. They fail to cure unemployment or create high-wage jobs. This has happened in Japan since 1990, and now in the United States and Europe since 2000.

Something new has to be tried—something based on common sense, something ethical, truthful, and straightforward.

SHORT-RUN REFORMS

What can we do immediately to revive the U.S economy? Let's start by exploring a simple idea: if you want the prosperity of the 1950s and the

1960s, then you have to adopt the economic policies, especially the wage and tax structure, of that period. This sounds like a sensible view, because such policies will revive demand, which is not only at the center of any advanced economy, but is also our main problem today. What do such policies call for?

1. Cut the Social Security tax as explained above.
2. Raise the corporate income tax rate from the current 34 percent to 45 percent, and eliminate the tax loopholes.
3. Raise the top-bracket individual income tax rate to 40 percent, and rescind the preferential treatment of dividends and capital gains.
4. Raise the minimum wage in steps to $8 per hour—to $6 immediately, followed by a dollar rise per year until it reaches $8. Furthermore, index the minimum wage to the GDP deflator, the price index incorporating all goods and services.
5. Enforce the antitrust laws vigorously to break up giant conglomerates like Exxon-Mobil, General Electric, AOL, WorldCom and other profitable companies that absorbed their rivals through mergers in the 1980s and 1990s.
6. Persuade other nations to adopt free trade, so that the trade deficit is eliminated, and America has balanced free trade.

Demand-Side Tax Cut versus Supply-Side Cut

This six-point program is needed to revive the comatose economy immediately. The first measure will trim federal revenue, but the next two will more than offset the revenue shortfall. During the 1950s, American corporations paid a quarter of the government's tax collection, compared to less than 10 percent today. Returning to that system would raise another $250 billion, more than enough to cover the payroll tax cut proposed above. The higher income tax will bring another $100 billion. So this is a program that will lower the government deficit.

This three-pronged tax overhaul may be called the demand-side tax cut, even though it will raise taxes on wealthy individuals and corporations. It will inject progressiveness to the tax system, which, along with the increasing minimum wage, will raise aggregate demand. Businesses will then respond by expanding their output as well as investment. Remember that according to history and logic a progressive tax structure raises GDP growth and nurtures investment.

Regardless of Greenspan's ideology, high corporate taxes do not discourage capital spending, which is spurred by consumer demand, as long as the tax burden is low for the poor and the middle class. Such was the case during the 1950s and the 1960s in the United States, Canada, and Western Europe. Of course, CEO compensation is adversely affected by corporate levies, but not investment. The tax overhaul as suggested above may be called the demand-side tax cut, even though it will reduce the budget deficit, because it will restore tax progressiveness and thus enhance aggregate spending. Once demand increases and new orders pile up, it will be foolish for corporations to hold back on investment just because their taxes went up. And if an investment slack does develop, new businesses will emerge to take advantage of rising consumer needs.

Contrast the impact of this program with that of the supply-side arm of Greenomics, which seeks to trim taxes paid by wealthy individuals and corporations to raise savings, investment, and GDP growth. However, it is simply impossible for pro-wealthy tax cuts to accomplish these goals. When top-bracket income and corporate taxes decrease, the federal budget deficit rises immediately by an equal amount. To finance its deficit, the government has to borrow back the same amount from the wealthy recipients of the tax cut. So the tax beneficiaries only have IOUs from the government, but no extra funds. How can they possibly enhance their savings, investment, and growth? Case closed.

But a demand-side tax reduction in a stagnant economy is beneficial to the public. A tax cut favoring the poor and the middle class also raises the deficit immediately. But then the government borrows idle funds of the wealthy and spends them; so overall demand increases by the spending rise of the tax-cut recipients. Recession and unemployment thus vanish in a hurry. The proposed demand-side tax cut clearly excels the recent Bush–Greenspan version, enacted in 2001, which amounts to the perversity of a tax cut and borrow-back policy by the government.

Balanced Free Trade and Other Measures

The enforcement of antitrust laws will expand business competition and improve the quality of goods made in the United States. It will enhance the demand for labor, generating a fall in unemployment and a rise in the real wage. *The irony of the current economic policy is that it expands foreign competition through increased trade but also permits the decline of competition by tolerating mergers.* The two contradict each other, and tend to crush labor demand. Mergers directly trim labor demand, while growing imports of labor-intensive goods do this indirectly.

We need true free enterprise, not free markets in name only. Declining business competition is one of the main reasons for the rise in the wage gap, inequality, stock market mania, the inevitable crash, and a prolonged downturn or stagnation in employment. Raising business competition to the level of the 1950s will be a step in the right direction. With the return of inter-company rivalry, product quality will improve and Americans will turn to homemade goods, reviving domestic industry in the process. This will also raise labor demand, employment, and wages and end the monopoly capitalism generated by Greenspan.

Finally, the sixth prescription offered above ensures that increased aggregate demand from reforms is not squandered on foreign goods. You may note that free trade raises the real GDP of every nation only if trade is in balance. It is true that during the 1990s the trade deficit actually stimulated American growth by lowering the rate of interest. But now the deficit is a huge drain on the nation's manufacturing sector as the interest rate has hit rock bottom. The federal funds rate is still one of the lowest in three decades, and could be kept at that level to prevent a major rise in the market rate of interest even if the trade deficit vanishes. In 2004 the trade shortfall of $600 billion was a one-for-one deduction from the GDP, that is, it lowered the GDP by $600 billion as well. This is a giant loss of production and resulting jobs.

Suppose it takes a company a maximum of $100,000 to create a high-wage job. The elimination of the trade deficit itself will increase U.S. GDP by $600 billion, which when divided by $100,000, yields 6 million. Thus the policy of balanced free trade will create at least 6 million new and lucrative jobs.

The trade-surplus nations—China, Japan, South Korea, and Singapore, among others—have not adopted free trade, because they have tied their currencies, loosely or tightly, to the dollar. Similarly, the European Union manages the euro to keep it from rising sufficiently. Free trade means the absence of government intervention in both the foreign trade and foreign exchange market. Paul Samuelson, a distinguished economist and Nobel laureate, along with his coauthor, Yale Professor William Nordhaus, write: "When a government fixes its exchange rate, it must 'intervene' in foreign exchange markets to maintain the rate. Government exchange-rate intervention occurs when the government buys or sells foreign exchange to affect exchange rates."[12]

This is precisely what the governments of China and Japan among others have been doing since 1990 to prevent an appreciation in the value of their currencies. They do not follow free trade, which is inconsistent with their intervention in the market for foreign exchange. They buy U.S. government bonds with dollars acquired from their trade surplus, and thus create an artificial demand for the greenback in world markets.

Normally, their increased supply of dollars would reduce the value of the currency around the globe until it significantly trimmed the U.S. trade deficit. Even with a shrunken manufacturing base, a sharp dollar depreciation would significantly cut the trade shortfall. But by purchasing federal bonds and thus increasing the demand for the greenback, foreign countries blunt this process. Japan and China together hold more than a trillion dollars of U.S. Treasury bonds. When supply and demand for something rise simultaneously, its price may be unchanged. That is why the dollar remains relatively stable in spite of the giant trade deficit. Thus, while the United States follows free trade, its trading partners do not. The trade deficit is now the biggest reason for the American economic malaise.

Owing to the intervention by foreign central banks, the dollar is not free to float in foreign exchange markets and find its value that will balance American trade. With a deficit as huge as that of the United States, the greenback should depreciate profusely until the nation's imports come close to exports. America should move toward balanced free trade, as only such trade brings lasting benefits to nations.

One way to accomplish balanced trade is to adopt a weak-dollar policy like the one that the G-7 nations pursued in 1985 under the Plaza Accord. The dollar depreciation at that time was somewhat effective in reducing the trade shortfall, because the U.S. manufacturing base was still alive, not comatose as today. Now, the dollar will have to depreciate a lot more than in the past to eliminate or even significantly prune the trade red ink. Thus, the G-7 nations and China should cooperate to bring about a sufficiently large depreciation of the dollar with respect to major foreign currencies such as the yuan, yen, and euro.

If such cooperation is not forthcoming then the United States will have to pursue unilateral policies that are consistent with WTO rules. In the past, nations adopted manufacturing tariffs and subsidies to balance their international commerce. Such measures, however, would violate international economic treaties today. But apparently exchange rate manipulation is not subject to WTO restraint, because almost every nation except the United States is doing it.

What can America do alone to ensure balanced free trade? The United States, like other nations, can tie the dollar to major global currencies, especially of those nations that have a large and persistent trade surplus. Take, for instance, the case of the Chinese yuan, which is currently tied to the dollar at a rate of 8.28 to 1. In other words, a dollar buys 8.28 yuan. Suppose the United States pegs the greenback to 6 yuan and makes this rate available only to foreign importers of goods. This will sharply increase Chinese imports from the United States, whose goods will become much cheaper in terms of the yuan. Instead of paying more than 8 yuan to the central bank and obtaining one dollar, a Chinese importer would prefer to pay just 6 yuan to the Fed and use the dollar to import American goods into China. The country would then import many more American cars, computers, airplanes, tractors, and so on.

The government of China should not oppose this policy, because Chinese exports to the United States would be unaffected, as a U.S. importer would still buy 8.28 yuan from the People's Bank of China and obtain Chinese goods as cheaply as before.

The United States could do the same thing with respect to other major currencies and revive its exports. Note that the pegged dollar rates would be available only to those companies that buy American goods and ship them abroad. The yen–dollar rate could be set at 80/1, that is, a Japanese importer could buy a dollar for 80 yen only, even though the government of Japan seeks to set a 105/1 rate. Similarly, the euro–dollar rate could be pegged at 1/1.6, i.e., a euro could buy $1.60 instead of the current $1.35. This way the U.S. trade deficit could be trimmed and even eliminated without curtailing American imports.

The United States would then have a two-tier system of exchange rates. One set of rates, to be fixed by the Fed or the U.S. Treasury, would apply to foreign importers of American goods, and another, to be determined by the global market for foreign exchange, would apply to all other international transactions such as U.S. imports, foreign investment, and worldwide tourism. This way the United States would not restrict its imports through dollar depreciation, but simply stimulate its own exports to bring about a balance in its global commerce. The policy would expand, not curtail overall world trade.

The Question of Outsourcing

The new millennium brought a new hazard to the U.S. economy. It is called outsourcing or offshoring—the direct export of high-tech as well as back-office jobs. Until recently the low-wage competition from abroad mostly afflicted the blue-collar or the unskilled workers, especially their wages. Not any more. Almost everyone can now see what globalization is doing to the nation's skilled as well as unskilled workers. Lucrative jobs are vanishing not just in auto, airplane, and textile manufacturing, but also in computers, software, telecommunications, and some service industries. High-tech is becoming low-tech, as far as real wages and employment are concerned.

Outsourcing hurts the relatively low-skilled worker, because routine, back-office work can now be performed by cheap labor outside the United States via e-mail and the Internet. All a U.S.-based company has to do is to hire people abroad, send them work instructions through e-mail, and receive their output back through the same medium. Outsourcing may also afflict a skilled worker equipped with a college education, as computer technology enables businesses to parcel out sophisticated work as well. The offshoring phenomenon is potentially explosive and could become an enduring economic nightmare, as new graduates, burdened by heavy student loans, are unable to find work commensurate with their education and skills.

In the past, what a computer engineer would contribute in the United States for a salary of $100,000 can now be done by an engineer in India, China, Pakistan, or Taiwan for just $20,000 a year. Some telephone operators answer the calls of American customers, but reside in Dhaka, Bombay, and Lahore. Some paralegals assist U.S.-based attorneys for $10,000 a year without setting foot outside the Philippines. Others live in Sri Lanka but are employed by American Express to answer the queries of their New York customers. This way, about a million U.S. jobs have been shipped directly to Asia, Africa, and low-wage European countries since the mid-1990s.

There is reason to believe that this trend will continue and could result in the export of 3 million high-tech positions in the next 15 years.

U.S. companies want to cut their costs as much as possible, maintain high profits, and richly reward their CEOs, and they see outsourcing as a lucrative option to trim their payrolls regardless of what it does to their nation's living standard. This, along with the huge trade deficit, is the main reason that George Bush became the first president since Herbert Hoover to see no rise in employment during his first term.

But there is nothing that the nation can do about outsourcing, because it is an integral part of the global economy and the WTO. Fortunately, it afflicts only a small portion of the labor force—less than 1 percent—and even the worst-case scenario does not see it rising to more than 2 percent of employment. Even if 3 million jobs are lost over the next 15 years due to outsourcing, the job loss would still be less than 2 percent of the labor force.

In any case, nothing can be done about outsourcing short of pulling out of the World Trade Organization and giving up the benefits of free trade, such as access to foreign oil and markets. As Ohio Representative Dennis Kucinich remarked, "The WTO, as long as we belong to it, will not let us protect the jobs. This is the reason why we have outsourcing going on right now. We can't tax it. We can't put tariffs on it."[13] The trade deficit is a much bigger headache, and currently afflicts almost 6 percent of GDP and hence employment. There is also something we can do about it, as explained above. But if outsourcing becomes a bigger headache, then the world would have to get together and rewrite the rules of globalization, incorporating the varied interests of affected nations.

Balanced Economy

In addition to balanced free trade, we should have a balanced economy. On its face, this statement appears naïve, for everyone likes the idea of balance. However, as we saw in earlier chapters, global economic ills have sprung from what may be called unbalancing economic policies that are periodically supplemented by fiscal and monetary expansion, which is a euphemism for new debt. Specifically, poverty, hunger, recessions, inflation, and depressions result when the government and private behavior create an imbalance in the labor market in the form of the rising wage gap. Once the labor market slips into imbalance, so do other sectors of the economy.

An important feature of a balanced economy is diversification, as opposed to specialization. Diversification tends to mitigate the labor-market distortion, which is a measure of the chasm between real wages and labor productivity. There is a well-known investment strategy: don't keep all your eggs in one basket. This is because if the basket were to fall, the eggs could all break at the same time. Thus, savvy investors diversify by parking their funds in a variety of assets. They purchase stocks, bonds, real estate, and gold; they buy shares and bonds of different companies and entities, and so on. By spreading their funds into a variety of assets, wise investors minimize their risk. If one asset declines in value, the other could rise, cut their losses, and maximize their gains.

A balanced economy operates in much the same way, and maximizes the living standard from the use of available resources. A diversified economy is far more stable and free from the scourge of speculative bubbles, market crashes, inflation, recessions, and depressions than a specialized economy.

The United States today has become a highly specialized economy, especially because of its trade deficit. The country hardly produces any manufacturing goods. In the 1960s, our benchmark decade for a healthy economy, nearly 30 percent of the labor force worked in manufacturing; today less than half of that does. The American economy was optimally diversified. We produced TVs, motorcycles, shoes, clothing, cameras, all sorts of spare parts, and industrial raw materials in vast quantities, and exported some of them. Today they are mostly imported, which hurts the working families. According to a *New York Times* editorial the GDP share of take-home pay is now the lowest since 1929. And the trade deficit is the chief culprit behind this wage debacle.[14]

The mushrooming trade deficit is destroying the dynamism of American industry and high-paying jobs. Balanced free trade, along with enhanced business competition through trust-busting laws, will go a long way toward restoring our economic balance. The United States is extremely vulnerable to troubles arising in its trading partners. If for some reason international commerce is disrupted and other nations are unable to supply industrial raw materials and spare parts, the American economy will come to a halt and face severe inflation.

The economic plan offered above is a win-win program. It has the support of history, logic, and, above all, common sense. It will bring about vast benefits to Americans including a reduction in the budget and trade deficits, a rise in the real wage of the vast majority of families, a lower tax burden for 80 percent of the people, and higher GDP growth. With its enactment the fruit of prosperity will be shared by all Americans, not just a privileged few. The rest of the world should also adopt a similar plan aimed at making the tax system more progressive.

ECONOMIC DEMOCRACY

In the long run, nations must escape the scourge of the rising wage gap, which is responsible for virtually every economic imbalance around the globe. An effective way to close this gap is to switch from the current factory system and move into what may be called economic democracy. At present, major stockowners run the companies. Such shareholders usually become CEOs or company chairpersons. They hire a group of executives, who in turn hire managers and production workers. There are thus two groups of employees in a firm—management and laborers—with diametrically opposite interests.

Management wants to squeeze the maximum effort out of employees, paying them the going wage set by the labor market. If the market is tight— that is, if qualified workers are in short supply—then their salaries reflect their productivity. However, if joblessness is high or work can be outsourced abroad, productivity considerations are set aside, and employees are usually paid far less than their contribution to the company.

When it comes to managerial salaries, labor market tightness matters little. They are set by executive cronies, using the back-scratching principle: you scratch my back, I will scratch yours. The result is that a CEO can now ask a ridiculous salary and get it. Such inequalities are not only unfair, they also help create economic imbalances. Pervasive inequality leads to insufficient product demand, forcing the government to resort to budget deficits that may be inflationary and waste resources. The Fed also has to lure the consumer into high debt. It is better to create a system where the consumer as a worker earns a wage high enough to meet basic requirements. There should be no need for the government and households to borrow to the hilt so that the economy functions smoothly, while the CEO wallows in luxuries.

In order to create a fair and efficient system, economic democracy should be established to supplement free enterprise resulting from high competition. In this system, company workers own the majority of shares; management is still in the hands of experts and professionals, but the board of directors is answerable to employees, not the CEO and outside shareholders. In fact, the board consists mainly of representatives elected by the workers. Such a body is not likely to approve of anything that increases the gap between wages and labor productivity.

During the 2004 campaign George Bush offered Americans a vision of an "ownership society," in which people are masters of their own destiny: they choose, among other things, their own health plans and partially manage their own Social Security accounts. His eloquent words were inscribed on a White House website: "If you own something, you have a vital stake in the future of our country. The more owners in America, the more vitality there is in America, and the more people have a vital stake in this country."[15] While the president focused on other ideas, it appears to me that economic democracy is by far the best way to fulfill his vision. In fact, this is perhaps the only way. A genuine ownership society is one in which the workers of a company own the majority of its shares so that the management of the enterprise is under their control. If such a system is established, it could be President Bush's finest legacy to the world—even though his version is far from the one described here. After all, he is the first one to popularize this phrase.

Low Inequality

Because of the democratic nature of this structure, the gap between worker and management salaries is likely to be reasonable. *Inequalities are automatically low in any democratic setup.* In the United States, the president earns $400,000 a year. He has perks similar to those of the CEOs, but receives a fraction of what some company officers make. This is because there is democracy in politics, but autocracy in corporations. Why else would top executives earn huge bonuses even when profits of their companies plunge? A non-performing chief executive in a democracy is usually booted out by the voters. He is not showered with privileges and outlandish severance packages, as happens with big business today.

Not only is economic democracy inherently fair, it is also innately more productive. Knowing that their efforts will be rewarded, self-employed persons work extremely hard. So will factory-owning workers. Wages will also be higher, although management salaries will be lower. Each employee will be paid a certain wage and a year-end bonus depending upon their efficiency and company profits. The same formula will apply to management salaries as well.

With companies still run by experts, productive efficiency will be at least as high as before. In reality, with employee ownership of the majority shares, productivity will be higher. Another advantage of economic democracy is its low level of unemployment. It is normal for all economies to go through ups and downs, but the ups and downs of capitalism occasionally get out of control and produce catastrophic inflation or depressions, culminating in high joblessness and despair.

Fair and Efficient

Today, when people are laid off, government spending increases to feed the unemployed. The government in turn raises taxes, so those employed end up supporting the unemployed. *Under economic democracy, no hardworking person would be laid off because all employees jointly own the company or at least its majority shares.* In a downturn, working hours and wages would be reduced for all. This way, everybody would share the pain, and few would feel the psychological trauma of being unemployed.

The current system is wasteful and debilitating for the jobless. Even today, the employed assist the unemployed through higher taxes. So the pain is shared even in the current system, although not equally, but there is a wasteful middleman collecting taxes to aid the jobless. This function will be unnecessary under economic democracy. There will be little wastage of capital and labor resources, because joblessness will be minimal.

Stability

With economic democracy, inequality is automatically low, so that consumer spending and aggregate demand are high. The government does not need high deficits to support high output levels and employment. A democratic system is inherently stable. When wages keep pace with productivity, both GDP and real wages grow apace, because consumer demand then keeps up with supply. With firms assured of a growing market, business investment also then expands rapidly; so does new technology, which in turn ignites productivity growth and real wages. In economic democracy, workers and hence consumers are in a win-win position, although stock markets and speculative manias are mercifully subdued. *A democratic economy is innately a high-growth and low-inequality economy.*

Economic democracy is practical only in large companies, such as General Motors, Wal-Mart, Microsoft, Sony, IBM, AT&T, Toyota, Mercedes-Benz, and so on. In big firms, at least 51 percent of the shares should be in the hands of employees, with the rest belonging to outsiders. The board of directors will then come mainly from workers. Medium-sized firms may also operate in this way.

In small companies, this system may or may not be practical. Those with less than a thousand workers may be individually owned or run as cooperatives, where shares may or may not be employee-owned. In a consumer co-op, some investment by employee members may be necessary. Otherwise, co-ops are run on the same democratic principles as medium and large companies.

Economic democracy will require State aid and commitment, just as political democracy once did. Even though the idea seems to be far-fetched today, it is the only way to produce a lasting solution for global economic dilemmas. As you saw in chapter 6, if the wage gap keeps rising, debt has to grow exponentially to provide jobs to the workforce, and that too at mediocre wages. It is simply impossible for debt to follow such a path. So economic democracy is inevitable in the long run. The question is whether or not it will materialize without a major economic calamity, leaving the world with no choice. The federal government can bring this about by targeting an industry's major firm, buying 51 percent of its shares in the stock market, and then selling them at subsidized rates to the firm's employees. The workers can buy the shares in installments, that is, a small fraction of their salary can be deducted every month to pay for their purchases. A model is then created in each industry. Once the model firm reveals its natural superiority in terms of efficiency, employee morale, and wages, other companies in that industry will follow suit and sell out to the employees.

The government could also use its tax revenue to buy shares from many firms and transform an entire industry into a democratic setup. The action may not involve huge outlays in a depressed stock market. This way, one by one, little by little, economic democracy will spread to all large and medium corporations.

When workers are majority owners themselves, there is no need for unions. Labor cannot strike against labor. Every employee will be paid a need-based minimum wage, plus a premium, depending upon education, experience, and skill, including a year-end bonus in proportion to profit. Hard work, innovation, and intelligence will be rewarded with extra bonuses, whereas lethargy, dishonesty, and inefficiency will be penalized through the loss of bonus, and, as a last resort, the loss of job. In short, there will be true free enterprise. In the rare case of job loss, the company will buy back the worker's shares at the current market price.

Mass Capitalism

We should not confuse worker management and ownership with socialism. The system is more like mass capitalism, because shares of Fortune 500 corporations will be majority-owned by a vast number of people. Unlike in socialism, in an economic democracy the state is not engaged in the production of goods and services. Once the new system is established, government intervention in the economy would be, and should be, minimal. In fact, the system will materialize the ideals cherished by most macroeconomic theories.

Economic democracy should please the classical and neoclassical economists because of its small government. The neo-Keynesians will be elated because of its low unemployment and inherent stability. Socialists will be ecstatic because of its low inequality. Even the chief executives will like it in the end because of its tendency to produce steady growth in profits and share prices without the ballyhoo and hoopla of the speculative bubble, followed by the inevitable crash. In short, there are few economic ills on earth that a democratic economy cannot heal. As mentioned above, it even accords with President Bush's vision of an ownership society.

When the world adopts the ethical system of economic democracy, its major economic troubles will vanish in a hurry. Otherwise, my other forecast made in my 1979 book, *Muslim Civilization and the Crisis in Iran*, could come true and convulse the globe. Remember that this forecast said: "It is now the turn of India and Islam to cause an upheaval in the Western world and Russia. It is the orient that is now poised to determine the future of the occident."

The Islamic world, as mentioned above, has already caused the downfall of communism. The downfall of capitalism could be next, unless the Western world adopts ethical ways in economics and politics. My 1979 prophecy is unfolding right before your eyes. The 9/11 massacre in 2001, the subsequent American pounding of Afghanistan and Iraq, and

Al Qaeda-supported insurgency in Iraq make it clear that Islam and the West could be embroiled for years to come until both cooperate for the good of the world. If you don't like any of this, then you have to adopt the ethical basis of economic democracy as soon as possible. A democratic economy would fortify capitalism and make it impervious to extraneous philosophies.

I am an economist as well as a forecaster. I now predict that most of the benefits promised by my economic plan will materialize within two to three years of its enactment. If not, the United States and the rest of the world will see more of what has transpired since the start of the new millennium—an employment and wage recession—for the rest of this decade. There is also a good chance that things could get really ugly before they get better. But we can avoid all this pain through timely reforms that materialize the cherished goal of economic democracy, which is likely to be established in some parts of the world by 2020, if not sooner:

> The goal of economic democracy
> Is to raise the living standard of all
> To erase poverty and unemployment
> For people big and small.

NOTES

CHAPTER 1

1. Alan Murray, "Passing a Test: Fed's New Chairman Wins a Lot of Praise on Handling the Crash," *Wall Street Journal*, November 25, 1987, p. A1; Martin Sosnoff, "Hands Off the Punch Bowl, Alan," *Forbes*, April 21, 1997, p. 392.
2. The Associated Press, "Fed: It Will Provide Sufficient Money to Banking System," messenger-inquirer.com, September 11, 2001.
3. *The Economist*, September 26, 1998, p. 72.
4. Bernard Baumol, "Is That Really You, Alan," *Time Europe*, March 20, 2002.
5. dailytimes.com.
6. Bob Woodward, *Maestro: Greenspan's Fed and the American Boom*, New York: Simon and Schuster, 2000.
7. Justin Martin, *Greenspan: The Man Behind Money*, Cambridge, Mass.: Perseus Publishing, 2001, p. 90.
8. Steven K. Beckner, *Back from the Brink: The Greenspan Years*, New York: John Wiley & Sons, 1996, p. 11.
9. Maggie Mahar, *Bull!: A History of the Boom, 1982–1999: What Drove the Breakneck Market—and What Every Investor Needs to Know about Financial Cycles*, New York: Harper Business, 2003. Also quoted in Paul Krugman, " 'Bull!' and 'Origins of the Crash': Executives Gone Wild," *New York Times*, February 8, 2004, p. 9.
10. Woodward, pp. 57–58.
11. John Cassidy, "The Fountainhead: Alan Greenspan Faces the Biggest Challenge of his Career," *The New Yorker*, April 24/May 1, 2000, pp. 162–175.
12. Greenspan's Testimony, "Economic Outlook and Current Fiscal Issues," February 25, 2004, www.federalreserve.gov.
13. Editorial, "A False Start on Social Security," *New York Times*, December 3, 2004, p. A22. In the fourth quarter of 2004, U.S. current account balance was in arrears by over $170 billion, which comes to $680 billion at the annual rate. Dividing this figure by 365 yields a rounded figure of $1.9 billion or approximately $2 billion per day.
14. Louis Uchitelle, "We Pledge Allegiance to the Mall," *New York Times*, December 6, 2004, p. C12.

CHAPTER 2

1. See the *Economic Report of the President*, Council of Economic Advisers, U.S. Government Printing Office, Washington, D.C., February 2004.

2. Keith H. Hammonds, "What's New on the Lecture Circuit; Big Bucks for Big Names in Business," *New York Times*, September 11, 1983, p. C15; Justin Martin, *Greenspan: The Man Behind Money*, Cambridge, Mass.: Perseus Publishing, 2001, p. 139.

3. Tamar Lewin, "The Quiet Allure of Alan Greenspan," *New York Times*, June 5, 1983, p. C1.

4. Steven Rattner, "Greenspan's Widened Influence," *New York Times*, March 10, 1981, p. D1.

5. Justin Martin, p. 145.

6. Lewin, p. D1.

7. David C. Johnston, *Perfectly Legal: The Covert Campaign to Rig Our Tax System to Benefit the Super Rich and Cheat Everybody Else*, New York: Portfolio, 2004, p. 120.

8. Deborah Rankin, "Personal Finance; Social Security Rises? Brace Yourself," *New York Times*, January 9, 1983, p. C19.

9. In effect, the legislation raised the economy-wide Social Security rates far and above those provided by the 1977 law, which itself had scheduled steep increases in those taxes. Tables N.1 and N.2 present all the tax rate changes that occurred in the 1983 legislation.

10. Francis X. Clines, "Pension Changes Signed into Law," *New York Times*, April 21, 1983, p. A17.

11. Phil Gailey, "Greenspan Urges Action on Deficit," *New York Times*, August 2, 1983, p. A10.

12. National Desk, "Excerpts from Final Report of the Commission on Social Security," *New York Times*, January 21, 1983, p. A12.

13. Spencer Rich, "House Hearings Begin as Social Security Plan Gains Backing of Aged," *Washington Post*, February 12, 1983, p. A6.

Table N.1. The FICA Tax Rate Schedule for Employees

Year	1984–2004			Previous Schedule		
	OASDI	HI	Total	OASDI	HI	Total
1984	5.7 %	1.3 %	7.0 %	5.4%	1.3 %	6.7 %
1985	5.7	1.35	7.05	5.7	1.35	7.05
1986–1987	5.7	1.45	7.15	5.7	1.45	7.15
1988–1989	6.06	1.45	7.51	5.7	1.45	7.15
1990 and after	6.2	1.45	7.65	6.2	1.45	7.65

Source: Social Security Amendments, 1983; www.ssa.gov/history.

Table N.2. The Self-Employment Tax Rate Schedule

Year	1984–2004			Previous Schedule		
	OASDI	HI	Total	OASDI	HI	Total
1984	11.40%	2.60%	14.00%	8.05%	1.30%	9.35%
1985	11.40	2.70	14.10	8.55	1.35	9.90
1986–1987	11.40	2.90	14.30	8.55	1.45	10.00
1988–1989	12.12	2.90	15.02	8.55	1.45	10.00
1990 and after	12.40	2.90	15.30	9.30	1.45	10.75

Source: Social Security Amendments, 1983; www.ssa.gov/history.

Table N.3. Operations of the Combined OASDI Trust Fund and the Federal Government in Selected Years: 1960–1983 (in Billions of Dollars)

Year	Fund's Deficit*	Fund's Assets	On Budget Deficit*
1960	−0.6	22.6	−0.6
1965	1.3	19.8	1.6
1970	3.9	30.1	8.7
1975	1.5	44.3	55.3
1976	3.2	41.1	70.5
1977	5.3	35.9	49.8
1978	4.1	31.7	54.9
1979	1.5	30.3	38.7
1980	3.8	26.5	72.7
1981	1.9	24.5	74.0
1982	12.1**	12.7	120.1
1983	−0.1	12.8	208.0
Total from 1975–1983	28.0	12.8	490.2

* A negative number means a surplus. The On Budget Deficit is the federal government deficit excluding the net income of the Trust Fund.
** For 1982, there is a mistake in the SSA table that I have corrected. This item in the SSA table displays a surplus of $200 million, whereas the OASDI Trust Fund faced a deficit of $12.1 billion that was made up by a loan from the Hospital Insurance fund.

Source: www.ssa.gov or Social Security Administration, *The Economic Report of the President*, 1997, p. 419.

14. Deborah Rankin, p. C19.
15. David R. Francis, "The Greenspan View of Social Security, Taxes, Deficits, Recovery," *Christian Science Monitor*, October 3, 1983, p. 19.
16. Editorial, "A Safe Harbor for Social Security," *Washington Post*, March 27, 1983, p. B6.
17. Harry Ellis, "Greenspan: Big Deficits Spawned by Breakdown in Fiscal Process," *Christian Science Monitor*, October 26, 1983, p. 3.
18. Jonathan Fuerbringer, "Delay on Increase in Benefits Asked," *New York Times*, January 3, 1985, p. A16.
19. Table N.3 gives you an idea of the extent of the deficit problem facing the OSADI trust fund and the federal government from 1960 to 1983. The cumulative Social Security deficit from 1975 to 1983 was $28 billion, compared to $490.2 billion for the federal government.
20. See Table N.3 and note 19.
21. See note 12.
22. Johnston, p. 120.
23. Juan Williams and Spencer Rich, "Social Security Rescue Plan Predicted to Pass Congress," *Washington Post*, January 17, 1983, p. A1.
24. David S. Broder, "Even More Compromises," *Washington Post*, January 26, 1983, p. A21.
25. Daniel P. Moynihan, "Conspirators, Trillions, Limos in the Night," *New York Times*, May 23, 1988, p. A19.
26. Anatole Kaletsky, "U.S. Compromise 'Breakthrough' for Budget Agreement," *Financial Times*, January 18, p. 1.
27. Associated Press, "Greenspan's Budget Ideas," *New York Times*, March 3, 1988, p. D9.

28. David E. Rosenbaum, "Fight Over Tax Cut Heats Up As Bush and Moynihan Dig In," *New York Times*, January 19, 1990, p. A1.

29. Andrew Rosenthal, "White House Hopes to Still The Siren Song of a Tax Cut," *New York Times*, January 17, 1990, p. A16.

30. Ibid.

31. Greenspan's Testimony, "Social Security Tax Cut," Federal News Service, February 27, 1990.

32. Quoted from Allen Smith, *The Looting of Social Security*, New York: Carroll & Graf Publishers, p. 19.

33. Ibid., p. 19.

34. Ibid., p. 21.

35. Ibid., p. 21.

36. Quoted from Scott Burns, "Hey Kid! Got $8.6 Trillion?" *Dallas Morning News*, July 6, 2004, p. D1.

37. William Grieder, *Who Will Tell the People*, New York: Simon and Schuster, 1992, p. 93.

38. David E. Rosenbaum, "Views Split over Effects of Tax Bill," *New York Times*, September 29, 1986, p. D5.

39. Ibid.

40. Max Mccarthy, "Greenspan Prescribes Bitter Pill to Cure Deficit," *Buffalo News*, July 24, 1994, Viewpoints Section, p. 11.

41. Greenspan's Testimony, "Social Security," federalreserve.gov, November 20, 1997, p. 1.

42. Greenspan's Testimony, "Social Security," federalreserve.gov, January 28, 1999, p. 1.

43. Ibid., p. 2.

44. Ibid., pp. 3–4.

45. Ibid., p. 3.

46. Jerome Tuccille, *Alan Shrugged: Alan Greenspan, The World's Most Powerful Banker*, New York: John Wiley & Sons, 2002, pp. 282–283.

47. Jeff Madrick, "Mr. Fixit," *New York Review of Books*, July 19, 2001, p. 1.

48. Ibid., p. 2.

49. Greenspan's Testimony, "Economic Outlook and Current Fiscal Issues," federalreserve.gov, February 25, 2004, p. 3.

50. Ibid., p. 3.

51. Ibid., p. 4.

52. Paul Krugman, "Maestro of Chutzpah," *New York Times*, March 2, 2004, p. A23.

CHAPTER 3

1. Jerome Tuccille, *Alan Shrugged: Alan Greenspan, The World's Most Powerful Banker*, New York: John Wiley & Sons, 2002, p. 84.

2. Ibid., p. 81.

3. Adam Smith, *The Wealth of Nations*, New York: Modern Library, 1937, p. 421. Also quoted by E. K. Hunt and Howard Sherman, in *Economics: An Introduction to Traditional and Radical Views*, New York: Harper and Row, 1975, p. 48.

4. Jeremy Bentham, "An Introduction to the Principles of Morals and Legislation," in A. I. Melden, ed., *Ethical Theories*, Engelwood Cliffs, N.J.: Prentice Hall, 1955, p. 341. Also see *The Internet Encyclopedia of Philosophy*, Jeremy Bentham, 1748–1832: Human Nature, iep.utm.edu.

5. Hunt and Sherman, p. 45.
6. J. C. Fite and J. E. Reese, *An Economic History of The United States*, Boston: Houghton Mifflin and Co., 1973, p. 355.
7. Alan Greenspan, in Ayn Rand, ed., *Capitalism: The Unknown Ideal*, New York: New American Library, 1967, p. 70.
8. Ibid., p. 67.
9. Ibid., p. 66.
10. Kathryn Kranhold, Bryan Lee, and Michael Benson, "Enron Rigged Power Market In California, Documents Say," *Wall Street Journal*, May 7, 2002, p. A1. Also see Bob Egelko, " 'Death Star' Trader Admits Manipulating California Market," *San Francisco Chronicle*, August 6, 2004, p. A1.
11. Tuccille, p. 84.
12. Greenspan, ibid., pp. 64–67.
13. Ibid., p. 118.
14. Ibid., p. 121.
15. Ibid.
16. Ravi Batra, *The Downfall of Capitalism and Communism*, London: Macmillan, 1978. Reprinted by Venus Books, Dallas, 1990.
17. Tuccille, p. 82.
18. John Cassidy, "The Fountainhead: Alan Greenspan Faces the Biggest Challenge of his Career," *The New Yorker*, April 24/May 1, 2000, pp. 162–175.
19. Alan Mayer and Jane Whitmore, "Greenspan—Atlas Jogs," *Newsweek*, April 24, 1975, p. 74; also quoted by Martin and Beckner, p. 12.
20. Tuccille, op. cit., p. 84.
21. Greenspan, p. 67.
22. Jack Kemp, "Lower Taxes, Higher Revenues," *New York Times*, February 11, 1996, p. A15.
23. For instance, in a speech before the Economic Club of New York, Greenspan described the British experience with wartime controls as generating the regulated economy, not a free-market economy. See, FRB Speeches, "*Current Account:* Remarks by Chairman Alan Greenspan," www.federalreserve.gov, March 2, 2004.
24. Greenspan's Testimony, "Semi-Annual Monetary Policy Report," FRB Testimony, federalreserve.gov, July 16, 2002.

CHAPTER 4

1. Larry Kahaner, *The Quotations of Chairman Greenspan*, Holbrook, Mass.: Adams Media Corporation, 2000, p. 223.
2. Robert Novak, "Master of the Fed Unchallenged," *Chicago Sun-Times*, August 30, 1999, Editorial, p. 29.
3. William Greider, "Greenspan's Con Job," *The Nation*, March 22, 2004. Dean Baker, an economist and co-director at the Center for Economic Policy and Research, calls Greenspan's actions a scam. See his "Greenspan's Social Security Scam," www.hnn.us; Krugman, as reported in chapter 2, is also critical of the maestro's actions.
4. David J. Miller and Michel Hersen, *Research Fraud in the Behavioral and Biomedical Sciences*, New York: John Wiley & Sons, 1992.
5. Roger Lowenstein, *Origins of the Crash*, New York: The Penguin Press, 2004.

6. Dan Ackman, "Wall Street Buys Peace," Forbes.com, December 20, 2002; Thomas A. Fogarty and Edward Iwata, "Links between Reports, Banking Fees Cited," *USA Today*, April 29, 2003, Money, p. 1.

7. Kent Conrad, "Supply-Side Daydream," *Washington Post*, August 15, 1997, p. A25.

8. Justin Martin, *Greenspan: The Man Behind Money*, New York: Perseus Publishing, 2001, p. 5.

9. Jerome Tuccille, *Alan Shrugged: Alan Greenspan, the World's Most Powerful Banker*, New York: John Wiley & Sons, 2002, p. 18.

10. There is a vast literature on the philosophy of Rand and Bentham. Two readable books are: Douglas G. Long, *Bentham on Liberty*, Toronto: University of Toronto Press, 1977; Alan Gotthelf, *On Ayn Rand*, Belmont, Cal.: Wadsworth/Thomson Learning, 2000.

11. Tuccille, p. 85.

12. John Cassidy, "The Fountainhead: Alan Greenspan Faces the Biggest Challenge of his Career," *The New Yorker*, April 24/May 1, 2000, pp. 162–175.

13. Martin, p. 46.

14. Ibid.

15. Ibid., p. 47.

16. Steven K. Beckner, *Back from the Brink: The Greenspan Years*, New York, John Wiley & Sons, 1996, p. 13.

17. Proxmire quoted from Tuccille, p. 115.

18. Ibid., pp. 117 and 123.

19. Ibid., p. 85; see also Martin, p. 99.

20. Tamar Lewin, "The Quiet Allure of Alan Greenspan," *New York Times*, June 5, 1983, p. C1.

21. The three letters appeared in *New York Times* in 1983 on June 19, sec. 3, p. 14, sec. 4, p. 20, and on June 26, sec. 4, p. 20.

22. Greenspan quoted from Martin, p. 103.

23. Erwin Hargrove and Samuel Morley, The President and the Council of Economic Advisers: Interview with CEA Chairmen, Boulder, CO: Westview Press, p. 451.

24. Martin, p. 140.

25. Tuccille, p. 127.

26. Alan Greenspan, "For a Large Corporate Tax Cut," *New York Times*, December 19, 1977, p. 31.

27. Thomas O'Toole, "Greenspan Predicts Inflation Upswing," *Washington Post*, April 10, 1978, p. D10.

28. Leonard Silk, "Economic Scene; The Candidates: Views Similar?" *New York Times*, September 10, 1980, p. D2.

29. Philip Shabecoff, "Jobless Rate Up Slightly; Economy Still Sluggish," *New York Times*, November 8, 1980, p.10.

30. Steven Rattner, "A Bold and Risky Venture," *New York Times*, February 19, 1981, p. A1.

31. Steven Rattner, "Greenspan's Widened Influence," *New York Times*, March 9, 1981, p. D1.

32. Tuccille, p. 114.

33. Phil Gailey, "Greenspan Urges Action on Deficit," *New York Times*, August 2, 1983, p. A10.

34. David Shriban, "$10.3 Billion in Spending Cuts Passed by House to Shave Deficit," *New York Times*, October 26, 1983, p. B7.

35. Edward Cowan, "Causes and Effects of Deficits," *New York Times*, December 28, 1981, p. D1; John M. Berry, "Not Even This Tight-Fisted President Can Stem the Red-Ink Tide," *Washington Post*, November 29, 1981, p. A15.

36. Louis Uchitelle, "Forecasts: Greenspan's Grades," *New York Times*, July 24, 1987, p. D1.

37. Martin, pp. 174–180.

38. Ibid., p. 210.

39. Ibid., pp. 196–197.

40. Woodward, p. 96.

41. *Time*, "Why We're So Gloomy," January 13, 1992, p. 34.

42. Keith Woolhouse, "Economy Enters New Reality," *Ottawa Citizen*, July 24, 1997, p. C3.

43. "Alan Greenspan's Brave New World," *Business Week*, July 14, 1997.

44. Woodward, p. 168.

45. Greenspan's Testimony, July 22, 1997, FRB Testimony, www.federalreserve.org.

46. Bob Woodward, *Maestro: Greenspan's Fed and the American Boom*, New York: Simon and Schuster, 2000, p. 195.

47. Greenspan's speech, "Is There a New Economy?" FRB Speeches, September 4, 1998, www.federalreserve.gov.

48. Ibid.

49. This is precisely what he had done after the 1987 crash—first he pumped money into the system, and then scooped it up once the crisis was over.

50. Woodward, pp. 221–222.

51. Greenspan's Testimony, "Social Security," FRB Testimony, www.federalreserve. gov, and Greenspan's Speech, "Challenges for Monetary Policy Makers," FRB Speeches, October 19, 2000, www.federalreserve.gov.

52. Burton Malkiel, "Remaking the Market, The Great Wall Street?" *Wall Street Journal*, October 14, 2002, p. A16.

53. Greenspan's Speech, "Structural Change in the Economy and Financial Markets," FRB Speeches, December 5, 2000, www.federalreserve.gov; even on June 10, 1998, the maestro had given credibility to security analysts by referring to them in his testimony before the Joint Economic Committee. But in a speech on March 26, 2002, to his alma matter, NYU, Greenspan finally saw through the analysts' inflation of projected corporate earnings.

54. Andrew Cave, "Fed U-turn Boosts Hopes for Rate Cuts," *Daily Telegraph*, December 20, 2000, p. 25.

55. Lowenstein, p. 211. See also Floyd Norris, "As Bull Market Nears a Birthday, Few Seem Ready to Celebrate," *New York Times*, September 24, 2004, p. C1.

56. John Crudele, "It's Time for Greenspan to Rescue the Market," *New York Post*, October 13, 2000; see also Cassidy, p. 163.

57. Lisa Singhania, "Investors, Federal Reserve Have Different Agendas," www.detnews.com, March 3, 2001.

58. Bill Bonner, "Today: Grand Illusion-II," March 16, 2001, www.tulipsandbears.com.

59. Tuccille, p. 231.

60. Ibid., p. 253.

61. Senate hearing, testimony of Chairman Greenspan, "Outlook for the Federal Budget and Implications for Fiscal Policy," Federal News Service, January 25, 2001.

62. Eric Pianin and Helen Dewar, "Senate GOP Tax Bill May Lead to Deal," *Washington Post*, July 28, 1999, p. A1, www.washingtonpost.com; see also www.wanniski.com, August 24, 1999; and *Village Voice*, August 10, 1999, p. 29.

63. Edmund Andrews, "Greenspan Throws Cold Water on Bush Arguments for Tax Cut," *New York Times*, February 12, 2003, p. A1.
64. David Rosenbaum, "Greenspan Says Tax Cut Without Spending Reductions Could Be Damaging," *New York Times*, May 1, 2003, September 16, p. A32.
65. Richard Stevenson, "Economic View: In a New Time of Global Turmoil, Greenspan's Experience Reassures," *New York Times*, September 16, p. C4.
66. "Notebook: US Stock Market Ignores Health Warning," *The Guardian*, April 23, 2003, p. 18.
67. "Heed Mr. Greenspan; The Federal Reserve Chairman Repeats his Warnings about a New Round of Tax Cuts," *Times Union*, May 3, 2003, p. A6.
68. Robert Novak, "Is it Goodbye for Greenspan," *Chicago Sun-Times*, February 24, 2003, p. 27.
69. Caroline Baum, "For Paul O'Neill, It's Always About the Truth," www.bloomberg.com, January 21, 2004.
70. Ron Suskind, *The Price of Loyalty*, New York: Simon and Schuster, 2004, p. 162.
71. Ibid., p. 291.
72. John Dickerson, "Confessions of a White House Insider," *Time*, January 11, 2004.
73. John Crudele, "White House May See Greenspan as Liability for Election," *New York Post*, March 30, 2004, p. 34.
74. Michael Lewis, "Did Greenspan Use O'Neill to Send Bush a Signal," www.bloomberg.com, February 5, 2004.
75. Senate Hearing, "Greenspan's Testimony: Federal Reserve Monetary Policy Report," Federal News Service, February 12, 2004.
76. "Social Insecurity; Cutting Retirement Benefits to Pay for a Tax Cut," *Pittsburgh Post-Gazette*, February 18, 2004, p. A20.
77. Martin Crutsinger, "Greenspan Urges Social Security Cuts," *Toronto Star*, February 13, 2004, p. E2.
78. House hearing, Greenspan's Testimony, "Current Fiscal Issues," Federal News Service, March 2, 2001.
79. Ian Williams, "Alan Greenspan and the D-Word," www.alternet.org, February 3, 2004.

CHAPTER 5

1. W. R. Cline, *International Debt and the Stability of the World Economy*, Washington, D.C.: The Institute for International Economics, 1983; Susan George, *A Fate Worse Than Debt*, New York: Grove Press, 1988.
2. Jerry Zeremski, "Greenspan Sees Gains from Mexican Trade," *Buffalo News*, March 26, 1993, p. 1.
3. Keith Bradsher, "Lately, a Much More Visible Fed Chief," *New York Times*, January 17, 1995, p. D1.
4. Bob Woodward, *Maestro: Greenspan's Fed and the American Boom*, New York: Simon and Schuster, 2000, p. 139.
5. Quoted in Enrique Rangel, "Mexico's GDP Shows 6.9% Slide," *Dallas Morning News*, February 17, 1996, p. F1.
6. Enrique Rangel, "Foreign Banks to Counter Gloom at Mexico Convention," *Dallas Morning News*, March 26, 1996, p. D2.
7. Senate Hearing: Greenspan's Testimony, "Federal Reserve's Semi-Annual Monetary Policy Report," Federal News Service, July 18, 1996.

8. James Cramer and Michael Sherrill, "Catching the Asian Flu," *Time*, November 3, 1997, p. 44.

9. Ravi Batra, *Stock Market Crashes of 1998 and 1999*, Richardson, Tex.: Liberty Press, 1997.

10. House Hearing: Greenspan's Testimony, "Long Term Capital Management," Federal News Service, October 1, 1998.

11. Lynnley Browning, "Tax Ruling Casts a Long Shadow," *New York Times*, August 30, 2004, p. C1.

12. Senate Hearing: Greenspan's Testimony, "The Global Economy," Federal News Service, September 23, 1998.

13. Woodward, *Maestro*, pp. 200–208; Justin Martin, *Greenspan: The Man Behind Money*, Cambridge, Mass.: Perseus Publishing, 2001, pp. xv–xvi.

14. Danny Kemp, "U.K. to Knight Greenspan," www.irishexaminer.com, August 8, 2002.

15. Ravi Batra, *The Crash of the Millennium*, New York: Harmony Books, 1999, pp. 134–142.

16. John Cassidy, *Dot.con: The Greatest Story Ever Sold*, New York: Harper Business, 2002, p. 189.

17. Floyd Norris, "As Bull Market Nears a Birthday, Few Ready to Celebrate," *New York Times*, September 24, 2004, p. C1.

CHAPTER 6

1. Robert J. Shiller, "The Mystery of Economic Recessions," *New York Times*, February 14, 2001, p. 17.

2. Robert Hall, "Struggling to Understand the Stock Market," *American Economic Review: Papers and Proceedings* 91, May 2001, pp. 1–11.

3. Economic theory frequently makes use of an economy where investment comes primarily from profits and consumption from wages. Such behavior is called the classical consumption function.

4. Ravi Batra, *The Great American Deception*, New York: John Wiley & Sons, 1996, ch. 4.

5. In other words, consumer spending = wages + consumer debt; and the demand formula becomes:

Demand = Wages + Consumer Debt + Investment + New Government Debt

6. You can easily confirm that without the new debt profits will be only $20.

7. For instance, suppose people save 10 percent of their wages, then the demand formula changes to

Demand = 90% of Wages + Investment + New Debt

The rest of the analysis remains the same. Things become more complicated, because you have to introduce a savings formula as well, but the conclusions will remain unchanged.

8. James K. Galbraith, "Greenspan Agonistes," February 2001, www.uttexas.edu.

9. Bob Woodward, *Maestro: Greenspan's Fed and the American Boom*, New York: Simon and Schuster, 2000, p. 195.

10. John Cassidy, *Dot.Con: The Greatest Story Ever Sold*, New York: Harper Business, 2002, p. 186.

CHAPTER 7

1. Edmund Andrews, "Report Finds Tax Cuts Heavily Favor The Wealthy," *New York Times*, August 13, 2004, p. 16.
2. See chapter 4.
3. GDP equaling twice the level of LIF net wages automatically means that the latter is half of GDP.
4. For instance adding the trade deficit will not change the formula because LIF consumption will still be half of GDP.

CHAPTER 8

1. House Hearing: Greenspan's Testimony, "Annual Economic Report," Federal News Service, February 24, 1999.
2. House Hearing: Greenspan's Testimony, "Monetary Policy Report," Federal News Service, July 18, 2001.
3. The normal practice to obtain real GDP is to use the GDP deflator, but the CPI is more familiar to the public. Theoretically, it makes little difference which price index is used to filter out the effect of inflation from the current value of GDP.
4. Alan Greenspan, "Economic and Budgetary Outlook," FRB Testimony, www.federalreserve.gov, October 8, 1997.
5. Alan Greenspan, "Technology and the Economy," FRB Speeches, www.federalreserve.gov, January 13, 2000.
6. Richard Stevenson, "Fed Chairman Discusses the 'Limits' to the Economy," *New York Times*, January 14, 2000, p. C2.
7. Senate Hearing: Greenspan's Testimony, "Nomination of Alan Greenspan," Federal News Service, January 26, 2000.
8. Aaron Zitner, "The Greenspan Green Light; Fed Chief Can Make or Break Next President's Economic Plans," *Boston Globe*, October 13, 1996, p. F1.
9. Larry Kahaner, *The Quotations of Chairman Greenspan*, Holbrook, Mass.: Adams Media Corporation, p. 133.
10. Jerome Tuccille, *Alan Shrugged: The World's Most Powerful Banker*, New York: John Wiley & Sons, 2002, pp. 225–226.
11. Paul Krugman, "America's Failing Health," *New York Times*, August 27, 2004, p. A21.

CHAPTER 9

1. James L. Rowe, Jr., "Economic Index Rises 0.7% in Feb., Points to Robust Growth in '86," *Washington Post*, March 29, 1986, p. A1.
2. Jane Seaberry, " '85 Economic Growth Slows To 2.3% Rate; Year Is Worst Since 1982; Inflation Put at 3.8%," *Washington Post*, January 23, 1986, p. A1.
3. Jane Seaberry, "Unemployment Rate Drops To 7.0 Pct. in November; Trade Deficit's Effects Seen Bottoming Out," *Washington Post*, December 7, 1985, p. A1.
4. Hobart Rowen, "2 Top Experts Disagree On Dollar's Next Course," *Washington Post*, May 14, 1984, p. D6.

5. Associated Press, "Greenspan Warns Protectionism Could Hurt Economy," USAToday.com, November 20, 2003.

6. House Hearing: Greenspan's Testimony, "Semiannual Report on Monetary Policy," Federal News Service, July 15, 2003.

7. Susan Harrigan, "Weak Dollar Helps Cut Trade Deficit," *Newsday*, March 3, 2004, p. A32.

8. Nell Henderson, "Greenspan Ties Budget Deficit to Trade Gap," *Washington Post*, March 3, 2004, p. E3.

9. Hobart Rowen, "Lower Dollar Alone Won't Cure Trade Ills," *Washington Post*, August 2, 1987, p. H1.

10. *The Economic Report of the President*, Council of Economic Advisers, Washington, D.C., 1996, p. 250.

11. Steven Cohen and John Zysman, *Manufacturing Matters*, New York: Basic Books, 1987, p. 3.

12. Floyd Norris, "Campaign Tactic: Blame Foreigners and Ignore the Trade Deficit," *New York Times*, August 20, 2004, p. C1.

13. See Ravi Batra, *The Great American Deception*, New York: John Wiley & Sons, 1996, p. 127, for an analysis of this view.

14. See the *Economic Report of the President*, 2004, p. 402, for the annual U.S. deficit on the current account. Adding the figure for 2004 to those available from the report approximately yields the figure of $3.6 trillion noted in the text.

CHAPTER 10

1. See *Forbes'* annual list of billionaires; *Business Week*, April 16, 2001, and Bruce Mcconnell and David Macpherson, *Contemporary Labor Economics*, 6th edition, New York: McGraw-Hill Irwin, 2003, p. 229.

2. The real production wage actually peaked in 1972 at $331.59 per week and fell slightly to $331.39 in 1973. Thus it is better to say that this wage peaked in the 1972–1973 period. However, many people hold 1973 as the peak year, as mentioned in the text.

3. See, for instance, Joseph M. Anderson, "The Wealth of U.S. Families in 1995; Report to Merrill Lynch," Merrill Lynch & Co. June 1, 1998, p. 1: "The average (median) U.S. family in 1995 had net financial assets of only about $1,000."

4. *Economic Report of the President*, Council of Economic Advisers, Washington, D.C., 1996.

5. Elizabeth Warren and Amelia Tyagi, *The Two-Income Trap: Why Middle-Class Mothers and Fathers are Going Broke*, New York: Basic Books, September 2003.

6. Lester Thurow, *The Future of Capitalism*, New York: Morrow, 1996, p. 21.

7. "CEO Compensation," Forbes.com, 2002.

8. Paul Krugman, "Inequality in America," Human Rights Monitor, October 20, 2002, p. 2.

9. Debra Watson, "Two Decades of Rising Inequality in America," *World Socialist Website*, www.wsws.org, June 8, 2002, and November 9, 2001.

10. Krugman, p. 3.

11. Since 200 percent is an unchanging number, it drops out of the GDP growth formula, which deals with the change in output.

12. Timothy Egan, "Economic Squeeze Plaguing Middle-Class Families," *New York Times*, August 28, 2004, p. A11.

13. *Economic Report of the President*, Council of Economic Advisers, Washington, D.C., various issues.
14. Bob Herbert, "An Economy That Turns American Values Upside Down," *New York Times*, September 6, 2004, p. A17.
15. Daniel Gross, "The Next Shock: Not Oil, but Debt," *New York Times*, September 5, 2004, p. 1.
16. Andreas Haufler, *Taxation in a Global Economy*, Cambridge: Cambridge University Press, 2001, pp. 13–17.
17. United Nations, *The World Economic and Social Survey*, New York, 1994, p. 3.
18. Junko Kato, *Regressive Taxation and the Welfare State*, Cambridge: Cambridge University Press, 2001, p. 5.
19. Steven Pearlstein, "Greenspan Out to Defend His Handling of Stock Bubble," *Washington Post*, December 22, 2002, p. A1.
20. Ibid.
21. House Hearing: Greenspan's Testimony, "Semi-Annual Report on Monetary Policy," Federal News Service, July 15, 2003.

CHAPTER 11

1. Bob Herbert, "Despair of the Jobless," *New York Times*, August 7, 2003, p. A23.
2. Ravi Batra, *The Downfall of Capitalism and Communism*, London: Macmillan, 1978, reprinted by Venus Books, Richardson, Tex., 1990.
3. Ravi Batra, *Muslim Civilization and the Crisis in Iran*, Richardson: Venus Books, 1979, p. 196. Briefly, my reasoning behind this forecast was:

   In the modern period . . . the West caused great commotion in the world of Islam and India. . . . Britain, France, Italy and even Russia had at one time captured or exploited the territories of the Ottoman empire. . . . It is now the turn of India and Islam to cause upheaval in the Western world and Russia.

4. Ravi Batra, *The Crash of the Millennium*, New York: Harmony Books, 1999, p. 144.
5. Ibid., pp. 145–146.
6. Ibid., pp. 152–154.
7. Ibid., p. 158.
8. Ibid., p. 182.
9. Laurence Kotlikoff and Scott Burns, *The Coming Generational Storm*, Cambridge, Mass.: MIT Press, 2004.
10. James Grant, "Blame Greenspan," *Forbes*, September 3, 2001.
11. Jeff Madrick, "The Bottom Line on Overhauling Social Security: Most Privatization Plans Involve a Decided Cut in Average Benefits," *New York Times*, December 23, 2004, p. C2. Also see Mark Hulbert, "In Great Expectations for Stocks, Danger for Pension Plans," *New York Times*, January 2, 2005, sec. 3, p. 6.
12. Paul Samuelson and William Nordhaus, *Economics*, 17th edition, New York: McGraw-Hill, 2000, p. 629.
13. Kucinich quoted from Mark Gongloff, "Outsourcing: What to DO?" *CNN/Money*, March 1, 2004, p. 1.
14. Editorial, "The Economy Unspun," *New York Times*, October 13, 2004, p. A34.
15. The White House, "Fact Sheet: America's Ownership Society: Expanding Opportunities," www.whitehouse.gov, 2004.

INDEX